Marriage on Trial

Society and Culture in the Modern Middle East
Series Editor: Michael Gilsenan

Marriage on Trial

A Study of Islamic Family Law

Iran and Morocco Compared

ZIBA MIR-HOSSEINI

I.B. Tauris & Co Ltd
Publishers
London · New York

Published in 1993 by
I.B.Tauris & Co Ltd
Victoria House
Bloomsbury Square
London WC1B 4DZ

175 Fifth Avenue
New York
NY 10010

This paperback edition published in 1997

In the United States of America
and Canada distributed by
St Martin's Press
175 Fifth Avenue
New York
NY 10010

A CIP record for this book is available from the British Library

A CIP record for this book is available from the Library of Congress

ISBN 1 86064 182 2

Typeset by The Midlands Book Typesetting Company
Printed and bound in Great Britain by
WBC Ltd, Bridgend, Mid Glamorgan

Contents

Preface

The relationship between law and society in the contemporary Muslim world is complex and multi-dimensional. This complexity reflects the tensions inherent in Islamic concepts of law, particularly those arising from the blurring of boundaries between the 'sacred' and the 'mundane'. Law in Islam has a transcendental dimension – in Muslim belief its source is divine revelation – but its prime purpose is that of moulding human reality.

Despite the fact that the centrality of law in Islam is widely acknowledged, little has been written on the interaction between law and actual practices, on the ways in which Muslims perceive and relate to legal injunctions for which divine and eternal validity are claimed. Existing studies, in concentrating on Islamic law from a legal point of view, or on customary practices from an anthropological point of view, do little to explain the processes by which Muslims translate their religious precepts into practice.

This book aims to break new ground in relating the traditions of Islam to the everyday lives of individuals. It explores aspects of marriage in law and in society in Iran and Morocco, two Muslim countries which follow different schools of Islamic law (Shi'a and Maliki respectively). Based on fieldwork in family courts and among litigants, it focuses on the dynamics of marriage and the consequences of its breakdown, as well as the way in which litigants manipulate the law in order to resolve marital difficulties. The book approaches Islamic law (the Shari'a) from an unorthodox angle. Its main focus is neither on the classical texts nor on modern legislation, but rather on the litigants, those who use the law. With this focus it goes beyond conventional Islamic law studies, which are largely textual, and shows how the law is interpreted and administered in practice. It also departs from another major trend in studies of Muslim institutions, which either deal with Islam and popular practices as two separate traditions, or confound them with a view to making ideological statements.

I should stress that I see this book as a contribution, not to 'legal anthropology' but to the 'anthropology of law', a distinction similar to that made by Richard Tapper between 'Islamic anthropology' and 'the anthropology of Islam' (Tapper n.d.). By 'legal anthropology' I mean 'anthropology – the study of culture and social relations – informed by a knowledge of law, or done by a specialist in law'. By 'anthropology of law' I understand 'the study of law – the production and administration of legal rules and order – informed by anthropological methods and insights, or done by an anthropologist' (cf. Geertz 1983; Rosen 1989). The necessity for such a distinction became evident to me from reviews of the manuscript of this book by readers who, unlike me, were trained primarily in Islamic law or Oriental Studies and who were disturbed by my 'cavalier treatment' of Islamic law, especially by my summarizing (in the Introduction) what they considered to be 'too complex to be summarized'. If this were a legal textbook, or even legal anthropology, I could accept such criticism; as it is intended as neither, I have no hesitation in standing by my summaries as both necessary and, I trust, reliable and adequate for the purposes of a study in the anthropology of law.

The book is divided into two parts and six main chapters, framed by an introduction and a conclusion. Each main chapter revolves around one category of marital dispute, examining one area of interaction between the Shari'a, the modern legal system and marriage, as revealed by that category of dispute cases.

The Introduction provides the necessary background elements for the book, it defines the aims and methods of the research and places Islamic law and its recent development in a historical perspective, with a view to showing the ways in which religious precepts and positive law continue to interact in contemporary Muslim societies.

Part One of the book is a general examination of the ideals and practices of marriage and divorce as reflected in Shari'a precepts, in the provisions of modern legal codes and in the contents of the actual marital dispute cases. Through analysis of the two dominant types of marital dispute, constituting the vast majority of all cases, the strategies of accommodation between these three levels are highlighted.

Chapter 1 provides an introduction to the courts, their procedures and dispute cases in Iran and Morocco. Its aim is to place the disputes first in their Shari'a context and then in the modern matrix of the legal systems of their respective countries. Two demands are central to every petition in both countries: the wife's demand for maintenance, and the husband's demand for her submission; I suggest that the reason for the predominance of these demands is to be found in the contractual aspect of marriage, whose salient features are the non-reciprocal and unequal rights and duties of spouses, and the absence of any kind of matrimonial regime. Legally speaking there is no common ownership of matrimonial goods. The rights and duties of each spouse are legally defined, thus each party can file a suit against the other if the terms of the contract are breached. Maintenance of the wife, incumbent on the husband, is the only element of marital obligation which is translated into positive law with the power of enforcement. The chapter shows how the underlying logic of marriage as a contract is used by women as an effective strategy to negotiate their marital terms.

Chapters 2, 3 and 4 focus on the dynamics of marital relations and their breakdown. Through the analysis of actual divorce cases, they show the contrast that exists between the theory and the practice of Islamic law. These chapters illustrate the ways in which social norms and customs modify men's Shari'a rights to unconditional divorce and polygamy, and highlight the ways in which these modifications determine court procedures and practices in each country. Chapter 2 deals with Iranian and Chapter 3 with Moroccan practices, Chapter 4 brings data from Iran and Morocco together in order to identify areas of tension between law and practice. The breakdown of marriage is dominated by two unresolved types of conflicts: those involving the matrimonial regime and those involving polygyny. Both stem from the contrast between the Shari'a model of marital harmony, based on male supremacy and viewed as static, and the actual dynamics of marital relations. These chapters show that marriage in Iran is not only more stable but has a more egalitarian character; a man's right to divorce is seriously curtailed by the way dower, an integral part of every Muslim marriage contract, is practised.

Part Two of the book is concerned with the tensions between the Shari'a, the modern legal system, and social practices. Tensions between the Shari'a and the modern legal system stem from the process of codifying Shari'a regulations and grafting them on to a modern legal system, giving rise to the existence of two parallel but distinct notions of legitimacy: Shari'a and legal. These tensions are manifest in disputes in which one of these notions of legitimacy is challenged. Petitioners manipulate the existing ambiguity as regards legitimacy in an effective way, to negotiate their terms of settlement, using the court as an arena. These disputes reveal the existence of another principle of legitimacy, which is defined by social norms and customs and is distinct from the Shari'a and the modern legal system.

Chapter 5 examines paternity and custody disputes, in order to explore the tensions that result from the co-existence of different legal and social constructions. There exist two different notions of legitimate paternity, that which is recognized by the Shari'a and one which is socially valid. Differences between the Shi'a and Maliki rites with respect to custody rights are reflected in actual patterns of child custody in Iran and Morocco. The chapter demonstrates the *de facto* negation of the Islamic ideals of the patrilineal and patrifocal model of the family. In Morocco, among the poor (who form the majority of those who resort to the court) family structure deviates from the ideal model in various ways. Here, dispute cases depict a matrifocal pattern which is striving to function and survive in a system dominated by a strong patrilineal and patriarchal ideology. Ironically, this ideology, which is embodied in the legal system, is the means of resolving marital disputes and the only legal recourse available to women.

Chapter 6 is concerned with another aspect of the tension, that which manifests itself in disputes over validity of marriage and divorce. I argue that these disputes have their origins in three different, but interrelated, constructions of marriage: those of the Shari'a, of the modern legal system, and of society at large. Disputes arise when these three constructions fail to concur. In the case of Iran, these disputes involve temporary unions, recognized only by the Shi'a, and the husband's right to resume marital relations within a certain period after divorce. In the case of Morocco, they involve a type of marriage which is socially valid but not recognized by the modern legal system, and the annulment of marriages which are legally valid but claimed to be invalid according to the Shari'a.

As will emerge in the course of these chapters, Iranian women enjoy a higher degree of legal and social protection than do Moroccan women. This finding of the study challenges the prevailing assumptions that the secularizing of the law necessarily enhances women's position and that a return to the Shari'a law limits women's choices and detracts from their position. To understand the implication of what these court cases reveal about family organization and the position of women in Iran and Morocco, and to bring their principal features out in relief, one needs to examine them in their wider socio-economic context. This is done in the Conclusion, which explores the ways in which the Shari'a model of family, and its differing interpretations by the Maliki and Shi'a schools, interact with the existing models among different socio-economic groups.

Ziba Mir-Hosseini
Girton College, Cambridge
December 1992.

Acknowledgements

I am grateful to a number of individuals in Iran whose understanding and support enabled me to pursue my research and attend court sessions at a most sensitive time, when Tehran was under Iraqi missile attack and academic research seemed an irrelevant luxury. In particular, the judges and court clerks of a number of Special Civil Courts in Tehran not only tolerated my presence in the courtroom but allowed me to gain insights into the intricacies of court files. Deeply indebted as I am to them and to numerous other officials and private persons, I regret that it is not appropriate to name them individually.

Fieldwork in Morocco was funded by grants from the British Academy, the Nuffield Foundation, the Wenner-Gren Institute for Anthropological Research, and the Institute for Intercultural Studies. Their generous support allowed me to give this study a comparative dimension. Peter Avery and Ali Bahaijoub helped me to obtain a visa for Morocco, at a time when my Iranian passport was a liability. Peter Taylor (British Council Representative), Edward Thomas (Executive Secretary of the Moroccan-American Commission for Educational and Cultural Exchange) and Mohammad Guessous (Head of the Department of Sociology at Université Mohammad V) provided letters of introduction in Rabat which made my presence less threatening to the Moroccan authorities.

Ernest Gellner introduced me to Moroccan academic circles, where I enjoyed searching discussions which not only enriched my experience of Islamic tradition but enabled me to come to terms with my own Islamic roots. I would particularly like to mention the following: Zuhur Alalawi, Abdelhakim Baakrim, Nourredin Affaya, Jamal Benomar, Rahma Bourkia, Anissa Benzakour, Mohammad Guessous, Abdallah and Miriam Hammoudi, Leila Hossini, Latif Jbabdi, Latifa Laghzaoui, Amina Lemrini, Jack Levert, Zeinab

Mi'adi, Fatima Mernissi, Abdurrazak Mouly Rchid, Rabia Naciri, Fatima Zahra Saleh and Khadija Tanana.

It is impossible to thank all those individuals who showed me such warm hospitality and friendship and shared their knowledge of Morocco during my year there, but I must mention my special debts to Fouzia Benyoub, Touria Elhatimi, Fayka Aouad and Somaya Majdoubi. I am also indebted to the following for their hospitality, friendship and intellectual support: Houria Affaya, Leila and Aziz Alevi, Oumama Aouad Lahrech, Fatima Belaoui, Fouad Benelkad, Mustapha Belouhlie, Issam Benzakour, Wafa Charkaoui, Jamal Elouadi, Radwan Halimy, Kazim and Fatana Shayesteh, Assia and Amina. Finally, without the help of Somaya Majdoubi, my research assistant, the data collected would have been less rich and my insight into Moroccan society much more limited.

The grant from the Nuffield Foundation also enabled me to consult sources in France, where I spent the spring of 1990 in Aix-en-Provence at the Institut de Recherches sur le Monde Arabe et Musulman. In particular, I would like to thank the following for their assistance: Maurice Flory, Michel Camau, Beatrice de Saenge, Bernard Botiveau, Lari Talha and Laroui Addi.

At Cambridge, a research fellowship at Girton College (1990–3) gave the space and time for writing this book. I would like to thank Esther Goody, Geoffrey Hawthorn, Martha Mundy, Helen Watson and Sarah Hobson for reading and commenting on various parts of this work. I am also grateful to two anonymous reviewers for their comments on the manuscript. My special thanks go to Bassim Musallam who read the whole manuscript and made many useful criticisms. My greatest debt is, however, to Richard Tapper, who read various versions of the manuscript and made generous and valuable suggestions. I am certain that without his comments this book would have been leaner and less elegant.

Finally, I should like to thank Esther and Jack Goody for their support and their encouragement throughout the years I have lived in Cambridge. Without them this study would have never been made, and to them I dedicate it.

Portions of Chapter 2 and Chapter 5 were previously published in different form as 'Divorce in Islamic Law and in Practice: the Case of Iran', *Cambridge Anthropology*, XI, 1 (1986); 'Contrast between Law and Practice for the Moroccan Family: Patriarchy and Matrifocality', *Morocco: Journal of Society for Moroccan Studies*, I, 1 (1991); and 'Women, Marriage and the Law in Post-revolutionary Iran', in ed. Haleh Afshar, *Women in the Middle East: Perceptions and Struggles* (London, Macmillan, 1993).

Note on Transliteration

Whenever possible, I have used the familiar English forms of Arabic and Persian words and names; otherwise, I have followed a modified form of the system of transliteration adopted by the International Journal of Middle Eastern Studies. Diacritical marks are used only in the Glossary and Bibliography. The letters *ayn* and *hamza* are indicated by '. Except for anglicized words, foreign words are italicized.

Introduction

In Muslim societies today, marriage is governed by religious precepts, embodied in modern systems of law. The relations between the precepts and the law are complex and further complicated by the distance between each and actual practice. This book discusses aspects of these relations through an analysis of strategies adopted by litigants in marital and child custody disputes in two Muslim countries: Iran and Morocco.

Law in Islam has two aspects: sacred and temporal. It is sacred in the sense that in Muslim belief its source is divine revelation and its prime purpose is that of mapping the route to salvation. The very term by which the law is called in Islam, the *Shari'a*, i.e., 'the right way', embodies this notion. Yet Islamic law, as we know it now, has also a distinct temporal aspect: it is the product of centuries of juristic interpretation; it rests on a well-developed legal theory and contains a varied body of positive laws.

The boundaries between the 'sacred' and the 'temporal' are particularly blurred in the case of family law, where the divine revelations were most abundant. Islamic family law is permeated with religious ideals and ethical values; it holds within itself a distinct model of family and gender relations. This model is claimed to be divinely ordained and, thus, immutable. Marital and other types of familial disputes heard in the courts are arenas in which tensions arising from the interface between the divine ideals informing the Shari'a model and the actual patterns of social behaviour come to the surface. Each dispute case is, in some ways, a microcosm of forces that shape the reality of Muslim life: the force of the sacred element in law; the modern legal system that embodies and enforces it; and

1

the way that individuals, be they judges or litigants, perceive and relate to both.

The book is thus concerned, in two specific settings, with confrontations that occur in myriad ways in the present Muslim world, between ideal and reality, tradition and modernity, religious blueprints and intimate human relations. The pronounced patriarchal character of Islamic law has been widely discussed in the literature on Muslim societies; I do not enter such a discussion here, although I do consider some of its contradictions and implications. The principal questions that I am concerned with are the nature of the relations between the concept of family in two schools of Islamic law and the actual family organization in Shi'a Iran and Maliki Morocco. What are the differences and similarities between the two schools? How do individuals, both men and women, relate to and make sense of the religious precepts that underlie every piece of legislation regulating their private lives?

My primary aim is to provide a detailed profile of the interactions between Islamic law and the social constructions of marriage and divorce. In so doing I attempt to look beyond the law, to examine the complexity of human relations, the very intimate exchanges that take place within marriage, and to explore the religious, social and psychological forces which influence and mould them. The law is unequal and gives men certain privileges over women. Two obvious examples are men's unilateral rights to divorce and polygamy. How does this inbuilt inequality affect the stability of marriage and the relations within it? How and to what extent is the inferior position of women in law reflected in social practice? In what ways and to what extent have modernizing processes, such as education and the growing economic independence of women, influenced marital relations?

Although answers to these questions are bound to be tentative and partial, I believe it is especially important to ask them in view of the recent resurgence of Islam as a political and social force, and the accompanying politicization of issues of law – all of which in themselves pose complex, yet urgent, problems of theory and practice.[1] On the one hand, both supporters and opponents of the various forms of Islamic resurgence, commonly referred to as 'fundamentalism', see implementation or reform of Islamic law as central for realizing their respective ideals. On the other hand, the impulse and manifestations of fundamentalism vary in different Muslim societies, for example as between Shi'ites and Sunnis and from one country to another; statutes and legal traditions also vary widely, as do economic and social conditions. We must ask, how do legal systems and actual practices differ within and between such societies, what are the tensions involved, and how may these differences and tensions best be explained?

But before attempting such questions, we first need to ask a more elementary one: why is it that the movement back to Islamic law has become one of the central issues in today's Muslim world? There is ample evidence that, despite the different forms which adherence to Islamic law has taken in recent years, law has come to provide a supreme validating ethos and legitimating device.[2] This is indeed reminiscent of its function during the formative period of Islam, when both the law and Islamic civilization were still inchoate. But there is a major difference: in the modern context the law can no longer distance itself from the state. The modern state not only does not allow such a distance but has used Islamic law as a means of political validation, as evidenced by the successful manipulation of Islamic law in recent years by several political leaders in the Muslim world.[3]

To understand the reasons behind these developments, we need to look at the nature and scope of law in Islam. In what follows I examine certain aspects of the concept of law in Islam as relevant to the problems addressed by this study. A thorough and balanced analysis of the topic requires a historical and analytical depth beyond the scope of this book. The ensuing account is both partial and selective; the aim is to place Islamic law and its recent developments in a historical perspective, and to show the ways in which religious precepts and positive law interact in modern Muslim countries. It is intended for the non-specialist; the specialist in Islamic law may wish to skip the next two sections.[4]

Islamic Law: a Historical Sketch

A historical perspective is essential to appreciate the current place of law in Muslim societies, and in particular to explore the dynamics of the changing relationship of law and society.[5] The nature of Islamic law is shaped by its history, and its history is inseparable from that of Islamic civilization.[6] Yet in conceptualizing Islam and its institutions, there is a tendency to overlook its tentative beginnings and see it as emerging intact in the form by which it is now characterized.[7] This disposition is particularly clear in those who ardently argue for the rule of the Shari'a. They tend to hold an idealized and totally ahistorical version of the development of the Islamic faith and its institutions, as though the last thirteen and a half centuries and intervening events do not exist or can be by-passed.[8]

From its inception, Islam has been both a political and a social order, to which the religious dimension of the faith was moulded. Its founder was both a prophet and an able statesman.[9] He not only brought a new faith to his people but created the community of believers, known in Islamic terminology as *umma*. In this community God was the ultimate authority and arbiter; and Muhammad derived his power from his divine office as the messenger.[10] What defined the *umma* was adherence to the Divine Law, which became the token of manifestation of the faith. Islam means submission, and a Muslim is a person who submits to the will of God, as revealed to Muhammad in what became compiled as the Koran. In this way the divine law became the backbone of Muslim society; it has continued to define and guide it ever since.

However, the complex structure of Islamic law, as we know it now, took shape during what is known as the formative phase of Islamic civilization. This phase started with the Umayyad dynasty (661–750) and covers the early part of the Abbassid era (750–1258). It was during this period that a gradual but enduring separation between the spiritual and temporal aspects of power came about, a separation that did not exist in the earlier period of Islam. Only the first four Caliphs, known as Rightly Guided Caliphs, partook in any of the Prophet's religious aura. They were all close companions of the Prophet, which assured the continuation of his guidance. Their rule (632–61) is regarded as the Golden Age of Islam, as an extension of the era when the Prophet was among the believers, and is very much idealized by the majority of Muslims. Yet this period was not free from internal struggles for power; the main division in Islam, that between Sunnis and Shi'as, has its origin in this period, involving a dispute over the succession. The Shi'as hold that the Prophet had chosen Ali, his cousin and son-in-law, as his successor; they reject the legitimacy of the rule of Caliphs and recognize a line of successors starting with Ali and continuing through his male offspring.[11]

In time, as the Prophet's successors, the Caliphs of Islam, lost their religious aura, the ulema (literally, those who possess Knowledge) came to represent the spiritual dimension of Islamic rule. These were private scholars, with no formal connections to the ruling apparatus, who derived their authority from their religious knowledge, especially from their role as guides to the Prophet's as yet unexplicated message. It was also during this phase that the need to elaborate a 'science of law' (*'ilm al-fiqh*) became more pressing. The Prophet was no longer among the believers to receive revelations corresponding to the new needs of the people. Yet the expansion of the faith and the demands raised by the conquest of new land necessitated a more elaborate system of law. Such a system of law, the ulema maintained, had to evolve and develop within the confines of the faith. Both its nature and its boundaries were already defined by the precepts preached by the Prophet: God is the ultimate ruler and legislator, and Muhammad is his last messenger, to whom the final commands were revealed. The task of the jurist then became that of discerning and expounding law from the divine commands.

From this emanates a distinction, central to the concept of law in Islam, between the Revealed Law (the *Shari'a*) and jurisprudence (*fiqh*). Shari'a is law in the sense that it contains a divine blueprint for mankind, for both this world and the other. It is in its most profound sense the all-inclusive law of creation: the Will of God for humanity. *Fiqh*, which contains the letter of the law, is, in Coulson's words, 'the whole process of intellectual activity which ascertains and discovers the terms of the divine will and transforms them into a system of legally enforceable rights and duties'.[12] *Fiqh* literally means understanding or knowledge, and the goal of Muslim jurists in developing what is now commonly termed Shari'a law was that of reaching an understanding of the divine will in order to help Muslims to keep to the 'right way'.

Yet Muslims do not normally distinguish between Shari'a and *fiqh*, especially at the popular level. Western usage of the term Shari'a law, initiated by colonial writers, was probably influenced by local perceptions of law. My own usage of these terms in the course of this study is blurred, as indeed are the boundaries between the Shari'a and *fiqh*. I neither raise the question nor enter any discussions as to whether *fiqh* is true to the essence of the Shari'a or not, which has been the centre of debates among Muslim secularists, feminists and Islamists. What is essential to note is that in Muslim consciousness these two are so much intertwined that to make any meaningful distinction entails the risk of questioning the very notion of a divinely ordained law.

In elaborating the law, the jurists were guided by two sacred sources: the divine revelations, compiled in the form of the Koran, and the precedents of the Prophet, known as the *sunna* (literally, practice). Since it was held that the Prophet was divinely guided, his sayings, actions, thoughts and decisions came to constitute the second source of guidance. These were transmitted orally and were later committed to writing in a body of literature known as *hadith* (tradition). The science of *hadith* was established, in which the texts (*mutun*) of these reports and the chains of transmitters (*isnad*) were scrutinized in order to ascertain their authenticity. Yet neither the Koran nor the growing literature of *hadith* could constitute a book of law; they merely provided divine guidance to which every ruling had to conform.[13]

To arrive at points of law, the jurists had to interpret these two divine sources and thus apply their own reasoning, which came to be known as the process of *ijtihad* (independent reasoning). In order to protect the divine properties of the law, to minimize the scope of human reasoning and to contain differences, jurist-theologians developed two major juristic methods, namely *qiyas*, analogical deduction, and *ijma'*, the consensus of jurists.

This is the orthodox theory of sources of the Shari'a and its development. It owes its formulation to Al-Shafi'i (770–819), regarded as the founder of Islamic jurisprudence. But, as Anderson points out, Schacht and others have shown that it is an idealized rather than a factual account: first, the science of *hadith* came to its full growth in the ninth century, almost 150 years after the death of the Prophet.[14] Thus the authenticity of many of the traditions that form the basis for a large body of the legal rules remains at best doubtful. Secondly, *sunna* (the practice of the Prophet), the raw material of *hadith* literature, in its broadest sense included the pre-Islamic customs of the Arabs as well as reforms introduced to them by the Prophet. Thirdly, other juristic devices were used, which afforded the jurists a wide scope for adapting the law to the exigencies of changing Muslim societies.

No doubt the actual processes of elaboration of the law from the divine sources were far more dynamic and complex than the account implied by the classical theory. Yet it was this ideological formulation that gained ascendancy and was transmitted to posterity.

What motivated these jurists was religious zeal to achieve an ideal, but it is important to stress that it was customary practices that provided them with the raw material upon which their Islamic ideal could be constructed.[15] Law-making entailed a process of Islamization, of permeating every act with what was felt to be the true Islamic spirit.[16] Naturally, different jurists invoked different points of law when faced with new problems in different contexts. This necessitated the introduction of other juristic devices and gave rise to different schools of law and legal thought which emerged in various parts of the Muslim world.[17] Although many schools of law came into being, the majority died out and only a few survived. Four schools established themselves among the Sunnis: Hanafi, Maliki, Shafi'i and Hanbali, named after their jurist founders. Today they are found in the following areas: Hanafi in the Middle East and India and Pakistan; the Maliki in North, Central and West Africa; the Shafi'i in East Africa and Southeast Asia, and the Hanbali in Saudi Arabia. Two schools dominate the Shi'as; the Imami or Ithna 'Ashari in Iran, Iraq and Lebanon, and the Zaydi in the Yemen.[18] It is important to stress that all these schools, Sunni as well as Shi'a, recognize each other's orthodoxy, although they differ from each other on certain legal points and postulates.[19]

By the beginning of the tenth century, the door of *ijtihad* (independent reasoning) was declared closed. The consensus of the jurists was that the law had reached its perfection, as all that could be deduced from the Koran and the *sunna* of the prophet had already been worked out. The rule of *taqlid* (imitation) replaced that of *ijtihad*.[20] This heralds a new phase when, at least in theory, the law becomes static and immutable. *Taqlid*, unlike *ijtihad*, entailed the unquestioning acceptance of the doctrines of the established schools and authorities.[21] In this way the dominant opinions within each school, which themselves were the product of *ijtihad*, came to be regarded as the letter of the law. These are contained in handbooks dating from the mediaeval period, and subsequent works derive their authority from them.

The doctrine of *taqlid* was adopted by almost all schools of law in the Sunni world, though the rule of *ijtihad* was preserved by the Shi'a schools and the Hanbali school of Sunni law, at least in theory.[22] Two points are important here. First, this was the state of affairs in theory; recent studies have shown that in practice the situation was much more complex.[23] Secondly, new and original thoughts were developed but they could only be freely expressed in the 'abstract and systematic constructions that affected neither the established decisions of positive law nor the classical doctrines'.[24] Schacht sees the consequent theoretical rigidity and immutability of the law as a factor that ensured the stability of the Shari'a over centuries in the face of drastic changes that were taking place in political institutions in Islam, although he admits that this also stultified the law, as the Shari'a became 'more and more out of touch with the developments of the state of society'.[25] In some ways, the ascendancy of *taqlid* over *ijtihad* marks a turning point in the continuing clash between 'idealism and realism' in Islamic law, a clash which, according to Coulson, was 'a natural and inevitable consequence of the basic tension between the two constituent elements of Islamic law: for divine revelation represents the fixed and constant factor, and human reason the variable and fluctuating factor, in Islamic jurisprudence.'[26]

This lasted until the mid-nineteenth century, when finally 'the idealism of the doctrine both in matters of substance and procedure, has perforce had to give way to the needs of state and society in practice'.[27] In 1850, the Ottoman authorities introduced extensive reforms which for the first time interfered with the substance of Islamic law in order to bring it into line with modern needs and contemporary issues. Since then, Islamic law has been subjected to reforms and amendments in every Muslim country. Although the impetus for and the processes of reform have varied considerably from one country to another, it can be said that all Muslim countries have followed one of the following three paths:[28] abandoning classical Islamic law in every sphere and replacing it by Western-inspired codes; retaining Islamic law in respect to family, inheritance, and religious endowments, while abandoning it in other areas of law; or preserving Islamic law as the fundamental law and attempting to apply it to the whole range of human relationships. A large majority of Muslim countries have chosen the middle path, where the Shari'a still forms the basis of family law, though reformed, codified and applied by a modern legal apparatus.

The situation is still far from settled. While until the late 1970s one could say that the dominant trend was toward the secularization of law, in 1990 this is no longer so. In both Sunni and Shi'a worlds a deliberate move towards purification and Islamization of the law can be discerned. In some countries, such as Iran and the Sudan, we are now witnessing a reversal of the process of secularization started in the early parts of this century. The return to Islamic law is seen as a way of asserting an Islamic and independent identity, an alternative to Western imported models.[29]

Islamic Law: Theory Versus Practice

Having sketched an outline of the evolution of the Shari'a, we can now examine those of its characteristics which are relevant to this study. What characterizes the Shari'a perhaps more than anything else is the distance between the ideal and the reality, between the law in theory and the law in practice.[30] In theory, the Shari'a is immutable and all-encompassing, regulating every aspect of life with no distinction between sacred and mundane. In practice, neither has ever been the case. Despite its doctrinal immutability, the Shari'a not only accommodated prevailing customs but developed legal devices for adapting itself to personal needs and circumstances.[31] The Shari'a has never been applied in its entirety. Long before the present century, it had been put aside in certain areas such as taxation and state organization, and it was only in areas of family law that it ruled supreme.[32]

A gap between law as an ideal system and law in practice is not peculiar to Islamic law. It has been noted in other societies and for other systems of law; it is even seen as an enduring feature of any legal system.[33] What is special to the Shari'a is the theoretical necessity for such a gap; since the Shari'a is regarded as the divine blueprint for human action, therefore, when it conflicts with legal practice, it is the latter that must be modified. In other words, it must be accepted that human practices not only are not uniform but often deviate from the divine blueprint. This gives the Shari'a a special configuration and has two consequences of major importance.

The first consequence is reflected in the legal nature and scope of the Shari'a rules. To ensure the viability of the Shari'a as a Divine Law, valid for all ages, the boundaries in law between the moral and the legal not only must remain blurred but must be capable of shifting. This accounts for the dual nature of many of the Shari'a rules: they can be both rigid and flexible, obsolete yet relevant.[34] Cognizant of this inherent duality, Muslim jurists, from the earliest times, have made a distinction between those aspects of the law regulating the relationship of a believer with God (*'ibadat*, ritual acts) and those regulating his relationship with others and with society (*mu'amilat*, contracts). While the primary perspective of Islamic law in the case of the former is eschatological, in the case of the latter it is sociological, dealing with issues of social intercourse and responsibility.

This perspective puts a large proportion of Shari'a subject matter beyond the domain of positive law, in the sense that it remains a matter between the individual and God, to be settled on the Day of Judgement (*al-akhira*). Perhaps it was precisely to contain the ensuing incongruities of such a stand, and to ensure the legal force of the Shari'a, that Muslim scholars divided all deeds into two broad categories: those which are forbidden (*haram*) and those which are permitted (*halal*). Permitted deeds are further divided into four sub-categories: those which are obligatory (*wajib*); those which are recommended but whose observance is not obligatory (*mustahab*); those which are neutral (*mubah*); and those which are disapproved, although not forbidden (*makruh*).[35] As is evident, only two of these categories (those which are obligatory and those which are forbidden) can be the subject of a substantive law, enforced by human courts. These acts embrace a small sphere of human action, while the majority fall in other categories, imputed with ethical and often religious values but legally neutral as the law remains silent about them. Yet behind the moral and ethical cloud that envelops each act, there exists an undisputable notion of legal validity.[36] For instance, men are given the right to divorce, though it is morally condemned (*makruh*) for a man to divorce without a valid reason. But what makes a divorce valid is the observance of the procedure set by the Shari'a, not the existence of a valid reason.[37]

The second consequence of the theoretical necessity for maintenance of a gap between ideal and reality is more political than legal. It ensures a voice for those who are in a position to define the terms of the divine law (the ulema) and checks the power of those who can enforce it. This fosters a peculiar type of tension between theory and practice, a tension which, although variable in time and space, is the corollary of the notion of the Shari'a as the manifestation of the Divine Will. It is precisely because this Divine Will needs to be discerned by human intellectual activity, and, more importantly, because it is enforced by human courts, that it is bound to bear the influence of the time and environment in which it operates.

The Shari'a and the Modern Nation-State

The intrinsic tension between religious ideal and positive law in the Shari'a has acquired a new dimension with the rise of Muslim nation-states in the present century.[38] Previously, the Shari'a managed, at least in theory, to avoid being identified with the temporal power. It was the state that accepted the Shari'a and, in part, derived its legitimacy and legal sanction from it, without having a direct say in shaping its method or influencing its decisions.[39] Though not applied in every sphere of law, the Shari'a remained nominally supreme everywhere in the Muslim world. It was recognized as the sacred law of the land without rival, at least at the ideological level.

The advance of nation-states in the Muslim world changed the scene. The governments of these states, unlike their predecessors, were in a position to effect a radical shift. They were not only influenced and guided by Western theories of government and sources of legitimacy but were also under internal pressure to modernize. It is essential to remember that at the turn of this century it was the secular outlook that dominated the intellectual and political scene in the developing Muslim countries, whether colonized or not.[40] And it was this outlook that informed the reforms, as evidenced by the enactment of modernist legislation. In almost every area of law, Western-inspired legal codes came to replace the Shari'a, considerably reducing its legal scope. It was only in the areas of family, inheritance and endowment (*waqf*) law that the Shari'a was retained.[41]

These branches survived for several reasons. First, they have traditionally been the most developed areas of Islamic law in which the ulema have the highest monopoly. It was, therefore, possible and more practical to introduce radical reforms in other areas where no rival jurisdictions existed. Secondly, in their modernizing schemes these governments were, either consciously or unconsciously, deploying the Western liberal distinction between public and private realms.[42] Family law could then be left in the hands of the ulema as it was deemed to be private and hence politically less significant. Thirdly, in this way the modernizing governments (or colonial powers) paid lip service to the Shari'a and avoided an open confrontation with its guardians.

Yet the Shari'a was not left intact. Through a series of legislations it was reformed and grafted on to modern legal systems, while through procedural rules the jurisdiction of its courts was severely limited. In this way the modern state steadily but firmly managed to extend its reach to the domains in which the Shari'a had ruled supreme for centuries. The extent to which any government succeeded in reforming the existing legal system was greatly influenced by the balance of power between conservative and modernist groups, which has remained fluid since then.[43]

Irrespective of the extent and method of reforms, the end result has been the creation of a hybrid family law, which is neither the Shari'a nor Western. Both the process of codification and the concept of a unified legal system which has the state as an enforcing authority behind it are alien to the Shari'a, for two simple reasons. First, the Shari'a in its classical form allowed fluidity in the demarcation between the moral and the legal aspects of human conduct. It was open to interpretation and capable of accommodating individual needs and circumstances. A glance at both mediaeval and contemporary legal treatises reveals that the basis of the system is more ethical than legal.

Secondly, the Shari'a was elaborated and transmitted by private scholars, based on the scholarly tradition within each school, with no direct access to judicial machinery. It is neither a case law based on precedent nor a formal legal code enforced by the state. Schacht sees its development as a 'unique phenomenon of legal science not the state playing the part of legislator'.[44] In its classical form, the Shari'a was binding primarily upon those Muslims who felt themselves in a direct relationship with God, regardless of territory and state. Even in the sphere of family law, where its hold and supremacy were uncontested, it afforded individuals a degree of choice. Here again its aim was to set 'concrete and material standards', and not to impose 'formal rules on the play of contending interests, which is the aim of secular laws'.[45] Its provisions were open-ended and flexible, with built-in mechanisms for avoiding a rule if it ran contrary to one's best interest. Examples of instances in which a rule could be circumvented are found in all areas of Shari'a law, including that of family law. In other words, a great many of its rules, including those regulating familial life, remained a matter between the individual and God, the ultimate authority. Perhaps its durability and hold can be partly imputed to the fact that there was little legal coercion to apply it. A greater portion of compulsion to conform came from one's conscience and social pressure; it was not enforced on individuals by the state.

All these factors changed totally when the Shari'a provisions became codified and enforceable by the state. As a result, not only has the traditional equilibrium between the Shari'a and the state-administered law been upset, but the Shari'a, for the first time in its history, has been given a definite legal force.

Family Law: the Last Bastion

An indirect repercussion of the political changes that resulted in state intervention in the Shari'a has been the transformation of family law into its last bastion. Two sets of factors have been at work. The first set comes from the place that family law occupies within the Shari'a. The provisions of the Koran were most abundant and explicit in the area of personal relationships, which are thus more closely intertwined with the 'sacred' in the law.[46] The second set of factors is a by-product of the process of secularization of Islamic law, an aspect of a wider process defined as 'officialization' or 'nationalization' of religion by the state.[47] The secularization of the law in other areas has had the effect of reinforcing the religious tone of those remaining branches still in the domain of the Shari'a. Paradoxically, it is precisely because there was little opposition to the abrupt abandonment of the Shari'a in other areas of law that family law became a sensitive and disputed issue. It is interesting to note that the ulema did not openly challenge the secularization of the law when governments started to introduce reforms which severely limited the scope of the Shari'a. Some felt that it was better to keep the Shari'a intact than to interfere with its substance by codification; thus its replacement was deemed a lesser evil. Others, with modernist views, favoured its incorporation and collaborated in its codification in the sphere of family law.[48]

It is only in the past two decades that attempts at further reform of the already codified family law have become a political issue, creating debates which are highly emotive and polarized. For Muslim traditionalists the Shari'a, now reduced to family law, is a sacred law upon which the most important social institution, the family, is founded. For secular modernists, the Shari'a as it stands is incompatible with modern life; they argue that Islam foresees and allows changes in family structure and relations, and that laws regulating them are not immutable. For feminists, the Shari'a is overtly discriminatory and unjust.

Today, the debate over family law is a sore spot in the Muslim psyche, revealing something of the ongoing struggle between the forces of traditionalism and modernism in the Muslim world.[49] There are two significant aspects to this debate. First, it is conducted almost entirely within the Islamic framework, indicative of the fact that the concept of an Islamic law is accepted as given. What the modernist movement objects to is not the postulate that Islam as a religion ought to regulate the sphere of law as well, but the traditional form of Islamic jurisprudence and the way in which the message of Islam has been interpreted by Muslim scholars.[50] Secondly, the debate has acquired a sharp political edge: in some instances the reforms introduced had to be dismantled either for fear of a religious backlash or in the hope of gaining political legitimacy and support.

This debate is the product of its time, bearing traces of the underlying tensions between differing world-views. At the root of the debate is the shift in the balance of power between religion and state, brought about by a host of factors, among them the bankruptcy of nationalist and modernist ideologies, as the regimes who adopted them failed to deliver their promises. Such a shift, as noted earlier, is no novelty in a Muslim scene where religious and political aims and claims are welded into a coherent system in which it is often difficult to discern the respective share of each. What is novel is the ways in which gender relations have now become an integral part of this politics, a reflection of the changed position of women in the Muslim world.[51] While in the earlier parts of the twentieth century the modernists had the upper hand and aimed to change the family in line with Western models, in its latter part it is the fundamentalists who have the upper hand and argue for a return to the traditional values and structures. At issue is the same question as that of women's emancipation: fundamentalists construe the abandonment of Shari'a family law as a threat to the Islamic order, an order which is distinctly patriarchal. Modernists see such an abandonment as a necessary step towards a more egalitarian society.

What the protagonists of this debate tend to ignore – and one of the theses of this book – is that it is an error to equate family law, as applied in today's Muslim societies, with the classical Shari'a. It is true that everywhere in Muslim countries (apart from Turkey) family law is derived at least nominally from the Shari'a, but it is equally true that its substance and its mode of application are no longer the same. The very premise of the debate is flawed, and it is bound to remain polemical unless it directs its attention toward suppressed questions, those which can provide it with an analytical basis. For instance, we know little of the ways in which Shari'a-based family law, this last bastion of the Islamic ideal of social relations, operates in today's Muslim world; whether indeed it has any significant relevance to the life of today's Muslims; and if it does, how far and through what processes it is translated into social reality.

The Anthropology of Marital Disputes

Implicit in the Muslim family law debate is the assumption that law shapes and controls behaviour and, thus, is capable of shaping social institutions. This is an old notion, shared by lawyers and policy makers. Law has often been used as an instrument of social change, although the results produced are at times unpredicted and negate the very intention of the legislator. There is another perspective, more anthropological, in which law is seen as an expression, a reflection of a particular social order. The two perspectives, however, are not mutually exclusive. Moore points out that 'law is both prescriptive and descriptive devices, i.e. [that] norms both reflect and direct social organization'. She further argues that law must be studied in this complex double image, as both directing and reflecting social organization.[52] Seen from this perspective the question then arises: 'when and under what circumstances does Islamic law direct, and when and under what conditions does it reflect?'

The 'resurgence' of Islamic law in the latter part of the twentieth century provides an opportune moment to explore some implications of this question. In Islam, law is assumed to direct but not reflect the social order; its very purpose is that of shaping society, leading it to the 'right way'. Thus we have a situation in which part of the legal process (law and its objectives) is 'fixed' and non-negotiable.[53] Yet paradoxically the process itself is highly negotiable, a fact which has been widely recognized. Flexibility and adaptability are two salient features of Islamic law, which have enabled it to be meaningful in a variety of cultural and social contexts from the outset. For instance Rosen, among others, sees the aim of Islamic law to be that of reestablishing 'the grounds upon which negotiation can proceed' and the role of the judge that of placing 'people back on the track of negotiating their own relationship'.[54]

One aim of this study is to identify the processes through which this negotiation takes place, processes which entail confrontations between the spheres of sacred and mundane. What makes the relationship between law and family special in the case of Islam is the myriad ways in which legal concepts and rules are defined and constrained by religious precepts. The fact that Muslims believe that these legal rules have their origins in the sacred sources (the Koran and the *hadith*) gives them a different kind of force and legitimacy. Therefore, another question that I believe needs to be addressed is the ways in which allusions to these legal concepts and rules are used and manipulated to legitimate or discredit behaviour.

A detailed study of marital dispute cases that make their way to courts provides a unique means of exploring the implications of these questions. Court cases represent instances in which other sanctions, religious, familial and social, have already been defied. The court system is used as the last resort. There is a great deal of stigma attached to bringing to the courts matters which belong to the private domain of the family; and here lies their unique significance. They provide insight into religious and legal precepts, as well as the personal considerations of those involved. Their analysis highlights the interplay between the three levels of reality in the realm of Muslim marriage: a sacred level embodied in the Shari'a; a legal level as reflected in modern legal codes and apparatus, which, although derived from the Shari'a, is distinct from it; and the existing practices as revealed in the choices that people make. As Moore points out, once a dispute reaches a point where it can no longer be settled between the parties but is going to involve others, 'the question of which "other" may have important effects not only on procedure, but on outcome'.[55] In this case the 'other' comprises a modern legal system empowered to uphold a model of family and familial relations with claims of divine validity.

The dominant approach in studies of Islamic law has been textual, focusing on the Shari'a texts and later on legislation.[56] Those with an anthropological approach, based on fieldwork, have focused on normative systems and the legal processes through which Islamic law is interpreted and applied.[57] The preoccupation with texts and procedure has precluded the search for more complex models of interaction of law with other social institutions. In recent years, the cultural dimensions of Islamic law have received some attention.[58] But the litigants, their perception of law, and their use of the system to meet their ends have remained generally neglected.

This study attempts to fill some of these gaps, examining the law from the perspective of those who use it.[59] Strategies adopted by litigants in the course of marital disputes give us insight into not only power relations in the family but how these relations are sustained or modified by the legal order. It is only through detailed case material that the interface between the individual and the legal form can be explored. Given that the Shari'a has always served as a frame of reference in which the past is formally invoked to legitimate the present, I believe this approach is the most appropriate.[60] It allows us to see not only ways in which religion and culture coalesce to shape the legal norms and legal forms but also how they reflect, mask, sustain or undermine the existing power structures within the family and society at large.

Methodology and Fieldwork

This study is based on materials collected in Iran and Morocco between 1985 and 1989. I began with research in the Special Civil Courts in Tehran in 1985. These are post-revolutionary courts, presided over by religious judges empowered to deal with familial disputes. My aim at the time was to examine the changes that were brought about as a result of the dismantling of the reforms introduced under Muhammad Reza Shah by the Family Protection Law of 1967, and the abolition of its courts.[61] I then became interested in the assumptions that lay behind the judgments; the different ways in which the judge and the disputing couples related to these assumptions; how the court system and its ideology were used by individuals to resolve their marital conflicts; in short, the rationale of the law, the workings of the legal apparatus, the nature of the conflicts, and the strategies adopted by those who resort to the law to break a marital impasse.

The case of Shi'a Iran could be regarded as too special and isolated in today's Muslim world: a country not part of mainstream Islam, which has experienced a revolution aiming to reverse the efforts of at least fifty years of secularization. To develop a comparative perspective, I decided to conduct a similar inquiry in a Muslim country following one of the Sunni schools of Islamic law. Morocco, which adheres exclusively to the Maliki rite, offered valuable points for comparison and contrast with Iran. In particular, the divorce rate in Morocco is high, while that in Iran is low. Situated in two geographical extremes of the Muslim world, the two countries belong to different cultural traditions. In addition, the fact that Morocco is one of the few remaining Muslim monarchies, the king claiming descent from the House of the Prophet, offered another point of contrast with Iran, previously a monarchy and now the first Islamic Republic. Whereas Iran has had no direct experience of colonization, Morocco was colonized by the French and gained its independence in 1954. Both countries have been experiencing rapid social change, in response to modernization and the influence of Western ideologies.

The legal systems of the two countries also present interesting points for comparison. In both, the Shari'a forms the basis of family law, now codified and implemented by a modern legal system.[62] Iranian family law, codified in 1935, was substantially reformed in 1967 and 1975. These reforms were partially abandoned after the creation of the Islamic Republic in 1979.[63] In contrast, Moroccan family law has remained untouched in terms of substantive law since its 1957 codification, which was a faithful translation of Maliki principles. I chose the largest cities in each country for my inquiry (Tehran in Iran; Casablanca, Rabat and Salé in Morocco). These cities are to a degree representative of the whole population as they are inhabited by migrants from other parts of the country, and all the regional groups are represented there. In addition, in large cities people tend to resort more often to formal legal systems for resolving disputes, formal and impersonal relations are more dominant, and familial and social sanctions can be more easily by-passed. In Iran, the capital city Tehran has a population of over six million. In Morocco, Rabat, the administrative capital, with its twin city Salé, have a combined population of less than one million, but Casablanca, the industrial capital, has a population of over four million.

Fieldwork in Tehran was conducted between 1985 and 1988, each year for a period of three months, and in Morocco for a total of eleven months between September 1988 and December 1989. I attended court sessions, had access to and examined current and closed (that is, completed) files, monitored the court registers, had discussions with judges and their assistants, and talked to marriage and divorce notaries and lawyers. In Morocco, the Chamber of Personal Status is a branch of the Court of First Instance with its separate filing and archive system, which made it possible to monitor the outcome of cases for any given year. I chose the year 1987 as a sample and examined all closed files for that year. In Tehran, the Special Civil Court is an independent body comprising various courts, each with its own separate filing and archive system. The outcome of cases for any given year cannot easily be monitored as there is no central archive of the closed files. Cases are indicated in a central register only when the petition is made. I monitored this central register. My quantitive data from Iran pertain therefore to current cases, and data from Morocco to closed cases of the year 1987. Court materials were supplemented by interviews with individual litigants whose cases I attended, and with others whose divorce took place without the intervention of the court, and by more general ethnographic data.

A number of personal factors may have influenced my research – my choice of topic, my perception of law, dispute cases and legal procedures and my interaction with the courts. My Iranian nationality made it possible to do fieldwork in post-revolutionary courts in Tehran, where my status as Sayyid (descendant of the Prophet) also afforded me a degree of acceptability; and being Muslim facilitated access to courts in Morocco. In Iran, fieldwork became almost impossible for non-Iranian anthropologists after the revolution. In Morocco, I was told that I was the first foreigner who was given access to the files of Personal Status disputes. Being a woman not only eased any political tension (women are not taken that seriously) but allowed me easy contact with women litigants, seeing the law from their viewpoint. Undoubtedly, all these factors, as well as my own experiences of two divorces under Islamic law, have tinted my perception of and interaction with courts and legal systems, which still are male domains.

In Tehran, where the judges are now appointed from among the clergy, well versed in the Shari'a but without much court experience, I found it difficult to explain my research objectives. Throughout my court attendance in Iran (spanning over seven years, from a short period in 1981, then from 1985 to 1988), despite my frequent explanations, I failed to convince any of the judges with whom I talked that studying court cases was a valid way of studying the Shari'a. It was seen as a futile way of attempting to understand Shari'a precepts and the law proper. I was told that if I wanted to study Islamic family law, then the court was not the right place to be: 'One studies it through authentic texts and with a *faqih* [Islamic jurist]'. Court cases, they maintained, misinform you about the Shari'a; they represent deviant cases, otherwise they would never have made their way to the court. If both parties acted in accordance with the true essence of the Shari'a, then there would be neither disharmony in marriage nor any problem in its dissolution. One judge, more sympathetic than others, concluded that I was a kind of law student, interested in legal process. He then assigned me the task of drafting court notes, the usual duty of the court clerk. This helped me a great deal to see the case from the court's viewpoint (or, more accurately, his), and I learned how to construct 'legal facts', how to translate the petitioners' grievances into court language, and how to discern the principles upon which the court operates. Later this duty became cumbersome as it prevented me from paying full attention while following the disputes during that session.

The fact that I failed to convince the religious judges in Tehran courts of the merits of a sociological approach is in itself indicative of their attitude to the Shari'a, an attitude which is more moralistic than legalistic. The situation was different in Morocco, where the judges operated within a unified secular court system and were graduates of modern law schools with knowledge of the Shari'a. Their approach was more legal and it was possible to discuss with them incongruities between law and practice, and often the ways in which the law could be amended in order to accommodate the changing situation.

In both countries, my presence in court was generally tolerated and at times welcomed. In Casablanca my access to the court files was severely limited, partly because the Court of First Instance was then going through a process of decentralization. The files were dispersed but I was allowed to attend sessions, read current files and monitor past court registers. However, a large part of the restriction imposed in Casablanca had to do with two court officials, one in charge of the filing system and the other secretary to the court president. Both men were very religious, and took an immediate dislike to my research; they saw it as irrelevant, and my approach and inquiries as Western-orientated and intrusive, and thus potentially anti-Islamic.

In Tehran, on only one occasion did my presence in the court prove to be disturbing. In 1985, at the end of one working day I found myself alone in the court room with a trainee judge who was from Qum and whose unfamiliarity with the court system was the subject of many jokes among the secular-trained court clerks. The court clerk had already left, knowing that the main judge was in a meeting, and the court attendant as usual had closed the court room. I was taking down notes from a file and the trainee judge was reading at the opposite end of the room, when suddenly he jumped up and ran towards the door, loudly cursing the devil and praising God. It was after he left the room that it dawned upon me why; a *hadith* had it all: the devil is always present whenever a man and a woman who are not *halal* (lawful) to each other are left alone. I inadvertently added to the already vast repertoire of jokes when I recounted the incident to the court clerk, who soon communicated it to his counterparts.

PART I

The Shari'a, Law and Social Practice:

Strategies of Accommodation

1

The Setting: Courts, Marital Disputes and Marriage

This chapter aims to establish a framework for the classification and analysis of marital disputes that make their way to courts, by first tracing their Shari'a origins and then placing them in the modern matrix of legal systems. In so doing it seeks to explore the assumptions behind the Shari'a notion of marriage; the adaptation of this notion by the modern legal system, as reflected in articles of the Iranian and Moroccan codes and the practice of their courts; and the different ways in which men and women utilize the court system to resolve marital conflicts, with the implicit aim of renegotiating the terms of their marriage.

The chapter comprises three sections. The first introduces courts and their procedures in Iran and Morocco. The second explores the legal basis upon which disputes are initiated by examining the rules governing marriage and its dissolution, and their underlying assumptions and implications. The third section first presents an overview of the range and type of marital disputes, and then proceeds to demonstrate how the contrasting realities of marriage in law and in practice render the court an arena for negotiations.

Legal Codes, Courts and their Procedures in Iran

Iranian family law has an uneven history.[1] Until the early decades of this century, the judiciary was the monopoly of the clergy, and family law was administered by the Shari'a courts, headed by judges trained in the Ithna 'Ashari school of Shi'a law. In 1927 Reza Shah Pahlavi initiated extensive legal reforms, aiming to create a totally secular judicial system, based on modern legal codes. Family law was codified between 1928 and 1935 as part of the Iranian Civil Code. Although in most areas of law the Civil Code shows the influence of European legal codes, in matters of personal status its provisions are, in effect, a simplification and codification of classical Ithna 'Ashari law.[2] The only major departures were those articles which set a legal age requirement for marriage, prohibiting the marriage of girls under 13 while requiring court permission for the marriage of those under 15.[3] Reforms were introduced through a separate legislation, known as the Marriage Law (*qanun-i izdivaj*), enacted in 1931. This made marriage subject to state provisions by requiring the registration of all marriages and divorces and denying legal recognition unless they were registered in civil bureaux. The law also enlarged the grounds on which women could initiate divorce proceedings and required such actions to be brought before civil courts rather than Shari'a courts.

More radical reforms were introduced in 1967 with the enactment of the Family Protection Law (*qanun-i himayat-i khanivada*). This law, regarded as among the most radical reforms of traditional divorce laws in the Muslim world, was a total departure from the Shari'a provisions.[4] It abolished the husband's rights to extra-judicial divorce and polygamy, and increased the age of marriage to 15 for females and 18 for males. It also established courts by the same name: Family Protection Courts. These new courts, headed by judges trained in modern jurisprudence, were empowered to deal with the whole range of marital disputes. In 1975, the Family Protection Law of 1967 was replaced by another law of the same title, which essentially retained the provisions of the earlier enactment. It increased the minimum age at marriage from 15 to 18 for females and from 18 to 20 for males; it introduced further modification in the areas of child custody and the financial maintenance of divorced wives. It also formally repealed all the prior laws conflicting with its provisions. Finally, the Family Protection Law of 1975 provided its courts with discretionary power to decide on the question of child custody, completely disregarding Shi'a provisions.

After its enactment in 1967 the Family Protection Law was opposed by various factions of the clergy, who regarded it as a violation of the sacred principles of the Shari'a.[5] In the early days of the revolution it was again strongly attacked by spokesmen of the Islamic Republic and declared to be non-Islamic. A return to Ithna 'Ashari provisions as embodied in the articles of the Civil Code in matters relating to the family was announced. Nevertheless, there followed an initial period of uncertainty. Family Protection Courts continued to operate until September 1979, about seven months after the Revolution, when the Special Civil Court Act was enacted.[6] This remains the only relevant legislation so far promulgated by the revolutionary regime with respect to family law. Its significance lies in the removal of family law cases from the ordinary civil courts – which dealt with such litigations under the Marriage Law of 1931 and subsequently under the Family Protection Law of 1967 and 1975 – and their relegation to courts presided over by religious judges.[7] The 'Special' in its title is indicative of its freedom from the law of evidence and procedure contained in the Civil Procedure Code. The Act itself is short, consisting of 19 articles primarily concerned with procedural rules; yet, at one stroke, it succeeded in dismantling a large part of the pre-revolutionary reforms, which were also effected through procedural devices.[8]

The Special Civil Courts of Tehran

The Special Civil Courts (*dadgah-i madani-yi khass*) are presided over by Islamic judges (*hakim-i shar'*), who are empowered to deal with the whole range of familial disputes. These are defined as disputes relating to marriage, divorce, annulment of marriage, *mahr* (dower), maintenance of wife and other dependants, custody of children, and inheritance.

In 1988, there were sixteen of these courts in Tehran, seven located in a building near the Ministry of Justice, close to the Bazaar in the centre of Tehran, and the rest scattered about the city. The head of the first court presides over all the others throughout the country, a factor which gives an additional centrality and weight to the first seven courts. These seven receive between 35 to 70 applications per day. The number of applications is highest on Saturdays and Sundays, and, as the week progresses, the flow of applications steadily decreases.[9] Two copies of an application form must be submitted to the General Office. There is a fee for each application, which the court can waive in the case of an applicant's destitution. It takes between a few days and a few months for each case to appear in court, depending on the nature of the case and the urgency required in dealing with it.

Each court has two officers: a judge trained in Islamic law in a seminary college (*hawza-yi 'ilmiyya*), and a clerk, a secular law graduate from a university; each has also its own secretariat (*daftar*). Five to seven cases are dealt with every day. The clerk processes applications at their initial stages and then refers them to the judge for the final judgment. Sessions take place in the judge's room where he sits behind an office desk, hears cases, engages in long discussions with the two parties and finally renders his judgment. Proceedings are informal and each case is presented by the litigants themselves, without the aid of lawyers. There is little emphasis on providing written testimonies. The court clerk keeps note of the proceedings of each session and of declarations made by each party, which are signed by them at the end of the session. These can serve as their testimonies if necessary. The court is bound to rule according to relevant articles of the Iranian Civil Code and post-revolutionary amendments to it.

I witnessed something of a gradual transformation in the structure and procedure of the Special Civil Courts of Tehran. In 1980, when I conducted a short period of fieldwork in one court, a secular judge was sitting next to the newly appointed religious judge. Decisions were made jointly, with the secular judge having a greater voice. At the time, the major preoccupation of the court was to offset the legacy of the Family Protection Law. Almost all its decisions involved authorizing the registration of men's second marriages or marriages of girls under the age of eighteen. The procedural rules of the Family Protection Law were more or less in effect and marriage registries declined to register such marriages. The court had to deal with each case individually. In 1985 when I resumed court attendance, a court clerk had replaced the secular judge; the clerk, unlike the secular judge, was subordinate to the religious judge and followed his instructions. Often a trainee religious judge, recently employed by the Ministry of Justice, sat in the court to be familiarized with the system. A large majority of cases involved divorce and there were no petitions for registration of second marriages, as rules of procedure had been amended to allow the registration of polygamous marriages (see Chapter 6).

Legal Codes, Courts and Their Procedures in Morocco

Moroccan family law has had a more even history. It was codified between 1957 and 1958 in the *Mudawwanat al-ahwal al-shakhsiyya* or the Code of Personal Status, commonly known as Mudawwana. The impetus for reform came second to that for unification; the aim of codification was to abolish the multiple customary codes and tribal councils that were encouraged under the French Protectorate.[10] The Mudawwana, derived from the Maliki school of law, successfully replaced the existing codes of personal status. Although marriage was subjected to state provisions which required registrations, the reforms introduced were not on the same scale as those effected in Iran in 1967 and 1975. They were more of a procedural nature, such as setting procedures for the registration of marriage and divorce and for the payment of divorce dues. In terms of substantive law, the reforms were confined to setting a minimum age for marriage (15 for a woman and 18 for a man); restricting the guardian's right of constraint (*jabr*) which suppressed a woman's right to refuse consent to her marriage;

and limiting the legal duration of pregnancy to one year. Despite several attempts at reform, the Mudawwana has remained intact since its codification; thus, unlike the Iranian case, there has been continuity.[11]

The Courts of First Instance in Casablanca, Rabat and Salé

The Chamber of Personal Status (*Ghurfat al-ahwal al-shakhsiyya*) of the Court of First Instance (*Al-Mahkama al-Ibtida'iyya*) deals with all familial disputes, which are defined in the same way as in Iran. Unlike in Iran, here the Chamber is essentially a civil court, governed by the same rules and procedures as other chambers, which are set by the Moroccan Civil Procedure Code. There are several judges serving in each chamber, empowered to rule according to the articles of the Mudawwana. In 1989, there were five judges in Casablanca, two in Rabat and two in Salé, who presided over the sessions and each dealt with a certain number of cases assigned to them by the president of the court. These judges were graduates of secular law schools; some had been trained in a Legal Institute, attached to the Ministry of Justice. Unlike in Iran, none of them was trained exclusively in *fiqh*.[12] Each chamber has its own secretariat (*daftar dabt*) which receives applications and is responsible for administrative duties such as sending summonses and notifying parties of the court decision. No special format is required and petitions may be submitted in any form. There is a fee for initiating a legal proceeding; this can be waived only in the case of an applicant's destitution, which entitles him/her to legal aid (*al-musa'ada al-qada'iyya*).

Litigation follows a more formal and lengthier procedure than in Iran. It usually takes some months for a case to appear in the court and then, depending on the type of case, several months or even years to reach the state of judgment. The court holds two types of sessions: Public (*jalsat al-'umumiyya*) and Inquiry (*jalsat al-bahth*). The Public sessions take place in the court rooms and last over an hour, during which between 30 and 40 cases are dealt with. The clerk calls out names, and parties present appear in front of the judge, who informs them of the progress of their cases, which often means telling them what document is needed. In these sessions women sit on benches on a different side of the court room from men. The two front rows are reserved for lawyers, who exchange documents with the judge.

Inquiry sessions take place in the judge's room, where the judge deals with a limited number of cases, not exceeding ten. Unlike the formal Public sessions, where the judge hurries through each case, Inquiry sessions are more relaxed and less structured. In both types of session a court clerk (*katib al-dabt*) sits next to the judge, keeping note of the procedures. There is a great emphasis on documentation and the contending parties are required to hand in their testimonies, necessitating the assistance of legal experts. As a result a large number of cases are represented by lawyers, especially during Public sessions where the parties themselves keep a low profile.

Court Files and Their Contents in Iran and Morocco

In both countries, each closed file normally contains the following documents:

1. A petition stating the case and demands made by the plaintiff (called *mudda'i* in Morocco and *khahan* in Iran). This not only reflects the grievances and demands of the petitioner but specifies the legal remedies sought. In Iran, the petition (*dadkhast*) must be written on a special form provided by the court's General Office. In Morocco, the petition (*maqal*) requires no special form. The style and wording of petitions vary considerably. Lawyers use a legal language; they first set the legal basis for the case and then list the demands in that light. Public scribes (see below) use a popular language: they first describe the marital dispute and its history, they then phrase the demands, using legal terminology.

2. A reply from the defendant (*muda'a 'alaihi* in Morocco and *khanda* in Iran), which sometimes takes the form of a counter-petition.

3. Documents submitted in support of the claims made, such as marriage or birth certificates, police or hospital reports (depending on the type of dispute).

4. The judgment (*hukm*) is the most informative piece of documentation in a file. It contains a summary of the case and its progress during the sessions, including the final demands made by the two parties, and the legal basis upon which the court decision was made. As a file very often contains two petitions, one made by the plaintiff and another made by the defendant, the judgment has two parts. In Iran the judgment is also referred to as *ra'i* (literally, opinion) and is often written by the court clerk under the direction of the judge, carrying his signature. In Morocco the judgment, drafted by the judge or his assistant, appears in the typed form.

After the judgment, petitions and counter-petitions are the next most informative documents. They can provide accurate clues to the social standing of the parties (often evident in their occupation, education and place of residence); to the marital history of each partner (for example the duration of the marriage, their ages, number of children and other marriages); to the nature and severity of the conflict, its underlying causes, and the role of the family in either causing or attempting to resolve it). Petitions also reveal something of the different but interacting realities of a marital conflict, that perceived by the law and that perceived by the spouses. They mediate between the two realms of the legal and social: through them actual marital tensions are translated into a legal language.

Parties to Disputes and Mediators

In both countries, the court is used as the last resort, when other attempts to resolve the dispute have already proved futile. There is a stigma attached to airing a private affair, such as a marital conflict, in public. Hence, the majority of those who come to the court are from the popular classes, where material needs outweigh the importance of honour, and among them women outnumber men. This is particularly true in Morocco, where the large majority of cases are initiated by women and revolve around maintenance claims. Other classes and men resort to court action when it is deemed to be an effective way of dealing with a marital impasse. This is more the case in Iran, because the intervention of the court is required when couples fail to agree on divorce.

On the whole, it is difficult to ascertain the social class of litigants during the court sessions. Great efforts are made by each party to appear poor and needy, with the aim of influencing the judge, who sets the amount of maintenance claimed. For the sessions, women take off their jewellery and dress shabbily; men underquote their earnings and hide their actual level of income. Sometimes, the files can provide one with an idea of their social and economic status on the basis of the following factors: occupation, education, place of residence, the nature of the dispute and the type of demands made. Not every file contains all this information; in some, the only data available are the names and addresses of the parties and the specific demands made.[13]

The conduct of men and women during court sessions varies greatly, reflecting their rights in law. In Morocco, where men can effect a divorce without court action, they are indignant when they are called by a judge to appear in court. A man will stand in front of the judge with his head up and argue his case, expressing fury at his wife's impertinence for petitioning against him. Women, despite comprising the bulk of petitioners, seem lost and hesitant; sometimes a woman will hand in a petition without a signature, written by a public scribe. When called to the stand, she will stand behind her husband

and keep her head and voice down. In Iran, where both men and women need a court's permission in order to register a divorce, the situation is rather different. Women appear confident and outspoken. Some of them do not hesitate to articulate their views on the injustice of a law by which they are treated as second-class citizens. This is largely the legacy of the pre-revolutionary reforms which provided a legal frame of reference in which women were treated on equal grounds with men.

In both Iran and Morocco, the majority of those who apply to the court are illiterate or, if literate, unable to express their grievances in legal language, in the form of a petition acceptable to the court. In both countries, there are professional 'petition writers', known as *katib 'umumi* (public scribe), who either sit outside the court with a typewriter, or have an office nearby. Some of them have a fixed corner in the court compound. For instance, in the Tehran court, one had a desk in the room in which tea was prepared; in the Rabat court, one had a corner in the central courtyard. They enjoy no formal attachment to the court but, over time, have acquired a sound knowledge of the law and the court system. They charge a small fee for their service, which includes writing the petition and giving advice to litigants regarding their suits. They thereby translate grievances into a courtroom language which is otherwise obscure to the majority of the population.[14]

In Morocco, the complexity of the court procedure, especially the heavy reliance on the provision of written documents, necessitates the expertise of professional lawyers. In many cases, a woman starts the case on her own and later engages a lawyer: the petition is written by a public scribe but the later correspondence is written by a lawyer. This reflects the fact that, as the case proceeds, the woman realizes that she cannot continue on her own. A substantial number of cases end in dismissal after a couple of hearings because they do not conform to the required legal format.

Taking on a lawyer serves different functions for different social groups. For the wealthy, often educated, it is a way of avoiding personal involvement in the court: the case is followed all the way through by lawyers without the attendance of the two parties involved. For the poor, often illiterate, it is a necessity in order to ensure that the case is heard by following the right format. But it does not deter petitioners, predominantly female, from attending court sessions and personally following their cases. Hiring a lawyer also validates a case; it becomes a declaration of the client's determination and confidence of winning the case: one would not pay such high fees if one was not sure of success. Spouses frequently intimidate each other by boasting about the skill and influence of their respective lawyers. This explains why even the very poor often resort to employing a lawyer, quite apart from the fact that they would have been lost in the labyrinth of the court system.[15]

In Iran, where familial disputes must be presented by the two parties personally, lawyers are of course absent. I have come across only two cases in which lawyers were engaged; in both instances it had an adverse effect and was looked upon unfavourably by the judge.

Marital Disputes and Their Legal Context

In both countries, the legal matrix within which marital conflicts are adjudicated is determined by articles of a modern code, which in turn are informed and legitimated by the Shari'a rules governing marriage and divorce. In this way, every marital dispute that reaches court has its *raison d'être* in an explicit or implicit violation of a Shari'a provision. Therefore, before discussing specific dispute cases, it is useful to delineate the salient features of marriage in Islamic law, and their reworking by the modern legal systems of Iran and Morocco.

It is important to stress, at the outset, that the following account neither aims nor claims to be an exhaustive summary of classical sources. Nor is it a critique of gender relations as perceived and constructed by Muslim jurists.[16] It merely examines these perceptions and constructions as they bear on marital disputes: they continue to define the legal reality of marriage.[17] I have relied specifically on those sources that were referred to during court sessions, either in petitions or in judgments. On Maliki law these include the works of Ibn Abi Zayd al-Qayrawani (d. 389/998) and Khalil Ibn Ishaq (d. 766/1374), popularly known as Sidi Khalil (Master Khalil). Both treatises, originally in Arabic, are also available in English and French.[18] On Shi'a law, Ayatollah Khomeini's treatise was the source frequently invoked, with occasional reference to Muhaqqiq al-Hilli (d. 676/1277) and Shahid-i Awwal (d. 786/1384), two prominent Shi'a jurists. Both sources are available in Arabic and Persian; sections of Khomeini's treatise have been also rendered into English.[19]

Marriage as Ordained: a Contract of Exchange

In both Shi'a and Maliki schools, in line with other schools of Islamic law, marriage is seen as a contract whose main function is to render sexual relations between a man and a woman licit.[20] Marriage is also seen as a religious obligation and is imbued with a host of ethical injunctions. This is particularly so because any sexual contact outside marriage constitutes the crime of *zina* (fornication) and is subject to heavy punishment.[21] Moreover, celibacy is condemned and is highly discouraged. In this way, marriage acquires a religious dimension: it becomes the means of preservation of morals and chastity through the satisfaction of sexual needs within the limit set by God.[22]

The boundaries between the ethico-religious and purely contractual bases of marriage are indeed blurred, both in law and in practice. In Islamic law, marriage is a contract, one of the very few that crosses the boundaries of its two main divisions: *'ibadat* (ritual acts) and *mu'amalat* (contracts). In spirit, marriage belongs to the *'ibadat*: it removes the sexual taboo between the sexes by making them licit (*halal*) to each other. In form, it comes under the category of *mu'amalat*: it is a civil contract and is patterned after the contract of sale, which has served as model for other contracts.[23] In practice, a marriage contract is enacted in a ceremony intertwined with religious symbolism and rituals such as the recitation of the *fatiha*, the first verse of the Koran, and the recitation of the formula is done by two religious functionaries, although the Islamic law does not positively prescribe any service.

In its legal structure, marriage is a contract of exchange with defined terms and uniform legal effects.[24] Its essential components are the offer (*ijab*) which is made by the woman or her guardian, the acceptance (*qabul*) by the man, and finally the payment of dower (*mahr* or *sadaq*). This is a sum of money or any other valuables that the husband pays or undertakes to give to the bride upon marriage. A woman has the right to refuse sexual access until she receives her dower in full. In the Maliki School, the importance of the exchange implied by the payment of dower is such that its suppression, or any conditions set in the contract that might lead to its obliteration, can render the marriage contract void.[25] In the Shi'a school, on the other hand, absence of a specified *mahr* does not void the contract but entitles the bride to a special type of *mahr* known as *mahr al-mithal*, the exemplary dower.

Shaykh Khalil, the most prominent Maliki jurist, sees the relationship of dower to marriage as follows: 'When a woman marries, she sells a part of her person. In the market one buys merchandise, in marriage the husband buys the genital *arvum mulieris*. As in any other bargain and sale, only useful and ritually clean objects may be given in dower.'[26] Such a conception is shared by the Shi'a jurists; Muhaqqiq al-Hilli, the most prominent, gives a very similar definition of marriage: 'a contract whose object is that of dominion over the vagina, without the right of its possession.'[27]

To identify certain similarities in the legal structures of marriage and sale contracts is not to suggest that Islamic law does conceptualize marriage as a sale.[28] Muslim jurists themselves have shown awareness of possible misunderstandings and are careful to enumerate the ways in which the marriage contract differs from that of sale.[29] In so doing they have gone as far as elevating marriage to the level of a religious duty, for which support is found in a number of Koranic verses and sayings attributed to the Prophet.[30] While employing the analogy of sale in discussing its legal structure, they did maintain that marriage resembles the sale contract only in form, not in spirit.[31] Even in statements such as those of Khalil and Hilli, it is clear that a distinction is made between the right over the person of the bride (which a husband does not have) and the right of access to her sexual and reproductive faculties (which he has). Such a distinction, as we shall see, has important implications for the rights and duties that marriage entails.

Marriage as Enforced: Rights and Obligations

Marriage, like any other contract, can be best understood by the rights and obligations that it creates between the contracting parties. In Islamic terminology, these are referred to as *ahkam al-zawaj*, the legal effects of marriage. With the marriage contract, a woman comes under her husband's *'isma*. *'Isma* can be translated as authority, control and protection: it entails certain rights and obligations for each party, some of them of a moral nature while others carry legal sanctions.[32]

Here again the boundaries between moral and legal obligations are hazy. In every treatise, any chapter on marriage includes a discussion of its religious merits and a list of moral injunctions that are incumbent on each spouse. Yet when it comes to the domain of positive law these moral injunctions are overshadowed by those elements of the contract that involve exchange. What separates the moral from the legal is determined by the 'purpose of marriage'. Here jurists generally agree that the prime purposes of marriage are the gratification of sexual needs and procreation.[33] Whatever serves or follows from the purpose of the marriage contract falls within the range of the duties of both spouses to be enforced. The rest, though still morally correct, remain legally unenforceable, left to the conscience of individuals. As will become clear in the course of the following chapters, since marriage is essentially a civil contract there remains some room for modifications, at both societal and personal levels.

A similar vagueness of definition is to be found in the modern legal codes of Iran and Morocco. This is not surprising since the marriage and divorce chapters of the Iranian Civil Code (ICC) and the Moroccan Code of Personal Status (MCPS) are in effect eclectic translations of dominant opinions on *ahkam al-zawaj* within Shi'a and Maliki jurisprudence respectively. Despite remaining faithful to the Shari'a conception of marriage and retaining its contractual nature, both codes have attempted to incorporate some of its moral aspects.[34] This is more so in the case of the MCPS, whose first article defines marriage as:

> A legal pact through which a man and a woman unite with the aim of establishing a durable and common conjugal life under the authority of the man on the basis of fidelity, purity and a desire to procreate and fulfil their reciprocal duties in security, peace and affection.

The ICC, on the other hand, does not attempt any definition of marriage, but directly sets out the rights and obligations created by the contract. This is perhaps due to difficulties involved in providing a definition that can cover temporary marriage, which is only recognized by the Ithna 'Ashari school. Temporary marriage entails neither living together nor procreation.[35] In spite of the code's silence, Iranian jurists give some definitions of marriage. For instance, in a legal commentary on the Civil Code, Imami, a secular jurist, defines marriage as 'a legal relationship established by *'aqd* (contract) between a man and a woman entitling them to sexual enjoyment'.[36] Muhaqqiq-Damad, a religious scholar and author of a recent book entitled *The Principles of Marriage and Divorce in Islam*, has modified Imami's definition in the following way: 'Marriage (*nikah*) is a legal-emotional relationship established through *'aqd* between a man and a woman, entitling them to cohabit; the dominant feature of this relationship is that of the right to sexual enjoyment from each other.'[37]

Despite their differing definitions of marriage, both codes agree as to the rights and duties that it gives rise to. These are expressed in a number of articles, and since these articles constitute the grounds upon which disputes are heard in courts, it is useful to outline them here. They fall into three categories.

1. Those which are reciprocal:
   - good treatment (Articles 1103 of ICC and 34/2 of MCPS);
   - cooperation in strengthening the foundation of the family and raising children (Articles 1104 of ICC and 1, 34/4 and 36/3 of MCPS);
   - inheritance from each other (Articles 940 of ICC and 34/3 of MCPS).
2. Those which are exclusively the wife's rights, and thus the husband's obligations:

- her right to refuse cohabitation prior to receiving her dower as stipulated in the contract (Articles 1085 of ICC and 21 of MCPS);
- her right to be maintained by the husband (Articles 1106 of ICC and 35/1 of MCPS);
- her right to control and dispose of her own wealth (Articles 1118 of ICC and 35/4 of MCPS);[38]
- her right to be treated equitably if she is a co-wife (Article 35/2 of MCPS);
- her right to visit and receive her close kin (Article 35/3 of MCPS).[39]

3. Those which are the husband's rights and the wife's obligation:
   - his right to contract four marriages simultaneously;[40]
   - his right to the headship of the family (Articles 1105 of ICC and 1 of MCPS);
   - his right to choose the place of residence and insist that his wife reside in the house chosen by him (Articles 1114 of ICC and 1, 34/1 of MCPS);
   - his right to his wife's obedience (Articles 1108 of ICC and 36/2 of MCPS);
   - his right to control her outside activities: he can prevent her from undertaking a profession or trade if it is not stipulated in the contract (Articles 1117 of ICC and 38 of MCPS);
   - his right to demand that she run his house (Article 36/4 of MCPS);
   - his right to demand that she shows respect towards his family (Article 36/5 of MCPS);[41]
   - his right to the termination of marriage (Articles 1133 of ICC and 82 of MCPS).

Two basic attributes of marriage in law can be inferred. First is the non-reciprocal and unequal emphasis in the rights and obligations of spouses. Each spouse has a separate sphere of duties and obligations. The only shared space is that involving the procreation and raising of children. Even here, according to ICC (Article 1176) a woman is not expected to suckle her child unless it is impossible to feed him otherwise.

The second attribute is the absence of any kind of matrimonial regime. There is no common ownership of marital goods. What a woman brings into a marriage remains hers and she has no right over the wealth accumulated during the marriage. The husband is responsible and must provide for her and their children, regardless of her or his financial circumstances. Such disparities in rights and duties are perceived and justified by modern Muslim writers as a natural result of the differing but complementary biological and psychological dispositions of men and women. A woman's economic autonomy, and the fact that she receives but is not required to contribute to the expenses of the household, are seen as proof of her high status in law and the esteem in which she is held by her husband.[42]

Both these attributes are the legal consequences of the Shari'a conception of marriage, dominated by two presuppositions: Women render their sexual favours; and in return they gain the right to maintenance. From this follows that which is binding on both of them; the rest is assigned to the domain of moral obligations. As we shall see in the next chapter, the Moroccan Code's attempt to give legal force to some of these moral obligations, such as cooperation between spouses, good treatment and mutual respect, proves to be ineffective.

Marriage as Terminated: Divorce in the Shari'a

Marriage can often be best understood by examining the rules and modes governing its dissolution: they not only tell us how marriage is defined, but reveal where the boundaries of appropriate marital relations are set. In both Iran and Morocco, despite reforms, the Shari'a perspective on divorce has remained intact and its rules continue to regulate contemporary divorces. It is therefore useful to examine them in some detail.[43]

Dissolution of marriage is permitted under four modes: *talaq*, or repudiation of the wife by the husband; *khul'* and *mubarat*, or termination of the marriage contract by mutual consent (initiated by the wife and accepted by the husband); *tatliq*, or separation by the decree of the court; and *faskh*, or annulment of the marriage contract.

To translate any of these forms as 'divorce' would be simplistic.[44] Only *tatliq* resembles divorce in the Western sense; the rest have different legal implications. However, *talaq* is conventionally used loosely in a general sense to cover all modes of dissolution of marriage, and I shall continue to use 'divorce' in the same sense.

Talaq *(repudiation)*

Talaq, in its specific sense, has often been translated as 'repudiation'. Legally, it is the absolute and exclusive power of the man to terminate the marriage, a right granted to him by a Koranic injunction.[45] He needs no grounds and his mere pronouncement of the *talaq* formula will result in the dissolution of the marital bonds; neither the consent nor the presence of the wife is required. *Talaq* is condemned by the Shari'a; a tradition has the Prophet referring to it as a lawful (*halal*) act which is most hateful to God. Yet it is effected with the utmost facility and classical Islamic law has made little attempt to contain *talaq*. In its legal structure, *talaq* is an act of *iqa'*, as opposed to marriage which is an act of *'aqd*. The difference between them is that *'aqd* is a type of legal act that involves the consent of the two parties, its formula containing the offer and acceptance; while *iqa'* is a unilateral act which acquires legal effect merely through the declaration of one party; in the case of *talaq*, the husband.[46]

The Shari'a recognizes two major forms of *talaq* procedures: regular (*talaq al-sunna*) and irregular (*talaq al-bid'a*).[47] In the regular forms the husband can only utter the *talaq* formula when his wife is in a state of purity (*tuhr*), between menses. The most approved form is known as *ahsan* (the best) in which the husband pronounces one *talaq* when the wife enters the period of purity, that is when she is free from her menstrual flow; he then abstains from sexual intercourse with her. Therewith she enters the period of waiting (*'idda*) which lasts three menstrual cycles. The marriage terminates only at the end of this period, during which he has the right to revoke his decision and take the wife back without any formalities. Another approved form, which is known as *hasan* (good), is a definite repudiation in which the husband repeats the *talaq* formula three times in the course of the wife's three purity periods. The third pronouncement has the effect of producing *talaq al-thalath* (literally, the triple repudiation). This creates a bar to marriage between the couple which can be removed only after she has contracted and consummated marriage with a different man who then releases her; its removal is known as *tahlil* (literally, solution).[48]

Irregular forms of *talaq* are referred to as *talaq al-bid'a*, a term which implies innovation, a deviation from the divine prescriptions. In these forms of *talaq* the above procedure, deduced from Koranic injunctions, is not followed. A husband can effect a definite and triple *talaq* by repeating the formula thrice in one session, or outside the purity period. Although these rules do not conform to the Koranic prescriptions, they have gained currency in practice.[49]

The Shi'a school shares the precepts of the Sunni schools on the issue of *talaq*. It differs on procedure by attaching more formality to it, recognizing only the regular forms of *talaq* as valid. It also requires the pronouncement of *talaq* to take place orally in the presence of two male witnesses; the exact term *talaq* or one of its derivatives must be used. The utterance of the formula is valid only if there is a definite intention on the part of the husband.[50]

Sections on *talaq* in the Iranian and Moroccan Codes reflect the above precepts. A man can repudiate his wife at will and does not need to produce any grounds (Articles 1133 of ICC and 44 of MCPS). Yet to do so he needs to follow the procedure which is set by the code; both codes have made validity of divorce dependent on following the procedure defined under the Regular Forms of *talaq* (Articles 1134 to 1142 of ICC and 44 to 52 of MCPS). In this way, both codes have attempted to limit a man's arbitrary exercise of his right to *talaq*; both the nature and the degree of these attempts will be explored in the next chapters.

Aside from procedure, both codes recognize two major types of *talaq*: *raj'i* (revocable) and *ba'in* (irrevocable). *Talaq al-raj'i* is a suspended form of repudiation in which the bond of marriage is not severed upon the pronouncement of the *talaq* formula; it becomes final only when the wife completes three menstrual cycles. During this waiting period, known as *'idda*, the wife cannot remarry and the husband has the right to return to marriage. She is, however, entitled to maintenance and in case of the death of one party the other's right to inheritance remains intact.

Talaq al-ba'in is an irrevocable repudiation in which the dissolution of marriage is final from the moment of the pronouncement of the divorce formula. Nevertheless the wife must observe the same period of waiting during which she is entitled to maintenance only if she is pregnant, though in the Moroccan Code she retains a claim to lodging. A repudiation is irrevocable only in the following conditions: if the marriage has not been consummated; if the woman is past her menopause; if the wife has not reached the age of menstruation; or if it is the third successive repudiation: the last creates the bar to marriage between the couple.[51]

Khul' *and* Mubarat *(divorce by mutual consent)*

These two types of dissolution of marriage, unlike *talaq*, involve the active participation of the wife. In *khul'*, separation is initiated by the wife, who secures the consent of her husband by offering him an inducement to release her. The Muslim jurists define *khul'* as a separation claimed by the wife as a result of her extreme reluctance (*ikrah*) towards her husband. An essential element of *khul'* is the payment of compensation (*'awad*) to the husband in return for her release. This can be the dower or any other form of compensation. Etymologically, *khul'* means to take off, for instance one's clothes, and hence 'to lay down one's authority over a wife'. This is also interpreted as an allusion to the Koranic metaphor which refers to husband and wife as clothing and covering one another. In this way, a woman expresses her reluctance to be close to her husband.[52] Another variation of this separation, in which the reluctance is mutual and the amount of compensation should not exceed the value of the dower itself, is *mubarat*, which denotes the act of mutual release.

Unlike *talaq*, these two forms of separation do not come under the category of unilateral acts (*iqa'at*). They come under *'aqd* (contract), as their essential prerequisite is the consent of the husband. In practice, all divorces by mutual consent are of the *khul'* type in both countries. The Moroccan Code does not mention *mubarat* but devotes five articles to *khul'* (Articles 61 to 65) in which it is stressed that if the wife has reached majority, she can perform a *khul'* without the consent of her guardian, and if she is poor, she cannot give as compensation to her husband something to which her children have also a right. The Iranian Code makes a distinction between *khul'* and *mubarat* (Articles 1146 and 1147), and recognizes them as irrevocable unless the wife claims back the compensation that she has paid (Article 1145/3).

Tatliq *(judicial dissolution)*

Tatliq is the outlet foreseen by the Shari'a in the event of a husband's refusal to release his wife from the bond of marriage. *Tatliq* requires the intervention of the court and the power of the judge either to compel the husband to pronounce a divorce or to pronounce it on his behalf upon the application of the wife. The facility and the grounds upon which a woman can demand the dissolution of her marriage vary in rites within the Shari'a. The Maliki rite is the most liberal and grants woman the widest grounds upon which she can initiate divorce proceedings. The Shi'a Ithna 'Ashari recognizes only one ground: the husband's impotence.[53]

Distinct from *khul'* and *tatliq*, both Maliki and Shi'a schools allow a woman to dissolve her marriage if the husband agrees to grant her such a right at the time of the contract or subsequently. This is done by inserting a stipulation in the marriage contract by which the husband authorizes the wife to release herself under certain conditions, for instance in the event of his marrying a second wife without her consent. This neither affects the husband's right to *talaq* nor enables the wife to dissolve the marriage by the mere occurrence of the inserted condition. The separation is effected by the judge as the wife needs to prove to the court that the stipulated condition was reached and then ask for a judicial dissolution.[54] As we shall see, in Morocco this principle, embodied in a special type of divorce recognized by Maliki law, has become more or less defunct in practice, whereas in Iran it has served as the basis for reforms.[55]

Faskh *(annulment)*

Faskh is different from other forms of dissolution of marriage so far dealt with, in both its legal structure and its effects.[56] It occurs under one of two circumstances: as a result of a fault in the marriage contract itself (either in its substance or in its form); or as a result of the absence or presence of a condition in one of the parties. The Maliki school admits only the first situation: a marriage is annulled when there is an irregularity in the contract itself, such as the absence of *mahr* or the couple being within the prohibited degrees.[57] The Shi'a school, in addition to the first category, allows annulment if there exists a physical or mental deformity in one of the parties. Consequently, the Iranian Code devotes an entire section (Articles 1121 to 1132) to *faskh*, which comes under Book Two, dealing with dissolution of marriage. On the other hand, the Moroccan Code refers to it only in passing and only in terms of its implications for the payment of dower and the validity of marriage (Articles 22 and 37).[58]

Although *faskh* like *talaq* is a unilateral act and comes under the category of *iqa'at* in Islamic law, it differs from it in five main ways. (1) It does not follow the formalities of *talaq*: the pronouncement of a certain formula, the presence of witnesses, women being in the state of purity. (2) Both parties have an equal right to seek annulment of the marriage. (3) The wife is not entitled to any portion of her *mahr* if annulment occurs before the consummation of the marriage; she is entitled to half of her *mahr* only if the annulment is due to her husband's impotence. (4) Although the woman needs to observe the same waiting period as in *talaq*, in *faskh* the husband has no right to resume marital relations within this period. (5) *Faskh*, regardless of how many times it happens between the same couple, does not create a temporary or permanent bar between them, whereas the third *talaq* creates the temporary bar and the ninth *talaq* creates a permanent prohibition.[59]

Having discussed the Shari'a rules regulating the dissolution of the marriage contract, we can summarize their salient features as follows.

1. Marriage can be easily ended, but the constructions of men's and women's rights in its termination are highly unequal.
2. In the Shari'a, the dissolution of marriages, unlike the making of marriage, is a unilateral act when it is desired by men.

3. Both the types of marriage dissolution and the nature of the payments involved suggest that a man's right to divorce emanates from his paying *mahr*. He has to forfeit what he paid as *mahr* if he takes the initiative to repudiate the wife; and he regains the *mahr* if the wife initiates the termination of the contract. Consistent with the logic of marriage as a contract, his right can be relinquished only through compensation; therefore the wife must pay in order to be on an equal footing with him.
4. The concept of a wife's right to alimony or any kind of support beyond the waiting period is absent. The man is required to provide maintenance only during the waiting period.

Marriage as Negotiated: an Overview of Court Cases

In practice, marriage involves a host of customary relations, obligations and duties, which go far beyond the Islamic conception of rights and duties outlined above. Yet it is this conception that provides the only legitimate framework within which marital disputes can be articulated and eventually adjudicated. In this way either the law must be circumvented or the definition of reality is subject to bargaining; either of which renders the court an arena for negotiations.[60] The strategies deployed to bridge the gap between law and reality reveal as much about the boundaries of law and practice as about the realities of marriage. Let us look at marriage through dispute cases.

To give an idea of the range and type of marital disputes that appear in the courts of Iran and Morocco, I have chosen one week's record of all familial dispute cases. Table 1.1 summarizes a week's cases heard in Public Sessions in the courts of Rabat, Salé and Casablanca; and a week's register of marital disputes in Tehran.[61] It covers all the cases that appeared in these courts during the chosen weeks and classifies the disputes according to type (the main demand) and plaintiff (man or woman).[62]

The table is not an exhaustive compilation of possible variations of marital dispute cases, but it presents an accurate synopsis of the range of disputes that the courts are likely to deal with in the course of a week. Before any examination of the data it contains and their implications, we need to look at the categories into which the courts have classified these disputes, and find out what they stand for.[63]

I. Maintenance (*nafaqa*) cases are initiated exclusively by women. They involve extant marriages in which women seek the enforcement of their right to maintenance. Cases classed as 'return to marital home' are exclusively brought by men. They are referred to in Morocco as *ruju' li-bait al-zawjiyya* (literally, return to marital home), and in Iran as *ilzam bi tamkin* (literally, enforcing

Table 1.1 *Marital Dispute Cases According to the Sex of the Petitioner*

Demand	Tehran (Feb. 88)	Rabat (Feb. 89)	Salé (April 89)	Casablanca (June 89)	Total
	Petitions made by women				
I. Maintenance (*nafaqa*)	43	39	48	52	182
II. Divorce (*talaq or tatliq*)	80	11	5	20	116
III. Divorce dues (*wajibat al-talaq*)	–	4	3	6	13
IV. Custody (*hadana*)	13	11	10	15	49
V. Return of goods (*irja' al-hawa'ij*)	3	4	4	12	23
VI. Dower (*mahr*)	5	–	–	–	5
VII. Proof of marriage (*thubut al-zawjiyya*)	6	–	–	–	6
Total women	150	69	70	105	394

Table 1.1 *continued*

Demand	Tehran (Feb. 88)	Rabat (Feb. 89)	Salé (April 89)	Casablanca (June 89)	Total
		Petitions made by men			
I. Return to marital home (*ruju'* or *tamkin*)	46	15	11	22	94
II. Divorce (*talaq*)	52	–	–	–	52
III. Divorce dues	–	4	1	4	9
IV. Custody (*hadana*)	5	1	–	2	8
VII. Proof of marriage (*thubut al-zawjiyya*)	8	–	–	–	8
VIII. Remarriage (*izdiwaj mujaddad*)	7	–	–	–	7
Total men	118	20	12	28	178
Total cases	268	89	82	133	572

obedience). They are in effect men's response to *nafaqa* claims made by their wives.

II.   Cases of *talaq* in Iran are demands to register divorce, which can be initiated by either men or women. Cases of *tatliq* in Morocco are brought exclusively by women, since a Moroccan man can initiate divorce and register it without either the consent of his wife or a court order.

III.   Cases of divorce dues (*wajibat al-talaq*) pertain to Morocco. They involve recent divorces effected by men, in which one party objects to the divorce dues set by the Notary Judge. Disputes of this nature in Iran involve extant marriages and come under demand for divorce, as a man needs the court's permission to register a divorce.

IV.   *Hadana* (literally, custody) cases are disputes over custody arrangements and payments. Unlike the first three categories they relate to marriages already terminated.

V.   Cases of *irja' al-hawa'ij* are brought by women demanding the return of the trousseau. They usually follow recent divorces or separations.

VI.   *Mahr* cases, which are brought solely by women, are relevant only to Iran. They stem from the particularity of practice in urban Iran, which enables women to claim their dower (*mahr*) whenever they wish.

VII.   *Thubut al-zawjiyya* cases concern disputes over the validity of a marriage; they can be brought by both spouses. In Iran they mainly involve the recognition of a temporary marriage and in Morocco that of an unregistered one. In Morocco, they also involve claims of paternity and are always brought by women, when a child is born in a non-registered union.

Table 1.1 reveals something of the dynamics of marital relations as defined by law and as articulated by men and women. In reading it, two points must be borne in mind. First, the classification of cases according to dispute category is fluid and subject to change; a case classified as 'maintenance' or 'custody' can involve other demands too. In fact, these entries show the possible stages through which a single marital dispute can go before it ends. A dispute commonly starts as a maintenance claim; it may then progress into a divorce petition and involve dower or other claims.

Secondly, the table must not be taken at its face value; it would be misleading to make any deductions about the cause and nature of marital conflicts on the basis of what the table reveals in terms of demands made by petitioners. These categories, rather than revealing the real nature of marital conflicts, reflect the legal avenues open for expressing grievances and seeking legal solutions to them. This factor also must be taken into consideration when comparing Iran and Morocco. Some differences, as will become clear, have their roots in the differing legal positions adopted by the Shi'a and Maliki jurists on certain judicial issues. These positions, which represented different shades of interpretation within the Shari'a, became ossified when opinion within each school was selected for codification.[64]

To highlight differences between Iran and Morocco, and then, within each country, the differences between men and women in terms of demands made, in Table 1.2 I have combined the data from the courts in Morocco into one group.

Table 1.3 relates dispute types to sex of petitioners, including only those disputes in which the marital link is not legally severed: cases such as a request for return of goods or child custody, in which the battle is extended beyond divorce, are excluded.

Two initial observations can be made. First, in both countries, women constitute the majority of petitioners, but by a much greater margin in Morocco than in Iran. Secondly, in Iran men and women appear to seek similar solutions to marital conflicts: both are more likely to ask for a divorce. This is not the case in Morocco where women's demand overwhelmingly centres on *nafaqa*.

To understand what these tables reveal about marriage and the legal system in each country, we need to by-pass dispute categories for the time being and explore the data from a different perspective, that of the litigants. What are these cases about? What do men and women aim to gain by bringing their marital problems to court? What aspects of marital rights and duties do they invoke? What role is played by legal rules and procedures in the articulation of marital conflicts in each country? What strategies are available to men and women in each country? Although these are the questions to be explored in the course of the coming chapters, some general remarks are in order at this stage.

Table 1.2 *Distribution of Cases by Country and Sex of Petitioner, based on Data in Table 1.1*

Petitioner	Iran		Morocco	
	no	*%*	*no*	*%*
Women	150	56	244	80
Men	118	44	60	20
Total	268	100	304	100

Table 1.3   *Distribution of Disputes in Extant Marriages by Country and Sex of Petitioner*

Type of dispute	Iran		Morocco	
	no	%	*no*	%
I. Petitioned by women				
Maintenance (*nafaqa*)	43	20	139	62
Divorce (*tatliq*)	80	37	36	16
II. Petitioned by men				
Return to marital home (*ruju'*)	41	19	48	22
Divorce (*talaq*)	52	24	–	–
Total	216	100	223	100

Nafaqa: *the ultimate strategy*

One important fact about marital dispute cases that needs to be borne in mind is that they have two interacting levels, or contain two agenda. That which is stated reflects the legal reality; that which is not articulated reflects the social reality. These two levels interact and define each other, but in petitions we come across only the stated one. This, as the above tables suggest, revolves around the question of maintenance (*nafaqa*) in the form of demands either to receive it or to be relieved from it. Two factors render a claim for *nafaqa* an effective strategy in the course of a marital dispute. First, *nafaqa* epitomizes the network of rights and obligations created by Muslim marriage. Secondly, it is the only element of marital obligation that is translated into positive law and has the power of enforcement.[65]

Legally speaking, *nafaqa*, a woman's right to maintenance, comes into effect when the marriage is consummated.[66] This right is absolute: it can neither be waived by agreement nor delegated. The husband remains responsible for his wife's maintenance even if he is without means and she can provide for herself. Both Shi'a and Maliki law agree on the basic components of *nafaqa*. These are: food, lodging and clothing; a woman acquires the right of possession (*milkiyyat*) only as regards food, and for the rest she has the right of use (*intifa'*).[67] There are, however, some minor differences. For instance, in Maliki law *nafaqa* includes medical care in case of sickness, while in Shi'a law, it includes only expenses related to minor illnesses.[68]

The rules that qualify and disqualify a woman for *nafaqa* revolve around the twin themes of sexual access and compensation.[69] A woman becomes entitled to it only after the consummation of marriage and she loses her right to claim it if she is in a state of disobedience (*nushuz*).[70] *Nushuz* literally means 'rebellion' and it implies the abandonment of marital duties. Interestingly, despite the fact that it is acknowledged that abandonment of marital duties can take place on the part of both spouses, in both Maliki and Shi'a sources the term *nashiza* (rebellious) is used only in the feminine form and in relation to maintenance rights.

Manifestations of *nushuz* are defined as acts which hamper the purpose of marriage, which is held to be that of sexual gratification and procreation. These acts can range from overt denial of sexual access to covert ones, such as not being physically available by leaving the marital home without the husband's permission; or not removing a condition which creates aversion in him. No other forms of rebellion, such as her refusal to do housework or her neglect of the husband and children, are mentioned as manifestations of a woman's *nushuz*.[71]

The modern legal codes of both countries have simplified the concept of *nushuz* and recognize abandonment of the marital home by either spouse as its manifestation. Although they agree on the principle that a disobedient woman is not entitled to maintenance, they differ on how this principle ought to be applied. The difference arises from a subtle legal point on the question of when *nafaqa* becomes incumbent on the husband, which goes back to the classical interpretations. There are two positions: first, *nafaqa*, like *mahr*, becomes incumbent on the man with the act of consummation. Only *nushuz* (the wife's non-submission) frees the husband from his duty to pay *nafaqa*, provided that she is capable of sexual access (that is, has reached puberty) and does not deny it. This position is adopted by the Maliki jurists and is also reflected in the Moroccan Code (Article 123). The second position holds that *nafaqa* becomes incumbent on the husband only as a result of the wife's submission, not simply as a result of the marriage contract (*'aqd*).[72] This position reflects the views of the majority of Muslim jurists and was adopted by Shi'a jurists and incorporated in the Iranian Civil Code (Article 1108).

These two positions have different legal implications, leading to two different procedures in dealing with *nafaqa* disputes. According to the Moroccan procedure, it is the husband who has to prove his wife's non-submission, as *nafaqa* becomes incumbent on him upon consummation. Therefore, as long as *nushuz* is not proved, a woman continues to have a claim to *nafaqa*. In the Iranian procedure, it is the woman who must prove her *tamkin* (submission), and she is not entitled to *nafaqa* unless her submission is proved, as *nafaqa* becomes

Table 1.4 Casablanca (Anfa Prefecture) 1987: Outcome of All Closed Cases Initiated According to Decision and the Sex of the Petitioner.[75]

Demand	Judicially decided				Not decided						Total	
	Accepted		Rejected		Withdrawn		Abandoned		Dismissed			
	no	%	no	%	no	%	no	%	no	%	no	%
Women	524	88	23	66	281	64	288	76	198	67	1314	76
Men	73	12	12	34	160	36	89	24	87	33	421	24
Total	597	100	35	100	441	100	377	100	285	100	1735	100
%	34		2		25		22		17		100	

incumbent on the husband only as a consequence of her submission. It is this difference that is partly responsible for the higher percentage of *nafaqa* cases in Morocco. A woman can claim it even if she has left the marital home, since the onus of proof of *nushuz* is on the husband. In Iran, a woman can claim it only if she remains in the marital home since the onus of proof is on her. To abandon the marital home without a Shari'a reason (*dalil-i shar'i*), means losing her claim to maintenance.[73]

Courts: arenas for negotiations

Another important fact about marital dispute cases, differentiating them from other court cases, is that a large majority of them never reach the state of judicial decision. This is not surprising, given that in a large majority of these disputes the marriage has already broken down and thus the hidden agenda is the negotiation of the terms of divorce. The case is withdrawn if the negotiations are successful; if they prove futile, the case is abandoned. Sometimes the best course of action is to abandon the case rather than take it to another stage. An examination of the closed files confirms these points. The following tables are based on data from Morocco; the Iranian situation, as will become clear in the next chapter, is quite similar.[74]

Table 1.4, based on data from Casablanca, shows the outcome of all cases that appeared in 1987. Cases are tabulated according to the sex of the petitioner and whether they reached a judicial decision or not. The former are in turn divided according to whether the court's decision was in favour, accepting their demands (*qabul al-talab*), or the court rejected the demand (*rafd al-talab*). Those cases which did not come to judgment fall into three categories: first, those in which an agreement was reached outside the court, and thus the petition was withdrawn (*tanazul*). These files contain a document indicating that the two parties made peace (*sulh*). Secondly, there are those instances in which the petitioner abandoned the case. When a litigant or his/her lawyer fail to appear in the sessions, the case enters the state of *tashtib* (cancel, cross out), which lasts for two months, at the end of which the judge annuls the case (*ilgha' al-da'wa*). Thirdly, there are the cases that were dismissed by the court either on the grounds of non-competence or because of the lack of a required document (usually the marriage contract); this is referred to as *'adam al-qabul al-da'wa* and is different from the other two categories of non-judged cases in the sense that it is the court that ends the case, not the petitioners.

As the table suggests, only 36 per cent of all cases reach the state of judicial decision, but among them the overwhelming majority (about 94 per cent) are decided in favour of the petitioner. Women not only outnumber men in all categories, but their petitions appear to have a greater chance of being accepted by the court (40 per cent as opposed to 17 per cent for men). On the other hand, a larger proportion of men (37 per cent as opposed to 21 per cent for women) tend to conclude the case by reaching a mutual agreement outside the court. This is referred to as *sulh* (literally, peace), which does not necessarily mean reaching a new balance in a marital relation; it often entails its termination.

Further evidence of the fact that the court functions as an intermediary is to be found in the relationship between the stage of a marital dispute and its outcome. The entries in Tables 1.5 and 1.6 have been arranged in a way to reveal something of the stage and severity of the marital dispute. These can be inferred from the date of the first petition and the wording of the demands. Specific demands that are made beside *nafaqa* qualify and add information to the general use of the term. For instance, cases which come under *nafaqa* and child custody payments involve disputes with a much longer history than those of *nafaqa* alone. The former indicate that the marital unit broke up some time earlier and the children are now with the wife. Cases in which the conflict is relatively recent (one criterion is the lack of prior court records) stand a greater chance of reaching settlement out of court. Cases with long-standing court records tend to reach a judicial decision, which often means that the conflict is not terminated but has been taken to another stage. This is especially true when a *nafaqa* demand is a cover for a divorce petition. On the other hand, petitions made shortly after the climax of a conflict – which usually coincides with the desertion of the marital home by one of the spouses – rarely reach judicial decision. This indicates the fact that the court order, or the very possibility of it, can precipitate the termination of a dispute.[76]

These tables reveal that the court system is used in different ways and for different purposes by men and women. The larger number of cases brought by women is a reflection of the unequal nature of marital rights and obligations. Women resort to court to improve their bargaining position *vis à vis* their husbands. Men come to court to offset – or preempt – their wives' actions. A woman's winning card is to demand maintenance and a man counters by demanding her submission, the only legal way of preempting or defying a *nafaqa* order. These strategies are often successful: 30 per cent of *nafaqa* and 42 per cent of *ruju'* cases ended in *tanazul*, withdrawal of the case, indicating that an agreement was reached outside the court.

The diametrically opposed nature of demands made by each party can be understood only in the light of the above. The wife states that she has been maltreated and forced out of the marital home;

Table 1.5 *Casablanca 1987: Outcome of All Closed Cases Initiated by Women According to the Main Demand Stated in the Petition.*

Demand	Judicially decided		Withdrawn	Not decided	Dismissed	Total	
	Accepted	Rejected		Abandoned		no	%
Nafaqa (maintenance)	133	7	219	218	159	736	56
Nafaqa and consummation of marriage	6	–	4	4	6	20	2
Nafaqa and separate housing	22	–	–	–	–	22	2
Nafaqa and good treatment	18	–	2	1	–	21	2
Nafaqa and childbirth expenses	35	–	4	7	4	50	4
Nafaqa and establishment of paternity	18	–	3	10	–	31	2
Nafaqa and remainder of dower	13	3	5	6	4	31	2
Nafaqa and divorce	53	5	35	33	21	147	11
Nafaqa and child custody payments	215	6	8	7	3	239	18
Custody	11	2	1	2	1	17	1
Total	524 (40%)	23 (2%)	281 (21%)	288 (22%)	198 (15%)	1314	100

Table 1.6 *Casablanca 1987: Outcome of All Closed Cases Initiated by Men According to the Main Demand Stated in the Petition.*

Demand	Judicially decided		Withdrawn	Not decided Abandoned	Dismissed	Total	
	Accepted	Rejected				no	%
Ruju' (return to marital home)	49	5	132	67	63	316	73
Seeking a solution	4	1	9	5	5	24	6
Payment reduction	9	6	12	13	25	65	15
Paternity denial	5	–	5	4	4	18	4
Visiting children	6	–	2	–	–	8	2
Total	73 (17%)	12 (3%)	160 (37%)	89 (20%)	97 (23%)	431	100

the husband denies her claims and says that she left of her own accord. To prove his good will, he must demand her return; to prove her sincerity, she must declare her willingness to go back, a token of her obedience. But how do judges reach a decision in the face of such conflicting claims?

In Morocco, the judge deals with each demand separately and accepts both demands ' if each party succeeds in providing the necessary proofs. Thus, the decision usually contains two parts: the first part orders the wife to return to the marital home and the other requires the husband to pay the *nafaqa* due for the period claimed by the wife. Neither claim precludes the validity of the other. This is not the case in Iran, where the validity of one claim excludes the other. As discussed earlier, this is due to the position adopted by the Iranian code which requires the wife to prove her submission in order to be granted a court order for *nafaqa*. In practical terms, this means that the court does not issue the order as long as the husband is successfully contesting it, thus *nafaqa* plays a different negotiating role.

Concluding Remarks

The law and court procedures not only define the nature of the dispute but determine who comes to the court and the demands that can be made. If we go back to the preceding tables and read them in this light, we can see that differences in dispute categories between Iran and Morocco reflect their differing legal realities. For instance, the higher percentages of men among petitioners in Iran is due to the fact that men cannot register a divorce without their wives' consent. This places them almost on the same footing as their wives in terms of the need to resort to court action. In Morocco, men are drawn to court only because of their wives' actions. Likewise the greater proportion of *nafaqa* cases in Morocco is due to the easier procedure for claiming it. The same logic applies to the absence of requests for divorce and permission to contract a second marriage by men in Morocco. Their legal rights to register divorce and subsequent marriages make such demands redundant.

Yet, in both countries, courts are used essentially as arenas for renegotiating marriage, especially by women. A court order can give them a degree of official power in relation to their husbands, a means of compensating for their inferior position in law. Such a bargaining card can be used for a variety of purposes: to secure housing separate from their in-laws; to send an erring husband a strong message; to prevent his taking a second wife or to exact revenge if he has done so; but most commonly it is used to induce a reluctant husband's consent to divorce. This is the topic of the next three chapters.

2

Legal Anatomy of Divorce:
the Iranian Case

Divorce is often a key to a deeper understanding of marriage. Legally, it is at the point of divorce that approved marital behaviour is rewarded and spouses who violate the norms are punished. Socially, divorce represents the point at which the inducements to leave prevail over the social and cultural forces that have so far kept the couple together. Personally, divorce represents the failure of a human relationship; it happens when the parties are no longer willing to negotiate. All these three levels – legal, social and personal – can be identified in divorce cases that appear in courts.

This chapter and the next examine the legal practice of divorce in Iran and Morocco through discussion of court procedures and divorce cases. They aim to portray the ways in which Shari'a precepts, which are now codified and applied by modern legal apparatus, find expression in social reality. The Iranian and Moroccan situations are discussed separately, for reasons which will become apparent. Legal practices and divorce patterns vary considerably between the two countries, despite the fact that their legal codes are both derived from the Shari'a.

Divorce in Law

In pre-revolutionary Iran, Shari'a rules of divorce were radically reformed. The Family Protection Law (FPL) of 1967 in effect abolished *talaq*: all divorces were decided by its courts, which issued the permits for their registration, known as Certificate of Impossibility of Reconciliation. In the absence of the mutual consent of the spouses to divorce, the court would issue the certificate upon the establishment

54

of certain conditions. Grounds available to men were the same as those available to women. The husband's failure to support his wife, his second marriage, or his failure to treat co-wives equally, gave the woman additional grounds for divorce.[1]

To avoid a total break with the Shari'a, which recognizes divorce as the exclusive right of men, those situations in which a certificate could be requested from the court were printed as stipulations in all marriage contracts. New marriage contracts were issued containing these conditions. In this way the reforms were given an Islamic appearance: a woman's right to dissolve her marriage was delegated to her by her husband at the time of marriage. As already mentioned, insertion of stipulations at the time of marriage is permissible under the Shari'a, provided that the essence of the contract is not violated. The marriage law of 1931 had also recognized stipulations in marriage contracts enabling a wife, in certain situations, to have the option of initiating divorce or divorcing herself on behalf of her husband. However, prior to the FPL, the insertion of such stipulations not only was optional but did not affect the husband's exclusive right to divorce.

Despite this attempt, the FPL never gained the approval of the clergy. In a ruling in 1967, Ayatollah Khomeini denounced its provisions as contrary to Islam and declared divorces issued by its court as void.[2] Not surprisingly, after the revolution the FPL was dismantled and was replaced by the Special Civil Courts Act, through which a return to Ithna 'Ashari law, as embodied in the articles of the Iranian Civil Code, was announced. Yet some elements of the reforms introduced by the FPL, particularly as regards divorce, have been retained. Passed in September 1979, seven months after the revolution, the new act allows a man to effect a divorce only when he has the consent of his wife; otherwise, a court's permission is required for its registration.

The evident contradiction between this provision and the classical Shi'a position – reflected in Article 1133 of the Civil Code, which states that 'a husband can repudiate his wife at any time he wishes' – is resolved by reference to a Koranic verse, which is stated in Article 3/2 of the Special Civil Courts Act. This article, which contains the only modification in terms of substantive law, reads:

> The divorce provisions are those contained in the Civil Code and Shari'a. But if a husband wishes a divorce in accordance with Article 1133 of the Civil Code, the court must first refer the case to arbitration, in conformity with the Holy verse: 'If you fear a breach between the two, bring forth an arbiter from his people and from her people an arbiter, if they desire to set

things right; God will compose their differences; surely God is all-knowing, All-aware.' Permission to divorce shall be granted to the husband, if reconciliation between the spouses has not materialized.[3]

Thus the new act, by requiring a man to obtain a court decree in order to be able to exercise his right to *talaq*, has in effect altered its extra-judicial nature; although it has not interfered with its unilateral nature. Men are still not required to provide grounds, whereas women can obtain a divorce only upon establishment of certain grounds.

At present, in terms of the grounds on which they can obtain a divorce from the court, women fall into three categories:

I. Those who married before the enactment of the FPL. These women seldom have any stipulations in their marriage contracts. Only in exceptional cases, and among the upper and educated classes, were stipulations inserted in marriage contracts before 1967. These usually gave women the power of attorney to divorce themselves if the husband took another wife, or gave the woman the right to choose the place of residence after marriage. Those women who have such stipulations can obtain a divorce if they are able to satisfy the court that their husbands have breached the conditions agreed at marriage. They constitute a very small minority. Those without any stipulations in their marriage contracts can dissolve their marriages only by establishing one of the grounds recognized by the Civil Code.

    The grounds for the annulment (*faskh*) of marriage are: a husband's inability to have normal sexual relations due to one of these conditions: impotency, eunuchism, removal of the penis (Article 1122); or his insanity (Article 1121) either at the time of marriage or subsequently (Article 1125). Grounds for divorce available to women are: her husband's failure to support her (Article 1129); and his ill-treatment to the extent that the continuation of marital life causes her *'asr va haraj* 'hardship and harm' (Article 1130).

II. Women who married between 1967 to 1982 (i.e. from the enactment of the FPL until the issue of the new marriage contracts). In the marriage contracts of these women, there is a stipulation conferring the right to divorce themselves on behalf of their husbands; having recourse to the court, they establish one of the grounds recognized by Article 8 of the FPL.[4] Every woman who married during that period is in possession of such a marriage contract and these stipulations are still recognized as valid by the courts.

III. Women who married after 1982, the year when post-revolutionary marriage contracts were issued. The marriage contracts of these women contain two main stipulations to which the husband consents by signing. The first requires the husband to pay his wife, upon divorce, up to half of the wealth he has acquired during that marriage, provided that the divorce has not been initiated or caused by any fault of the wife.[5] The court decides whether or not the fault of the divorce lies with the wife. The second stipulation gives the wife the delegated right to divorce herself after recourse to the court where she must establish one of the conditions which have been inserted in her marriage contract, namely:

- The husband's failure to support her or to fulfil other compulsory duties for at least six months.
- Husband's maltreatment (of the wife) to the extent that the continuation of the marriage has been rendered intolerable for her.
- Husband's affliction with any incurable disease that may endanger her health.
- Husband's insanity in cases where the Shari'a does not allow the annulment of marriage.
- Husband's failure to comply with a court order to abstain from an occupation which is repugnant to the wife and her position.
- Husband's sentence to a prison term of five years or more, or failure to pay a fine which results in his imprisonment for a period of five years or more.
- Husband's addiction to anything harmful, which in the court's judgment is detrimental to family life and renders the continuation of marital life difficult for the wife.
- Husband's desertion of marital life without just cause for more than six months. The court decides on the question of his desertion and on the acceptability of the excuse.
- Husband's conviction for any offence or sentence including *hadd* (fixed Islamic punishment for certain crimes) and *ta'zir* (discretionary punishment awarded by the *Hakim-i Shar'*, Shari'a judge) that is repugnant to the family and position of the wife.
- Husband's failure to father a child after five years of marriage.
- Husband's disappearance and the failure to find him within six months of the wife's application to the court.
- Husband's second marriage without the consent of the first wife or his failure to treat co-wives equally.

These stipulations, which are now printed in every marriage contract, are not valid unless they bear the husband's signature under each clause. The husband retains the right to refrain from signing anything he perceives as unacceptable. This is in conformity with the Shari'a mandate of divorce: a man is free to repudiate, to delegate or refrain from delegating this right. As we shall see, his signature under each clause does not have much effect on the woman's right to obtain a court divorce. As to the recent stipulation which entitles women to half of the wealth acquired during marriage, none of the branches of courts that I attended came across any dispute pertaining to this. In the court files, I came across a few marriage contracts in which the husband had refrained from signing that stipulation.

Divorce in Practice: the Court Procedure

A large majority of divorces take place without recourse to the court: a divorce can now be registered when there is mutual agreement between the couples. The cases with which the courts deal are thus those in which couples have failed to reach an agreement. In these cases, while one party is adamant about divorce, the other is resistant. I recorded 264 such instances: 171 are direct demands for divorce, the other 93 are presented in the guise of requests by women for maintenance or by men for their wives' return to the marital home. Table 2.1 summarizes these cases according to the sex of the petitioner and the type of complaint.

These cases can be divided into two broad categories: those in which one party is genuinely resisting a divorce and wants to salvage

Table 2.1 *Marital Dispute Cases According to Title of Demand and Sex of Petitioner, Tehran 1987*

| Petitioner | Title of demand | | | | | |
| | Divorce | | Maintenance or return of the wife | | Total | |
	no	%	no	%	no	%
Men	66	39	42	45	108	41
%	61		39		100	
Women	105	61	51	55	156	59
%	67		33		100	
Total	171	100	93	100	264	100
%	65		35		100	

the marriage; and those in which both partners are willing to terminate the marriage but have failed to agree on the divorce settlement. It is, however, difficult to ascertain to which category a case belongs. Petitions reveal little of the true motivations or the actual dynamics of the marital conflict itself. Couples throughout the court hearings hold on to their positions and play their negotiating cards; they rarely say anything which reveals their true intentions. Nevertheless, it can be said that a large portion of the 66 cases where divorce is demanded by men belong to the first category. In some of these cases the couple are still cohabiting; in others, the wife is willing to continue the marriage and it is the husband who has left the marital home. Similarly, most of the 42 cases of 'return of the wife' belong to the second category; in these cases the marriage has already broken down and the issue is that of reaching a financial settlement. The same type of generalization cannot be made regarding cases where divorce is requested by the wife; as we shall see, these cases are more complex.

Divorce petitioned by men

As Table 2.1 suggests, 41 per cent of all cases are initiated by men, of which 61 per cent are direct demands for divorce and the remaining 39 per cent are demands for restitution of marital rights, which are in effect men's negotiating strategy. Given that men are not required to provide grounds, it appears paradoxical that a higher percentage of them resort to deploying strategies (39 per cent of men as to 33 per cent of women). Two factors are responsible for this. First, in practice men need to satisfy the court that their actions are not based on caprice. The court seems to require them to produce grounds similar to those stipulated in their marriage contracts, entitling their wives to a judicial divorce. Second, the financial consequences of a divorce are different if the husband can prove that it was provoked by his wife. Not only does a disobedient wife lose her claim to maintenance but also, if a divorce results from a wife's failure to comply with her marital duties, the husband is not required to pay for her maintenance during the *'idda* period that follows every divorce.

Not surprisingly, 92 per cent of men gave their wives' 'lack of obedience' (*'adam-i tamkin*) as reasons for seeking divorce. The wording of these applications indicates the husband's dissatisfaction with marital life, what he terms 'disobedience'. The term encompasses a wide range of wifely conduct. Some men referred to abrasive language and insolence; some mention excessive autonomy: leaving the house without his prior permission, lending money without his knowledge, insisting on working despite his opposition; some men complain about neglect of the household chores or of the children, or about bad cooking; and, finally, a few hint at sexual insubordination.

Upon receiving a man's application, the court gives him a date, usually not later than three months ahead, on which to present his case. He is asked to come to the court with his wife. The court also delivers a writ to the wife, notifying her of his action and requiring her to attend the session. In some cases it is through this writ that a wife first learns of her husband's intentions or is forced to take seriously his frequent threats of divorce. Very often she comes to the court as soon as she is notified, long before the appointed session. Carrying the writ, she protests, cries and finally seeks advice as to how she can prevent her imminent divorce. Being aware of a man's inability in the pre-revolutionary period to effect a divorce without establishing recognized grounds, a woman often asks: 'Can he really divorce me without my consent?' When she is told that now he can, a second question follows: 'Can't the court stop him?' She is informed that divorce is his Shari'a right, but he must also honour his obligations to her in full. His obligation to her consists of providing *nafaqa* for her, as long as the marriage is extant, and paying her *mahr* and three months' maintenance upon divorce. She is advised that the court can bring an action against her husband if he has breached his duties, namely if he has already left the marital home or stopped supporting her.

If this is the case – which it usually is, or so she claims – the wife, in retaliation, files a complaint against him for failure to support her (in other words, demanding maintenance). Her application is then given priority and is processed within a week. Her husband is summoned to the court; if he comes and fails to refute his wife's claim, he is required by the judge to pay *nafaqa* to his wife there and then, unless he can prove to the court that he has been paying it. He can do this either by providing receipts for his payments to the wife or by bringing witnesses attesting his claim. His failure to comply with the court order can incur the recently ordained penalty: a maximum of 74 lashes.[6] He is exempted from this penalty if he satisfies the court that his non-payment of *nafaqa* is due either to his destitution or to his wife's disobedience. Her desertion of the marital home is the only evidence accepted by the court as proof of her disobedience, provided that this action was not prompted by fear of her husband. Faced with the penalty, husbands often pay or pledge to pay the sum within a week to the court, which subsequently hands it over to the wife. The judge determines the amount, taking into account the income of the husband and the length of time prior to the case when the wife was left without maintenance.

The day that the couple appear in the court, their file usually contains two applications: one a petition for divorce by the husband,

and the other a claim for interim maintenance by the wife. At first the court clerk endeavours to reconcile the pair, speaking to each spouse separately, trying to persuade them to reach a compromise. This process can last for hours or even a couple of hearings, during which the couple are sent out of the court room to discuss the matter and reach an agreement. If his efforts fail, the clerk will prepare a signed statement containing the couple's grievances and demands. At this stage, the judge intervenes. He too attempts a reconciliation by putting forward conditions that each might observe and by reminding them of their Islamic obligations towards each other as husband and wife. The judge reminds the wife of her husband's right to divorce and that she can prevent it only through compromise. He also tells the husband that if he insists on divorce he must first honour his obligations to her, namely her *mahr* and three months' maintenance after divorce.

If the court's initial attempts to reconcile the spouses fail, it refers the case to arbitration. Each spouse is asked to introduce an arbiter within a week and may be required to sign a document promising to comply with the arbiter's report. The arbiters must try to reconcile the spouses outside the court in a cordial fashion, and submit a written report to the court within two months, reflecting their assessment of the nature of the marital dispute and of the possibility of reconciliation.

All the cases where divorce was sought by the husband were referred to arbitration, with the exception of three cases in which the husband's stated reason for divorce was his wife's barrenness; here, the court issued the decree upon receiving a medical certificate substantiating his claim. The court may withhold a decision upon the recommendation of arbiters. The attempt to reconcile the spouses is sometimes successful, thus rendering the case closed. Where, however, the husband insists on divorce, arbitration attempts achieve very little, as the following case illustrates.

Case No. 1: Tehran, Divorce Petitioned by a Man

In June 1986 Hamid, a taxi driver aged 42, submitted a petition to divorce his wife, Mahin, a housewife aged 30. The couple had been married for 15 years and had two children: a boy aged 13 and a girl aged 11. In his petition, Hamid cited his wife's bad temper (*bad-akhlaqi*) and her abrasive language (*bad-dahani*) as reasons for seeking divorce. He also mentioned that three years ago he reached a point when he 'had no other choice than taking a second wife': he could no longer endure Mahin's bad temper and needed comfort.

Mahin's account, to be found in the notes taken during the first hearing, revealed a different story. The second wife, a divorced woman, was a friend of Mahin who used to frequent their house. Mahin's husband had been carrying on an affair with her friend for a while prior to contracting a marriage in secret. When Mahin learned of this, she was dumbfounded; she protested, and was supported by her family as well as his. After pressure from kin and friends, Hamid finally gave in and divorced the second wife (who gave her consent). A month later, he revoked his decision and returned to the second marriage, again in secret. When Mahin learned about this she objected but this time he told her, 'Either accept it or I'll divorce you.' But Mahin did not give up, nor did he. The second wife was now pregnant and he was threatening Mahin with divorce. In this session, which was held in August, Mahin declined to give her consent to divorce. She said that, because of her children, she was willing to continue her marriage; but insisted that he should divorce the second wife. The judge referred the case to arbitration.

The arbiters succeeded in reconciling the couple and Hamid promised to divorce the second wife. In order to oblige him to keep to his word, the arbiters suggested that he should sign a document in the court to that effect. Upon receiving the arbiters' report, the couple were summoned to the court. In the notes of this session, held in October, there is a document in which Hamid pledged to comply with his marital obligations and keep his word to divorce the second wife.

Three months later, Mahin came to the court to seek advice. Her husband not only had not divorced the second wife but had stopped paying maintenance for the past two weeks. The judge advised her to file a suit for *nafaqa*, which she did.

Hamid was summoned to the court within a week. This time he was defiant, expressing his intent to divorce Mahin. He said that it was a man's right to divorce if he was not happy in a marriage. He refused to pay *nafaqa* and was not impressed by the threat of 74 lashes. He was not salaried, so the court could not issue an order to deduct maintenance from his earnings. Mahin was advised to pursue her demand: he would pay when he realized that she was serious and prepared to have him punished. She did not take the advice; she feared that it might further alienate him.

I have no further information on this case. In summer 1987, when I resumed my court attendance, I learned that, since neither Hamid nor Mahin had pursued their respective demands, the file had been closed. When I asked the judge as to the likely outcome, he said, 'Either they have come to their senses and carried on their union or she finally agreed to go with him to register a divorce.'

Although the court cannot deny a divorce requested by the husband, it can delay its registration. In some courts, one gains the impression that the judge is reluctant to come to a decision where the husband fails to provide grounds indicative of the breakdown of the marriage. Of course, the procedure of each court depends largely on the attitude of its judge. In one court, the judge referred each case only once to arbitration and, upon the receipt of the report, issued the document enabling the husband to register the divorce. In another court, the judge used every possible device available to delay what he considered to be an unjust divorce and made sure that the wife was duly compensated. The following case illustrates the processes involved and modes of redress available to women.

Case No. 2: Tehran, Delaying a Divorce

The couple had been married for four years and had a son, aged three. Majid, the husband, was 30 years old; he worked in a tailor's shop, where he met his second wife whom he married in secret in December 1986. In April 1987, he filed a petition to divorce his first wife, Homa, four years older than him. In his petition, he cited Homa's disobedience and her 'bad mouthing' as reasons for divorce, without mentioning his having taken a second wife. The court set the date of the first hearing for July.

Upon receiving the court's writ, Homa came to the court and immediately filed a counter-petition in which she claimed that her husband had abandoned her and that he had not paid any maintenance since he left. This petition was dealt with prior to the July session; Majid was summoned to the court and claimed that he had paid Homa 7000 tomans only a month before. She denied this and spelled out her complaints: that he no longer came home; that he had taken a second wife without her knowledge, let alone her consent; that he had shamed her in front of everyone. He was asked whether he could provide proof of payment. He said that he had never thought of taking receipts from his wife, adding that it was not the maintenance that Homa was after: she was angry at his remarriage and wanted revenge. The judge said that it was her right to be maintained and fixed 9000 toman for three months. He refused to pay and said that in his eyes she was no longer his wife and he wanted to register a divorce. A bitter row broke out between the couple. He remained adamant in his refusal to pay and so did she in demanding her right. The judge sentenced him to the penalty of 50 lashes and sent the case to the executionary body.

In July when the couple appeared in front of the judge, Majid was extremely angry and dismissed any idea of reconciliation, saying, 'I accepted 50 lashes but not this woman.' Homa, on the other hand, adopted a mild tone, saying, 'I am not objecting to his taking another wife; if Islam allows him to do so, who am I to object; but Islam also gives me rights.' She then burst into tears and said that he had taken away her three-year-old son, accusing her mother-in-law of conspiring to ruin their marriage. The second marriage could not have taken place without the aid of his mother, who never approved of Homa because of her previous marriage and her age. Despite the obvious hostility between the couple, the judge referred the case to arbitration and the couple were asked to introduce two arbiters within a week.

In September, in a hearing to deal with another maintenance petition made by Homa, Majid refused once again to pay. The couple started insulting each other and a fight broke out between them. The judge, annoyed, ordered them out of the courtroom, saying that their case would not be dealt with unless they learned to respect the court. They were ushered out by the court attendant to the corridor, where Homa's mother and sister were awaiting her. At the very end of the court session, after the court clerk and I had mediated on their behalf, the judge agreed to allow the couple back into the court. The judge told them that no decision could be reached until he had received the arbiters' report. The judge reminded the husband that by law he was required to pay the maintenance that he owed his wife. Majid still refused; the judge said that he must prepare himself for another sentence and asked the clerk to prepare the necessary documentation. At this point, Majid relented and asked to telephone his brother to bring the money.

At the final hearing, held in November 1987, having received the arbiters' report indicating that there was no possibility of reconciliation, the court issued the order enabling Majid to register the divorce.

In effect, the penalty of lashing is involved only when there is extreme acrimony in the course of a marital dispute, in which the wife is more keen on exacting revenge than on salvaging her marriage. Interestingly, out of eight cases in which a husband received corporal punishment because of non-payment of his wife's *nafaqa*, six involved his second marriage. The pressure to divorce the first wife is usually exerted by the second wife, while the husband's financial inability to support two households is another contributing factor. In some cases, like that of Majid and Homa, the husband remains adamant about not fulfilling his marital duties, epitomised in the payment of *nafaqa*, even at the expense of being flogged.

In short, the outcome of divorce cases initiated by men is determined by two factors: the husband's financial situation and the judge's evaluation of the marital problem (which is partly influenced by the arbitrators' reports). As we have seen, neither arbitration nor the threat of 74 lashes seem to deter a man who is determined to divorce. Arbitration attempts were successful in less than 5 per cent of these cases. The threat of corporal punishment has little impact in salvaging the marriage; it is more likely to fuel the conflict.

Divorce petitioned by women

In the court room, women base their applications on grounds cited in their marriage contracts.[7] This also is true of those women whose marriage contracts do not contain any stipulations (that is, those who married before 1967). The judge is now empowered, on the basis of Article 1130 of the civil code, to issue a divorce if the wife can establish grounds analogous to those inserted in recent marriage contracts. According to this article, which was amended in 1982, a judge can either compel the husband to allow a divorce, or act on his behalf, if marriage entails *'asr va haraj* (hardship and harm).[8] This is a Shari'a concept which allows the sanction of a rule to be lifted when adherence to it creates hardship. In the sphere of marriage, its implication is that, for a woman, remaining married is the rule as long as her husband desires it; to be released from a marriage she needs to prove that its continuation is causing her harm. This is the rationale upon which divorce grounds available to women under the Ithna 'Ashari law were enlarged in post-revolutionary Iran. Stipulations inserted in marriage contracts are to be seen as means of identifying and listing those circumstances which can render marital life intolerable to the wife.

The grounds upon which a woman bases her application influence both the speed at which her case is dealt with and its outcome. In cases where the establishment of the grounds is simple and straightforward, the court issues the divorce without more ado. Otherwise, all depends on the husband's goodwill, or on the judge's assessment of the marital dispute. Aware of this, women attempt to tailor their grievances to those acceptable to the court, an exercise known in Persian as producing a 'court-favoured reason' (*dalil-i mahkama-pasand*); although few of them succeed in gaining its favour.

Out of 105 women who requested divorce, 33 based their application on the husband's addiction to drugs; eight on the husband's desertion of the marital home; three on the husband's mental condition, resembling insanity; three on the husband's sterility; 22 on the husband's failure to pay maintenance; and 36 on maltreatment.

The ground most readily accepted by the court is drug addiction, provided it involves the husband's conviction and imprisonment: this condition was fulfilled in only 11 of the 33 cases brought under this category. In all these cases, the husbands were in prison; some were already convicted and others were awaiting trial. In one of these cases, the couple had a previous file in the court containing a signed document wherein the husband pledged to give up his addiction, conferring on his wife the right to divorce herself if he resumed his old habits. Upon his second arrest, the wife approached the court, demanding a divorce. He attended the session in the custody of a prison officer and pleaded to be given another chance, saying that he wanted to keep his marriage. The wife remained adamant, and the court, on the basis of the previous agreement between the spouses, issued the document enabling the wife to register the divorce. In the other ten cases, husbands also appeared in the court; they were informed that because of their addiction, the court was empowered to issue the divorce if they refused to reach an agreement with their wives. In all these cases, the court technically was competent to issue the divorce without the husband's presence, although in actual fact it was reluctant to do so and tended to encourage the spouses to reach a mutually agreeable settlement. In the remaining 22 cases, having failed to prove their husbands' addiction, women combined this claim with that of non-support.

Similarly, in only three of the eight cases where women based their case upon their husband's desertion of the marital home, was their evidence accepted. In all three cases, the husbands had already left the country after the revolution for political reasons. The women claimed that they had already asked for and been refused their husbands' consent. Having investigated the women's claim through witnesses, correspondence between the spouses and a report from the Ministry of Information and other relevant departments, the court issued the document enabling the registration of the divorce in the absence of the husband. This document also contained a summary of the court's efforts to establish the husband's flight. In the remaining five cases, the husband's desertion of the marital home happened after he took either a second wife or failed to secure the his wife's consent to a divorce; they all involved claims for *nafaqa* and were sent to arbitration (I have no further information on the outcome).

Cases in which non-support is the stated ground are varied and complicated; claims for maintenance are symptoms of a deeper disharmony. Eight out of 22 such cases involved the husband's remarriage. In all these cases, wives demanded their *mahr* (see below for implications) as well as claiming past maintenance. They appeared to be determined to retrieve all that was due to them in case they should be divorced by their husbands at the instigation of the new wives. In some, women claimed that their husbands, by not providing for them, were pressuring them to consent to a divorce *khul'* (forfeiting their rights). Four of these women, upon realizing the futility of their efforts to get viable maintenance for a long period, finally reached an agreement with their husbands and consented to divorce; the remaining cases were referred to arbitration.

Maltreatment is the most difficult ground to establish, yet it is the most common, constituting 34 per cent of all cases. This is so because it is the only option left when a woman fails to establish any of the above grounds. Here all depends on the judge: the amended version of Article 1130 of the Civil Code provides him with discretionary power to withhold or issue a divorce requested by women. The extent to which 'harm' can be a viable ground for divorce rests entirely on the judge's values and outlook. As the following two examples illustrate, he decides which kind of physical and mental cruelty are harmful to which kind of people.

Case No. 3: Tehran, Divorce Petitioned on Grounds of Harm

This case involved a young middle-class couple, who had been married for four years and had a son aged two. The husband, Amir, was 33 years old; he was a journalist with a university degree and worked for several papers. The wife, Mina, was 23 years old; she came from a wealthy merchant family and had a high school diploma.

She made her first petition in March 1985, in which she requested a divorce on the ground of harm. In her petition she enumerated ways in which her marriage was causing her harm: her husband, being a nervous and suspicious man, beat her regularly and locked her out of their flat. Twice, she had to spend the entire night in the parking space, as he would not let her in and she could not go out without her veil.[9] In February 1984, she had finally reached the limits of her tolerance; she had taken her child and returned to her father's house. She neither demanded maintenance nor claimed her *mahr* (300,000 tomans); she merely wanted a divorce.

The first court hearing, held in June 1985, resulted in reconciliation. Amir admitted that he had done her wrong and earnestly requested to be given another chance to correct himself. The court's notes of that session contain the following agreements: (1) both spouses pledged to cooperate and respect each other; (2) the wife undertook to perform her marital duties; (3) the husband undertook to perform his marital duties; (4) the husband pledged, from that moment onwards, never and in no circumstances to beat his wife; (5) in the course of a binding contract performed in the court (see below), the husband gave the wife the power to effect a *khul'* divorce, without requiring his presence, after proving to the court that he failed to keep one of the above pledges.

With the judge's encouragement and the above legal assurance, Mina's father agreed to let her go back to her husband. Things remained much the same in her marriage and Mina returned to her father's house in less than a year. She filed another petition for divorce; this time she claimed her *mahr*, and started receiving it in instalments: 3000 tomans had been deducted from his salary from December 1985.

The court heard the case in February 1986. Amir denied her claims of maltreatment. He said that their marriage was like others which had their ups and downs, and what Mina claimed to be maltreatment was in fact 'things that go on in every marriage'. He then accused Mina's parents of interfering with their marriage: they gave her undue support. He made a court demand for her return to the marital home. Mina refused, saying that she feared for her life and did not trust him any more. The judge asked her to substantiate her claims of maltreatment either by means of witnesses or by a medical report. Mina failed to do so and the court referred the case to arbitration, urging them to reach an agreement. The arbiters failed to reconcile the couple. Their report contained the details of a session held outside the court: Mina and her father were insisting on divorce; she was willing to forgo her dower if the husband agreed to a divorce. Amir rejected this proposal and stated that he wished to continue the marriage. Shortly after this session, he took the son (aged three) away from her, on the pretext of a visit to the grandparents. He refused to let her see her child, using this as a strategy to bring about reconciliation.

When the couple appeared for their third hearing, September 1986, Mina was clearly disturbed by her separation from her child and demanded that the court intervene. Amir said that, since his son was now over two, custody belonged to the father, and if she wanted her child then she should return to her marriage. She refused and accused him of blackmail. He told the court that it was he who had been blackmailed: she had claimed her *mahr* and he was paying it out of his meagre salary. He then went into a long account of the hardship that this caused him, how she came from a rich family and had no need of money, all the while hinting at the possibility of a bargain: she could have her son back if she gave up her claim to her *mahr*. The court reminded him that it was her right to claim her *mahr* and that he must pay; and reminded her that her husband now had priority in the custody of their son and nothing could be done about it. The session ended with no definite conclusions.

Later, I learned that they had reached an agreement out of court, he had given the child back, and she had frozen the *mahr* claim. In this way Amir succeeded in thwarting her efforts to negotiate a divorce via the court. Mina was left without any leverage in negotiating her release: if she resumed her claim of *mahr*, she risked losing her child. Neither could she claim *nafaqa*, as she was now in a state of *nushuz*: she was the one who had left the marital home.

The court issued its decision on 17 March 1987 in which it rejected Mina's demand for divorce because of the insufficient proof, and she was ordered to return to her marital home.

Mina made an appeal; and the appeal decision, dated 20 September 1987, confirmed the first judgment.

On 26 September 1987, upon Amir's request, the court issued an order in which Mina was required to comply with her marital duties (*tamkin*) and return to the marital home.

On 28 October 1987, Mina submitted a new petition, this time to another court, demanding divorce on the grounds of harm. This resulted in another round of court hearings during which she again failed to convince the court that the continuation of the marriage was causing her harm. Neither the medical report that she produced nor the testimony of her witnesses were accepted. The medical certificate, testifying that her hearing was impaired as result of a blow, was dismissed as the court accepted Amir's claim that it was dated three months after she had left him and that nobody saw him hitting her. The testimony of her two maternal uncles, that they saw her bruised shortly after her second return to her father's house, was challenged. Amir argued that these were fabrications, part of the plot to destroy his marriage. He said, 'None of them have seen me beating my wife, so how could they attest that her bruises, if they ever existed, have been caused by me?'

The court reached its decision after three sessions. The judgment dated 19 July 1988 read as follows: 'As regards the petition submitted by the wife, Mina, against her permanent husband Amir for divorce, since the wife has not submitted any convincing reasons for her demand and since the husband has not agreed to her request, the court rejects her demand on the basis of *al-talaq bi yad man akhadha bi al saq*, (a saying attributed to the Prophet, which literally means: divorce is in the hand of the one who took the calf, that is, divorce is the man's right).[10]

I have no more information on this case.

Case No. 4: Tehran, Another Variation of Harm as a Ground

This case involved another middle-class couple, married for five years. Both were now architects; they had met and married as students in America. Shortly after their child was born, the wife, Nazi, came to Tehran for a holiday, with her new-born baby.

In her petition to the court, Nazi gave incompatibility and a gradual deterioration of marital conditions as the main reasons for seeking a divorce. She referred to her husband's excessive domination; that he did not even let her mother her child and wanted to take over. She stated that while in the United States she had to work in a restaurant owned by her husband. She found this unbearable as it was not in line with her training and social standing.

The judge required her to bring witnesses confirming her claims. Nazi produced four witnesses: all of them knew the couple in the United States. They all attested that she had been working as a cashier in his restaurant; that this was not compatible with her family standing and education; that she had been unhappy there.

She was granted a divorce at the third hearing on the grounds of harm.[11]

These two cases illustrate how difficult and yet how easy can it be to obtain a divorce on the grounds of 'harm'. The way that harm is defined and the grounds needed to establish it may vary from one judge to another, yet there is a certain rationale behind each judge's decision which is uniform. All are guided by the assumptions stemming from the Shari'a conception of marriage. As we have seen in Chapter 1, the marriage contract establishes the man's authority over his wife. It is his duty to provide for her and it is hers to submit to him. Thus it becomes his prerogative to chastise a disobedient wife, and hers not to go out to work. This explains why, in the first case, the wife's grievances against her husband (being physically and verbally abused, locked in the house, and unable to see her parents) were regarded as insufficient grounds for divorce; and why the plight of a Muslim woman who, because of her marriage, is forced to work in the land of infidels, was accepted as a sufficient proof of 'harm'.

In theory, the husband's right to chastise his wife is limited. On the basis of a Koranic injunction, the jurists recommend that the husband should first try to subdue her gently, using the stick and the carrot: to persuade her, to scold her, or to deprive her of his bed. He should administer physical punishment only as the last resort. Yet, in practice, the line between chastisement and harm remains arbitrary, as in Mina's case. The court disregards psychological cruelty and requires tangible evidence of physical violence, such as a broken arm or a police report after a fight – a doctor's certificate is not accepted on its own. Establishing harm by means of witnesses is also difficult. A man's own kin are rarely prepared to betray him, and he rarely dares to be cruel to her in the presence of hers. The structure of houses and the style of life in certain quarters of Tehran provide a degree of privacy, impeding the neighbours from observing what is going on inside the home. Harm, thus, can be a viable ground only if the woman is subjected to an extreme form of marital cruelty: such cases constitute a very small minority indeed and I came across only two in the Tehran courts.

Negotiating Divorce in the Courts

Irrespective of the grounds upon which a divorce is sought and regardless of who initiates the proceedings, the court appears reluctant to allow it. Instead, it directs all its efforts towards encouraging the couple to reach a compromise. The judge uses every device to facilitate this. He may appoint another set of arbiters; or he may secure the wife's position by making any promises made by the husband legally binding. In order legally to oblige a husband to comply with assurances made in court, he is often required to delegate to his wife an unconditional right to divorce herself in case he resumes his previous conduct. This is done through a contract referred to as *'aqd-i kharij-i lazim* (literally, binding outside contract), that is, a binding contract which is made between the spouses in the court, but outside the marriage contract. In such a contract the husband delegates to his wife the right to divorce herself. It is carried out in the following manner by the court clerk. He takes a cigarette or something else which belongs to the husband and gives it to the wife while repeating the following formula: 'I am selling you this cigarette on behalf of your husband; during this transaction, he agrees to the following conditions and authorizes you to divorce yourself on his behalf should he breach any of the conditions stated in the document signed by him.' In return, the wife gives the court clerk some money which he hands to the husband to complete the transaction. The clerk then prepares a document containing all the conditions that have been agreed upon by the spouses. This document then becomes binding for the two parties; should the wife establish that the husband has breached any of its conditions, she can acquire a divorce.

This symbolic transaction is necessary in order to give legal validity to an agreement reached to settle a marital dispute. Only in the course of another transaction can new conditions be set or modifications be made to the conditions inherent in the original marriage contract. Over 20 per cent of women petitioning for divorce had court files containing such an agreement, indicative of their previous court attendances. It is one way of giving the wife permission to effect the divorce in the absence of her husband's consent. It also acts as a safeguard against a husband's possible claim that his consent was obtained under pressure.

This court agreement is often the first official step towards a divorce by mutual consent (*khul'*); it is always preceded by a long period of argument, negotiation and bargaining between the spouses. What plays a crucial role in this process is the institution of *mahr*, especially the way it is practised in urban areas. No adequate understanding of divorce in Iran is possible without taking into account the role and place of *mahr*.

Theory and practice of mahr *(dower)*

Mahr is an integral part of every marriage contract in Islam: there can be no marriage without it. It is also called *sadaq*, an Arabic term which implies 'friendship'; in English it has been rendered 'dower'; hence a gift that the bridegroom offers to the bride upon marriage. *Mahr* becomes the exclusive property of the bride after marriage and she is free to dispose of it in whatever way she wishes. There are two types of *mahr*. In *mahr al-musamma* (definite *mahr*), as the name implies, the exact amount of *mahr* is agreed upon prior to marriage and is specified in the marriage contract. In *mahr al-mithal* (exemplary *mahr*), the amount is not specified in the marriage contract, and it is determined later on the basis of the bride's personal qualities, her family position and the amount of *mahr* prevailing among her people.

There is a general consensus among different rites within the Shari'a on the basic assumptions that lie behind *mahr*. It is, as suggested earlier, a corollary of the exchange element of the marriage contract. This view is underlined by the way that *mahr* is defined, as the price (*'awad*) that the man pays for exclusive rights to the sexual and reproductive faculties of the woman, analogous to the price paid in the contract of sale. Modern writers, however, regard *mahr* as an expression of a woman's worth, which can also give her economic security.[12] The rules regulating *mahr* negate this view: it is linked merely to the act of consummation, not to any other aspect of the marriage. For example, a woman becomes entitled to *mahr* only after consummation of marriage; she can refrain from sexual submission unless she receives her *mahr* in full. But once she has begun performing her marital duties of her own free will, she can no longer make her performance contingent on receiving her *mahr*, although her claim to it remains intact (Article 1085 of ICC). If the marriage is annulled before consummation, she is not entitled to any portion of her *mahr* but she is entitled to half of it if she is divorced before consummation (Articles 1085 and 1092 of ICC).

Despite the uniformity that exists among all the schools within the Shari'a on the rules governing the institution of *mahr*, Muslim societies vary greatly with respect to its practice.[13] In some cases, *mahr* is divided into two portions, the 'prompt' portion which is paid at the time of marriage, and the 'deferred' portion which is payable only upon divorce. In others, the wife has no control over her *mahr*, as the entire amount is received at the time of the contract by her father who might or might not use it for providing her with a trousseau for her wedding.

In Iran, there is a wide disparity between the legal and social constructions of *mahr*. Legally a woman can demand her *mahr* whenever she wishes. She merely needs to produce her marriage contract and register a request; the husband is then obliged to pay it either in instalments or in cash, depending on his means.[14] In marriage contracts, the phrase *'ind-al-mutalaba* (literally, upon request) is always written next to the amount of *mahr*, rendering it 'prompt' as opposed to 'deferred'. Only in exceptional cases, where *mahr* is a piece of land or property, are conditions for its transfer to the bride specified. The Civil Code devotes an entire chapter (Chapter 7) to *mahr*, relating its payment only to the act of consummation (Articles 1092, 1093, 1098, 1099 and 1101). In practice, such a linkage is never made: neither side, at the time of its stipulation, expects it to be paid to the bride. This is reflected in a Persian saying which is often referred to by the bride's side: 'Who has ever given or received [*mahr*]?' (*Ta bihal ki dada ki girifta?*).

What distinguishes *mahr* from other prestations at the time of marriage is that its value is always beyond the immediate financial means of the groom. This is essential in order to ensure its role as a safeguard for women in marriage. Discussing and reaching an agreement on the amount of *mahr* comprises the most important part of the lengthy negotiations between the families before the wedding. The bride's side proposes and demands a high *mahr* while the groom's side strives to modify it. Each side makes promises and gives assurances; and *mahr* becomes the yardstick of their sincerity. The bride's family argues, 'We won't give away a girl like this,' without a guarantee, a pledge; while the groom's side reminds them, 'A high *mahr* cannot bring marital happiness.' What prolongs the process of negotiation is the awareness on both sides that, despite all the maxims and assurances, *mahr* is not a legal fiction; a woman can and will claim it when she needs to.

Although marriage customs and prestations vary considerably within the country, it can be said that in urban Iran (especially in Tehran), it is the groom's side which bears the greater part of the wedding expenses.[15] These include holding a wedding reception, which often takes place in the bride's house, or these days in a hotel; buying jewellery and clothing: a gold ring, the wedding dress and its accessories, as well as other sets of garments. The bride brings a trousseau (*jahiz*) comprising furnishing for the house that the couple eventually establish. She also receives jewellery from both sides, from her own kin as well as his, which is neither written down in the marriage contract nor regarded as part of her *mahr*. It is only customary to write in the ring that the groom gives the bride and a set of matching mirrors and candle-holders, which decorate the *sufra-i 'aqd* (ceremonial cloth on which bride and groom sit when the marriage formula is recited).

In rural Iran and among recent migrants to town, *mahr* is overshadowed by another type of payment known as *shirbaha* (literally, the price of milk), which is paid by the groom's father to the bride's father to provide her with a trousseau. If the marriage is registered, the actual amount of *mahr* written in marriage contracts is minimal; it is a matter of complying with the conditions of validity of the marriage contract. With increased urbanization, *mahr* is gradually acquiring importance at the expense of *shirbaha*.[16] Among recent migrants it has now become a matter of prestige, a sign of urbanity, for families to stipulate a substantial *mahr* in the marriage contracts of their daughters.

The value of the *mahr* varies with the social class and wealth of the families. As marriages are usually arranged, the amount of *mahr* is often agreed upon by the parents of the spouses. Its value has increased significantly in recent years. Inflation in the country is partly responsible for this increase. Nowadays, with the depreciation of the Iranian currency, gold coins are stipulated in the contracts as *mahr* instead of currency. In 1974, only 9 per cent of women who married in Tehran during that year had a *mahr* of more than 100,000 tomans. The corresponding percentages for 1977, 1979, 1980 and 1981 were 23, 39, 45 and 52 respectively.[17] Apart from inflation and the depreciation,[18] another reason for the increase in the value of *mahr* is undoubtedly the recent changes in family law which resulted in the reinstatement of man's traditional right to arbitrary divorce and polygny. Thus, once again, the important function of a high *mahr* as a safeguard for women in marriage was brought into relief. Before the revolution of 1979, in marriages among 'modern' (that is, educated and Western-influenced) couples, only a minimal amount of *mahr* was stipulated, that is a gold coin, or a volume of the Holy Koran. For such couples, *mahr* was an outdated institution, indicative of the purchase of women through marriage. The FPL, by granting equal rights to both spouses in matters of divorce and child custody, further encouraged this modern tendency, as women felt that they no longer needed a substantial *mahr* as a safeguard. Women whose 'modern' marriages break down regret not having stipulated a significant *mahr* in their marriage contracts. In one case, a woman whose 'romantic' marriage broke down was furious about her *mahr*, which was a ton of jasmine. She said that the idea of a ton of jasmine as *mahr* was romantic at the time of her wedding, although it was of no use after she was divorced by her husband. She believed that if her *mahr* had been high enough her husband would have thought twice before divorcing her to marry another woman, or at least she could have been compensated or exacted revenge by forcing him to pay afterwards.

Women may demand payment of *mahr* for two apparently contradictory purposes: to prevent or delay an unwanted divorce; or to bring about a divorce. The processes involved in each can be best examined through the analysis of two divorce cases in which *mahr* was used as the main bargaining strategy.

Case No. 5: Tehran, *Mahr* as a Deterrent

Hassan, a government employee, applied for a divorce in November 1985, seven months after the marriage. In his application the stated reason for his decision was 'incompatibility'. The court notified Nahid, the wife, a teacher, and set the first hearing for December 1985. At this session Nahid, who was pregnant, declined to give her consent. The court subsequently referred the case to arbitration.

The report of the two arbiters was in favour of the wife. The first arbiter, Nahid's brother, blamed Hassan and identified his sudden second marriage as the cause of marital conflict; and added that he was under pressure from the second wife to terminate his first marriage. He declared Nahid to be blameless and willing to continue the marriage. The second arbiter,

Hassan's brother, confirmed his counterpart's report and added that reconciliation was possible but more time was required to bring it about.

During the second session, in March 1986, the wife again refused to agree to a divorce. This session lasted for two hours, at the end of which the wife declared that she would concede a divorce only if she received her *mahr* in full (250 gold coins). She knew that Hassan was unable to pay the 250 gold coins, a substantial sum well beyond his means. He accused her of blackmail and asked to pay in instalments, to which Nahid did not agree. Yet she took no action to recover her *mahr* through either the court or a marriage registry office. The court urged the couple to resolve their dispute in an amicable manner, stressing its reluctance to set another session unless they reached a prior agreement with respect to the *mahr*. Hassan, however, demanded another hearing.

They came to the court again in October 1986. This time, in addition to her *mahr*, Nahid claimed interim maintenance for herself from November 1985, the date that Hassan left the marital home, and for the new baby, who was born in June. The court sanctioned her right to maintenance, as she was willing to comply with her marital duties and it was the husband who had abandoned the marital home. But she took no further action. The court took Nahid's refusal to file a suit for maintenance against Hassan as indicating her desire to placate the husband, and was convinced that there was still hope for reconciliation. The judge decided to refer the case once more to arbitration. The new arbiters confirmed the report of the previous ones and declared that the wife was not at fault; she was even willing to accommodate her husband's second union, but since he was insistent on divorcing her she demanded that her rights be honoured, a reference to her demand for payment of the *mahr*.

Meanwhile Hassan, in his frustration, wrote to the three eminent Islamic jurists (*ayatollah 'uzma*) of the country. In his letter, he stated his case and enquired whether it was within the court's power to prevent him from divorcing his wife on the basis of his inability to pay her dower in full. All the three jurists (one of them was Ayatollah Khomeini) in their separate replies to this judicial query (*istifta'*) stated, 'A man's inability to pay dower does not interfere with his right of divorce; he can pay the dower in instalments according to his means.'[19]

Hassan forwarded copies of the *istifta'* and the responses to the court, demanding another hearing. The court set a session for

June 1987. As Nahid did not appear, the hearing was postponed to August, but again she failed to appear in this session. The court then sent a notice to Nahid, indicating that if she failed to appear for the third time, the court would render its decision without her presence.

The final session took place in November 1987, during which three agreements were reached: (1) Nahid gave her consent to be divorced; (2) Hassan in return agreed to give her the full custody of their son, who was now 2 years old; and (3) he agreed to pay the dower in monthly instalments as well as a monthly amount for the maintenance of the child. She also claimed past maintenance and another monthly instalment was set. The court's order, which enabled Hassan to register the divorce, contained all these agreements and became binding on the two parties.

This case, owing its prolongation to the sympathy of the judge for the wife and her tactful appeal to the court ideology, clearly demonstrates the role of *mahr* as both deterrent and compensator. Although *mahr* cannot prevent a divorce, as confirmed by the decree of the three eminent jurists, it can provide women with a degree of compensation in the face of it. It is evident that, contrary to what the wife maintained throughout the court case, she was negotiating the terms of her divorce rather than salvaging her marriage. In doing so, she used her right to *mahr* effectively to achieve her goals: to obtain the custody of her son and as a kind of alimony. Both would have been denied to her under a normal divorce.[20]

Sometimes women use their claim to *mahr* in order to make a point and offset some of the disadvantages that a particular marriage entails. The following case demonstrates some of the processes involved as well as the limitations when a woman uses her *mahr* to this effect.

Case No. 6: Tehran, *Mahr* as Incentive

The case was petitioned by Sima, a 45-year-old former entertainer, against her husband, Ali, 52 years old and a merchant in the Bazaar. Ali had another wife to whom he had been married for 27 years. By his first wife, he had four grown-up children, three of whom now lived abroad.

The date of the permanent marriage contract was May 1982, but the couple had contracted a temporary marriage 17 years before, which they continued until the permanent contract was made. They had a son who was 14 years old. The marriage contract contained a special stipulation according to which the wife had the right to choose the place of residence, and the stipulated *mahr* was 200 gold coins.[21]

Sima made her first petition for a divorce in February 1983, less than a year after transforming her union into a permanent one. In the petition, which she wrote herself, she stated that Ali had maltreated her, beating her to compel her to forgo her *mahr*. She was constantly troubled and provoked by her in-laws, allegedly at the instigation of the husband. She cited as evidence harassment by the brothers of her co-wife. Twice she was taken to the police station and once she became the victim of a conspiracy, resulting in her being unjustly convicted. The petition, though graphic in details of her suffering, gave no clue to the real causes of the dispute.

At the first hearing, held in April 1983, Sima reiterated her demands for divorce and her *mahr*. Ali refused to agree to divorce, saying that he loved his wife and his child and was willing to continue the marriage and meet her lawful demands. He agreed to pay maintenance but she insisted on receiving her *mahr* in full, and threatened to file a suit demanding her 200 gold coins. She declared that her *mahr* was her right and she would not compromise it. But she wanted to use it for charitable purposes, namely to give it to the Imam's account (a special account for the poor in the name of Ayatollah Khomeini).[22]

At the second hearing, in June 1983, she repeated her demand and stated that Ali was causing her numerous problems and was constantly pressuring her to forfeit her *mahr* in return for a divorce, but she wanted a 'correct and Islamic' divorce in which all her rights were honoured. Meanwhile, she had obtained a court order enabling her to confiscate a portion of Ali's property equivalent to the value of her *mahr* (this was necessary as he was not salaried).

At the third hearing, December 1983, in addition to her *mahr*, she demanded *nafaqa* (maintenance) for the past 17 years, from the date of their temporary union, claiming that all those years he had failed to provide for her.[22] The court issued its decision in March 1984, rejecting her demands both for divorce and for past maintenance. Her claim for past maintenance was rejected on the grounds that a temporary wife is not entitled to it unless it is stipulated in her marriage contract. Her claim for divorce was rejected because the court found her claim of harm and non-support insubstantial. She was ordered to show obedience (*tamkin*) and to continue her marriage. But the court required the husband to pay a monthly amount of 3000 tomans for her maintenance and set instalments of 7000 tomans for paying off the *mahr*.

Three months later, she wrote again to the same court and repeated her grievances. Her letter was a long and dramatic account of her suffering at the hands of her husband and the relatives of his first wife. Her only demand was to be justly (without forfeiting her *mahr*) released from an intolerable marriage. In support of her case, she provided quotations from the sayings of the Prophet and the Shi'a Imams on a man's religious obligation to treat his wife well and not to keep her against her will in marriage. She also quoted from a recent speech of Imam Khomeini to the effect that in reaching a decision a judge must be mindful only of God and the Koran, and not be influenced by other factors. She renewed her pledge to give her *mahr* to the poor and included a receipt for three instalments that she had donated to the Imam's account, and stated that she had so far not kept any of her *mahr* for herself.

At the fourth hearing, October 1985, Ali was still refusing to agree to divorce and Sima was not prepared to relinquish her claim to *mahr*. She made more financial claims: expenses that she had incurred for their son, presenting a receipt for a motor-cycle that she had bought him. At that session Ali handed her a cheque to cover the purchase. Faced with her threats to take legal action, he also agreed to pay 200,000 tomans of her *mahr* in cash and stated that he wanted to keep the marriage and was willing to meet her reasonable demands. On the basis of the agreement reached during this session, the court issued its second decision. Her demand for divorce was rejected again, and the previous agreement was reaffirmed: Ali to pay 10,000 tomans per month (3000 for *nafaqa* and 7000 as instalment of *mahr*). This judgment was dated November 1985 and was the final one.

By March 1988, when I came across this case, Sima had received about 400,000 of her *mahr* and was coming to the court each month to get her cheque (the husband was required to hand it in to the court at the beginning of each month). She was unhappy that the court had evaluated her *mahr*, 200 gold coins, on the basis of the official rate for gold coins which was much lower than its market value.[24] She had no intention of either forgoing her *mahr* or relinquishing her demand for divorce. The husband also knew that either way he had to pay, so he preferred to keep her in limbo in the hope that she might finally relinquish her demand.

This case represents an instance of excessively bitter marital conflict, with *mahr* occupying a central role. The way that Sima used *mahr* in the process of negotiations is exceptional in the sense that divorce seemed not to be her priority; she persistently refused to compromise and forgo her *mahr* in return for her release from the marital bond. There are certain facts about this case which make it atypical. First, Sima's life style, her code of morality and sense of honour were not shared by the vast majority of married women: she was a dancer in a night-club in pre-revolutionary Tehran, not a respectable position for a woman. Secondly, the union deviated from the culturally and socially accepted model. It started as a temporary marriage, which is not socially considered a proper marriage. It was only later that Sima acquired the respectable status of a permanent wife, when their only child was already fourteen years old. The reason for this transformation is not reflected in the court file, and she was evasive when I asked her. But it is certain that the acrimony started shortly after the permanent marriage contract was made. It created a chain of actions and reactions which culminated in her imprisonment and her first petition only eight months after the permanent marriage. Sima's high *mahr* provided her with a bargaining position for negotiating the terms of her marriage, if not her divorce.

These two cases represent extreme examples of the two principal ways in which *mahr* is used.[25] They might be isolated but they highlight the contrast between the theory and practice of *mahr* and the ways in which the resultant tension can be manipulated by each party.

Both cases illustrate the existing disparities between social and legal conceptions of *mahr*. In law the payment of *mahr* is merely linked to the act of consummation whereas in social practice the question of its payment arises only in the instance of divorce. The court is bound to enforce the legal position, which is derived from the Shari'a, as reaffirmed by the judicial decree of the three eminent Ayatollahs. Yet in its practice the court seems to act in accord with the social norms: in both cases, though in different ways, judges made a link between *mahr* and divorce. In the first case the woman gained the judge's sympathy, and as a result the divorce was substantially delayed, because the wife was using her *mahr* as a trump card in accordance with one of its perceived functions: to safeguard the wife's position in marriage and to control the husband's capricious impulses. In the second case, it was the husband who gained the judge's sympathy as the wife was not using her *mahr* in accordance to another variation of its popular function: to free her from an undesired marriage. She could not receive her *mahr* and demand a divorce at the same time. Her unwillingness to forfeit her *mahr* in return for a divorce convinced the judge that her real intention was not freeing herself but abusing her right to *mahr*. In the first case, the court considered the claim for *mahr* 'legitimate' and in the second case 'illegitimate'. Despite this, when it came to the question of a final decision, the court had to comply with the legal reality and keep the question of *mahr* separate from that of divorce. In the first case, the court could not prevent the husband from divorcing the wife and in the second case it could not prevent Sima from receiving her *mahr*, although she was not granted a divorce.

Both cases, in different ways, reveal the complexity of women's motivations and how the law and the court's ideology can be successfully manipulated to achieve their objectives. In the first case, by having the weight of the court's support on her side, the woman achieved her objectives: to gain full custody of her son without compromising her *mahr*. In doing so, she embodied the wifely ideals of patience, endurance and willingness to compromise to keep the family together. In the second case, although Sima overtly defied the wifely ideals, she also achieved her goals: to gain respectability for her unorthodox marriage, to settle a score with her husband, and to retaliate against the attacks of her co-wife. She did so by appealing to the revolutionary ideology (donating payments of her *mahr* to the Imam's fund) and successfully manipulating the disparity between legal and social constructions of *mahr*.

A large majority of court cases lie between the two extremes represented by the above cases. Depending on who is seeking the divorce, one of the parties agrees to a compromise and the matter is settled. All the court cases where divorce is sought by women also involve claims of *mahr*. A large majority of them result in divorce by mutual consent (*khul'*) in which the wife forfeits her *mahr*. Very often the mere threat of a claim for *mahr* is sufficient to induce the husband's consent; but if necessary she takes her threats one step further and files a suit against him. In negotiating their divorce, the couple often go to such extremes in their respective positions that it becomes difficult to ascertain their real intentions, something which continually puzzled me during my early court attendances. The judge and the court clerk, however, are aware of these factors and they are able to control or end the pretence on either side. Sometimes the court itself takes advantage of the situation created by the bargaining spouses to convince the pair of the advantages of reaching a compromise.

Whatever the compromise and its dynamics, the fact remains that rarely do women get any portion of their *mahr*, unless the husband is adamant on divorce (as in case No. 5) or the wife is prepared to remain in a state of limbo (as in case No. 6); both are exceptional. There are two interrelated factors responsible for this: the legal processes involved in retrieving the *mahr*, and the social position of court clients.

Women who come to the court can be divided, roughly speaking, into two categories. First are those who seek a divorce; they very often enjoy the support of their natal families or are economically independent. These women often belong to upper or middle strata of the society, where divorce is neither so stigmatized nor the women's options so limited. They are prepared to forgo their *mahr*, which is often substantial, in order to be released from an undesirable marriage, as reflected in another Persian saying about *mahr*, 'I release you from my *mahr* to free my life' (*mahram halal janam azad*). In addition, it is only by forgoing all or part of her *mahr* that a woman can obtain a final divorce (*ba'in*). Otherwise, the court issues the permission to register a revocable divorce (*raj'i*) in which the husband retains the right to take her back during the *'idda* period (see case No. 20, Chapter 6).

The second category are those women who seek to deter a divorce requested by their husbands; a large majority of them belong to the lower strata and lack the economic means to sustain their independence after divorce. These women approach the court to make their husbands pay maintenance and are very reluctant to forgo their *mahr*. Although the amount of their *mahr* is negligible in comparison to that of women of the first category, it represents their only compensation. Yet very seldom do they get any portion of it. There is little that a woman can do to retrieve her *mahr* when her husband is without property or a regular salaried income, which is the case among the poor. Although the law regards *mahr* as a man's debt to his wife which must be paid upon demand, irrespective of their marital situation, unlike other types of debts, the failure to pay *mahr* does not incur imprisonment. A wife can file a suit against her husband, claiming her *mahr*, but in order to retrieve it she must produce evidence of her husband's financial ability: for instance, if he has a car or a house, it can be confiscated by the court to pay off the *mahr*; if he is a salaried employee, a monthly amount is deducted from his salary.

This is borne out by the fact that over 50 per cent of all divorces for any given year registered in Tehran are *khul'*, in which by definition the wife forfeited her *mahr*.[26] Likewise, in only three out of 93 cases of divorce initiated by women did the wife receive a part of her *mahr*, although all claimed it. In some cases, in order to hasten their divorce women forgo their *mahr* even though they might have received it if they pursued the matter. In one of these cases, the wife was seeking the dissolution of her marriage because of her husband's mental condition resembling epilepsy. She produced a medical certificate attesting her claim. She had also claimed her *mahr*, consisting of twenty-five gold coins, and had already received three instalments by monthly deductions from his salary as a government technician. The husband explained that his extreme reluctance to divorce was related to the expenses incurred by him at the time of the marriage and his fear of not finding another suitable wife. The judge replied that if his wife could prove that he had suffered even one of his fits, the court would annul the marriage, in which case the husband would be required to pay the entire *mahr* as well as three months' maintenance. The judge reasoned with him that it was in his interest to reach a compromise with his wife since she remained so adamant. Finally, the couple did reach a compromise: the wife forfeited half of her *mahr* and the three months' maintenance, and the husband consented to a divorce. Two other cases involved divorce prior to consummation, thus the wife had a claim to half of the *mahr*. Here again, the couple reached a compromise and the wife received a portion of her *mahr*, less than what she was legally entitled to claim.

3

Legal Anatomy of Divorce: the Moroccan Case

In Morocco, dissolution of marriage is regulated by the provisions of the Code of Personal Status (Mudawwana). These provisions, derived from Maliki law, are outlined in Book 3 of the code, which recognizes three modes of dissolution and devotes a separate chapter to each. These are: *talaq*, rendered 'repudiation' in the French translation of the code; *tatliq*, translated as 'divorce'; and *khul'*, translated as 'repudiation by means of compensation'.[1] Here, I shall be dealing only with the first two modes of dissolution, since *khul'* entails mutual consent and obviates the intervention of the court.

Divorce cases that make their way to the courts are exclusively initiated by women. A man can effect a divorce without going to court and without the consent or even the knowledge of his wife. He simply needs to register it. Yet, in Courts of First Instance, there is a category of dispute in which, although the marriage is already terminated by the husband, the marital conflict is not over. It has extended beyond the divorce and is now expressed over the issue of 'divorce dues'. These disputes come under Demand for Revision of the Order of the Judge of Notary (*talab ta'an fi amr qadi al-tawthiq*); and in effect can be treated as instances in which divorce is initiated by men. In Rabat Court, they comprised the following percentage of all marital disputes: 10.8 in 1985; 8.9 in 1986; 9.9 in 1987 and 7.5 in 1988.

The analysis in the following section is based on the closed files for the year 1987. Out of 1898 cases of marital dispute in that year, 189 were initiated by men who sought to reduce the dues set by the Notary Judge when they registered their *talaq*. The files on 164 such cases were clear enough for me to analyse them. Before doing so, let

84

us first look at *talaq* and its procedure in Morocco and the nature and composition of the 'divorce dues' which form the legal basis for these disputes.

Divorce Effected by Men: *Talaq*

In Morocco, a man's right to *talaq* has remained intact, although the rules governing its procedure have been modified.[2] These modifications, outlined in Chapter 1 of Book 3 of the Code, are:

1. Requiring the registration of *talaq* (Article 48).
2. Narrowing its validity; certain repudiations are now invalid: those pronounced during intoxication or under compulsion, in a fit of violence or in anger (Article 49); those pronounced during the wife's menstruation (Article 47); and those by means of an oath, that is, a husband's swearing that henceforth his wife is unlawful to him or that if she commits or abstains from a certain act she will be divorced (Article 50).[3]
3. Abolishing triple repudiation by means of a single formula; every *talaq* constitutes a single divorce unless it is the third consecutive divorce (Article 51).
4. Recognizing every repudiation as revocable (*raj'i*) unless it results from a third consecutive repudiation or a *khul'* arrangement (Article 67).
5. Requiring a man to pay a consolation gift (*mut'a*) whenever he repudiates his wife, thus providing a kind of compensation for the wife (Article 60).

For a *talaq* to be legal, it must be registered by two notaries (*'udul*) who might operate from their own office (*maktab al-'udul*) or from the Court of Notaries (*mahkamat al-tawthiq*).[4] To repudiate his wife, a man needs to present his Personal Status Booklet and the marriage certificate, on the back (or underneath) of which the *talaq* declaration is drafted (Article 80). This declaration must specify *talaq* type (revocable or irrevocable) and whether it has taken place in the presence of the wife (Article 81). If the wife is present, *talaq* becomes *huduri* (literally, in her presence), otherwise *talaq* is *ghiyabi* (literally, in her absence), which is the case in the majority of *talaqs*.

I came across the following categories used by notaries, covering all possible combinations of divorce types.

● *Talaq raj'i ghiyabi awwal* (or *thani*) is, literally, the first (or second) revocable repudiation in the absence (of the wife). This means that the husband repudiated the wife, in her absence, for the first (or second) time. The divorce becomes final only after the expiry of the waiting period, during which he has the right to resume marital relations.

- *Talaq raj'i huduri awwal* (or *thani*) is, literally, the first (or second revocable repudiation in the presence (of the wife). It differs from the former only in that the wife is present when the repudiation is effected.
- *Talaq al-thalath* is, literally, the third divorce. This divorce is irrevocable and can be either *huduri* or *ghiyabi*. After the expiry of the *'idda* period the couple become forbidden to each other.
- *Talaq al-khul'*. This, as we have seen, is a kind of divorce by mutual consent in which the husband receives compensation for agreeing to release the wife. By definition, *khul'* is a *huduri talaq* as the presence of the wife or her guardian is an essential part of the contract.
- *Talaq qabl al-bina'*, literally, divorce prior to consummation. This type of divorce is irrevocable, and the divorce dues are reduced.
- *Talaq al-mumalik*, literally, possessed. This is an irrevocable divorce in which the husband specifies that he wants the repudiation to be final. It is one of the irregular forms (*talaq al-bida'*) which has endured in practice despite being disregarded by the code in 1957.[5]

When I asked the judges in Court of Notaries about this form of *talaq*, they all told me that, in Maliki law, *mumalik* is a form of irrevocable *talaq* in which the husband gives the woman the option of divorcing herself if a certain stipulated condition in the marriage contract is breached, for example his taking a second wife.[6] They then added that *mumalik*, as practised now, is a type of *talaq* in which upon the husband's demand the divorce becomes final (*ba'in*). Such a divorce is distinct from *talaq thalath* as it does not in itself create a temporary bar between the couple, unless it is the third successive divorce. Only the irrevocable element has survived from the original *mumalik* in Maliki law. But instead of giving women the option of divorce, men are given the option of finalizing the repudiation by using a distorted version of the original *mumalik* formula. This distortion, I believe, has its origins in a pronounced reluctance to insert conditions in the marriage contract, which would enable women to use the option of divorce. This attitude is still very prevalent among present day *'udul*; some told me that they would never agree to contract a marriage with such a stipulation, as it sets a shaky foundation for the union. It seems probable that in time this has led to the disappearance of that element of *talaq*

Table 3.1 *Distribution of Types of Talaq, Salé and Rabat, 1987*

Town	Revocable raji'i		Irrevocable mumalik		khul'		qabl al-bina		thalath		Total
	no	%	no	%	no	%	no	%	no	%	
Rabat	433	21	564	28	723	35	292	14	47	2	2059
Salé	741	45	84	5	623	37	171	10	42	3	1661
Total	1174	32	648	17	1346	36	463	13	89	2	3720

al-mumalik which restricted men's power in marriage.[7] *Mumalik*, as practised in today's Morocco, is an example of how a Shari'a rule which was meant to afford women easier access to divorce can be modified in time to give men a freer hand in disposing of their wives.

There are no accurate statistics on *talaq* types. My own data are insufficient to make any valid generalization: in only 27 out of 164 cases that I analysed, did the file contain a divorce document. Thirteen of these *talaqs* were revocable, of which five were of the *ghiyabi* type; 14 were irrevocable, of which six were of the *mumalik* type, four were divorce prior to consummation, one was third divorce; and the remaining three were irrevocable divorces issued by the court upon the woman's demand. When I asked the notaries, they maintained that most divorces are revocable (*raj'i*); yet the only statistics that I could obtain are more in line with my own data. Table 3.1, based on all divorces registered in 1987 in the Courts of Notaries of Salé and Rabat, clearly suggests the prevalence of the irrevocable type of divorce.[8]

The difference between Rabat and Salé is more a reflection of the practice of their respective Courts of Notaries than of any significant difference in the nature and severity of marital conflicts, leading to a final type of divorce. Salé's lower percentage of *mumalik* divorces, outlawed by the Moroccan Code, is due to the fact there is a greater degree of conformity to articles of the code.[9]

Divorce dues

Whenever a man repudiates his wife, the notaries who draft the document send a copy to the Court of Notaries where divorce is registered (some of these notaries are stationed in the court itself). Upon registration, the couple are summoned to the court in order to set the divorce dues. During a short and informal session held in his room, the Notary Judge determines the divorce dues (*wajibat al-talaq*), comprising five types of payment to which every repudiated wife is entitled. These payments are listed here and discussed in more detail in the context of dispute cases which involved their modification.

1. *Mut'a*, literally, consolation gift, applies to all cases.[10]
2. *Nafaqat al-'idda*, literally, 'waiting period maintenance'. This maintenance is either for three months or until delivery if the woman is pregnant.
3. *Nafaqat al-awlad*, literally, 'children's maintenance'. This applies only if there are children from the marriage.
4. *Nafaqat al-mahal al-sukna*, literally, 'place of residence maintenance'.

An amount is fixed only if the repudiation is revocable and the wife is living outside the marital home during the waiting period (she has the right to remain in the conjugal home until the divorce is finalized).

5. *Kali' al-sadaq.* This is the deferred portion of dower, the exact amount is as written in the marriage contract.

The order on which these payments are recorded is referred to as *amr qadi al-tawthiq* (The Order of the Notary Judge; ONJ). Article 179 of the Moroccan Civil Procedure Code requires its immediate execution. This means that a man has to pay there and then or within ten days. It is only later and through normal legal channels that he can object to the amount fixed by the judge. This is done by filing a petition to the Court of First Instance within a month of its issue. I recorded details of 164 of these files, as summarized in Table 3.2.

Table 3.2 *A summary of Outcome of ONJ According to Sex of Petitioner, Rabat, 1987.*

| | Decided | | | | Not decided | | | | |
| | Accepted | | Rejected | | Withdrawn | | Abandoned | | Total |
	no	%	no	%	no	%	no	%	no
Men	84	70	19	16	10	8	7	6	120
Women	30	68	10	23	3	7	1	2	44
Total	114	69	29	18	13	8	8	5	164

These files have two distinctive features. First, men petition a large majority of these disputes (120 cases or 73 per cent) whereas women constitute the bulk of petitioners (80 per cent of all marital disputes).[11] Secondly, not only does a high percentage of them reach the state of judgment (87 per cent), but a significant number of them are rejected; the corresponding percentages for all marital disputes are respectively 36 and 2 per cent.[12] The reasons behind this are two-fold: the relevant sections of the code, and thus the court procedures, are clear-cut; and the parties are less inclined to use the court as a means of bargaining their terms. The repudiation has relegated negotiations to the domain of post-marital relations, which are reduced to pecuniary issues. What either party can object to is only the amount set by the Notary Judge; men naturally demand a reduction and women demand

Table 3.3 *Accepted Demands According to Type of Payment and Petitioner, Rabat 1987.*

	Mut'a (consolation gift)	Nafaqat al-'idda (waiting period maintenance)	Nafaqat (maintenance for children)	Total
Men	63	44	45	84
Women	13	16	19	30
Total	76	60	64	114

an increase. Table 3.3 summarizes the outcome of those cases in which three types of payment were modified.

The entries in this table are not mutually exclusive: they are arranged to show the frequency of the payment type whose modification is demanded. Most disputes involve the reduction or increase of more than one type of payment; and among them *mut'a* occupies a central place (75 per cent of men demanded its reduction). This is a consolation gift that the husband is required by law to give to his repudiated wife. Payment of *mut'a* was non-existent in Morocco prior to 1957; it is among the reforms introduced by way of rendering obligatory a Shari'a recommendation which had only a meritorious character. The justification for obliging a man to compensate his wife upon repudiation is derived from a number of Maliki commentaries on two Koranic verses.[13] The rationale for this payment, as the judges interpret it, is to appease the wife and to alleviate the pain that the divorce has caused her; *mut'a* here means appeasement.[14] Notary Judges told me that the determining factor in fixing the amount is the 'harm' (*darar*) inflicted on the wife due to repudiation. The harm is assumed to be greater if the husband's action was based on caprice; it is less if she was at fault or if she gave her consent.[15] They added that in theory no other factor, such as the length of marriage or the wife's economic situation, should influence the amount of *mut'a*, although the judge needs to be mindful of the husband's finances and the woman's social situation.

Aware of the rationale behind the determination of the value of *mut'a*, men and women argue their cases differently. The reasons given by men can be divided into three: (1) financial, including a wide range of considerations for contending that the amount set is out of proportion to their earnings; (2) familial obligations, including responsibility for another wife and another set of children, or for their aged parents and siblings; (3) playing down the degree of harm caused by the repudiation. It is through the arguments put forward in such cases that one can gain an impression of what were the tensions and the causes of conflict which led to the husband's decision to use his power of *talaq*.

The husband attempts to convince the court that the wife was responsible for the break-up of marriage, thus the harm caused was minimal. In five cases, the husband argued that, since the wife was previously married and divorced, the second divorce could not be considered as causing serious harm. This argument, in a distorted way, reflects the premium placed on virginity: the harm had already been done by the first divorce. In three cases, the husbands argued that according to the Shari'a, *mut'a* should be one quarter of *sadaq* and thus protested at the unreasonableness of the amount set by ONJ.[16] In other applications, men simply pleaded for the reduction of *mut'a* on the basis of their low income and their responsibility towards their other wife, and their aged parents.

Conversely, women endeavour to show the harm that the divorce caused them and the arbitrary nature of their husband's action. They stress the fact that they stand little chance of remarriage, given their age, their not being virgin and having the custody of their children. Women gave the following causes for their repudiation: the husband's remarriage and bringing the second wife to the house; his irresponsibility, drinking and gambling.

The court pays little attention to the arguments of each party, which are always diametrically opposite; and it does not concern itself with establishing the truth of these claims. What appear to influence the court's decision are the financial situation of each party, the duration of marriage and the possibility of the woman's remarriage. A man is required to prove to the court that his earning level is low, that he is unemployed and does not own any property; his repudiated wife needs to provide evidence refuting his claim. Contrary to what is held in theory and was articulated by Notary Judges, the woman's income does affect the outcome of the cases that reach courts of First Instance. In cases where women were employed and earned a regular income (always government or salaried), the *mut'a* was reduced; conversely, in cases where women were unemployed and the duration of marriage was long, *mut'a* was increased by the court. A comparison between the original amount of *mut'a* set by ONJ and its modification by the judgment of the Court of First Instance (Table 3.4 and Figure 3.1) shows that the court has reduced the very high payments and increased the low ones. The revised *mut'a* is more evenly distributed and has a lower average.

Table 3.4 *Original and Revised Mut'a Awards, Rabat 1987*

Original award (in dirhams)	No of cases	Mean change	No of cases un-changed	No of cases raised	Mean size of raise	No of cases reduced	Mean size of reduction
0– 999	24	+331	15	9	+883	0	–
1000–1999	29	+66	20	4	+992	5	–410
2000–2999	24	–304	13	0	–	11	–664
3000–3999	28	–568	15	0	–	13	–1223
4000–4999	14	–1343	5	0	–	9	–2088
5000–5999	20	–1195	6	0	–	14	–1707
6000–6999	4	–1000	3	0	–	1	–4000
7000–7999	5	–2000	2	0	–	3	–3333
8000+	5	–4200	2	0	–	3	–7000
Totals	153	–595	81	13	–	59	–1745

	Lowest	Highest	Mean
Original:	300 dirhams	10,000 dirhams	2894 dirhams
Revised:	300 dirhams	10,000 dirhams	2305 dirhams

Figure 3.1 *Distribution of Sizes of Original and Revised* Mut'a *Awards, Rabat 1987*

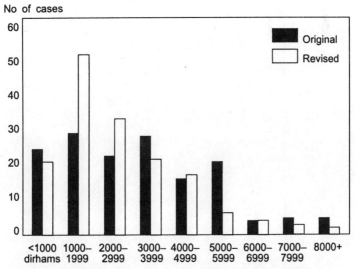

Figure 3.2 *Distribution of Original and Revised* 'Idda *Awards, Rabat 1987*

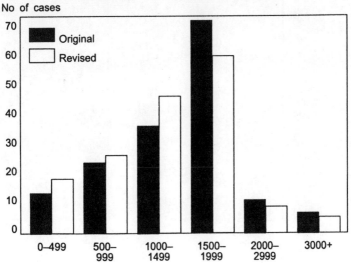

Table 3.5 *Original and Revised 'Idda Awards, Rabat 1987*

Original award (in dirhams)	No of cases	Mean change	No of cases unchanged	No of cases raised	Mean size of raise	No of cases reduced	Mean size of reduction
0– 499	12	+167	7	4	+538	1	–150
500– 999	22	+5	15	3	+533	4	–375
1000–1499	34	–72	18	2	+800	14	–289
1500–1999	72	–98	51	3	+633	18	–496
2000–2999	9	–528	3	–	–	6	–792
3000+	6	–333	4	–	–	2	–1000
Totals	155	–91	98	12	+604	45	–475

	Lowest	*Highest*	*Mean*
Original:	150 dirhams	4,000 dirhams	1341 dirhams
Revised:	150 dirhams	4,000 dirhams	1213 dirhams

Table 3.6 *Original and Revised Hadana Awards, Rabat 1987*

Original award (in dirhams)	No of cases	Mean change	No of cases un-changed	No of cases raised	Mean size of raise	No of cases reduced	Mean size of reduction
0– 99	7	+389	–	7	+389	–	–
100–199	11	+166	6	5	+366	–	–
200–299	23	–61	9	8	+209	6	–43
300–399	47	–35	19	2	+175	26	–76
400+	18	–5	9	3	+167	6	–98
Totals	106	+40	43	25	+283	38	–74

	Lowest	Highest	Mean
Original:	75 dirhams	600 dirhams	298 dirhams
Revised:	125 dirhams	900 dirhams	323 dirhams

Figure 3.3 *Distribution of Original and Revised* Hadana *Awards, Rabat 1987*

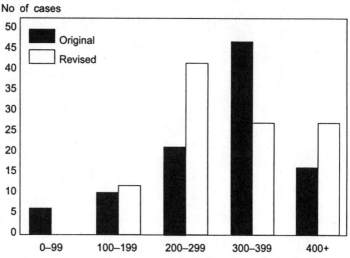

The court requires the same kinds of proofs to be provided for revising the two other payments: *'idda* and *hadana*. Tables 3.5 and 3.6, and Figures 3.2 and 3.3 show how the court modifies these payments. The *'idda* payment is the wife's maintenance during the waiting period, and *hadana* is applicable whenever there are children and when the wife has the custody.[17]

As these tables and figures suggest, the court has tended to decrease the *'idda* but to increase the *hadana*, although in both cases their main function is to modify the extreme original payments. In 15 cases the wife was pregnant and claimed for the maintenance to be extended until delivery, which was granted when she provided a medical certificate attesting her pregnancy. Some of these cases also involved other claims such as expenses incurred for delivery or acknowledgment of the child's paternity (see Chapter 5).

Kali' al-sadaq, (literally, the remainder of dower) is the only payment which is not modified. The reason for this lies in the contractual aspect of marriage. Like *mahr* in Iran, *sadaq* in Morocco is fixed at the time of the marriage and becomes an integral part of the contract, therefore it cannot be subject to any modifications. Although there are almost no disputes involving *sadaq* in Moroccan courts, it is essential to look at this payment in more detail and compare it with *mahr* in Iranian marriages.

Moroccan practice of dower (sadaq)

The rules pertaining to *sadaq* are to be found in Chapter 4 of the Mudawwana. It defines *sadaq* as 'any valuable that the husband offers to the bride, indicative of his desire to contract a marriage and establish a family' (Article 16). No limit is set for the value of *sadaq* (Article 17), which becomes the exclusive property of the bride upon marriage (Article 18). *Sadaq* is payable either upon marriage or later (Article 20), in which case the wife has the right to refuse consummation until she receives it (Article 21). In case of her repudiation prior to the consummation of marriage, she is entitled to only half of the agreed *sadaq* (Article 22). Finally, in case of dispute over the payment of *sadaq*, a woman's claim is believed if the marriage is not consummated, otherwise the man's claim will be accepted (Article 24). Although these rules do not differ from those contained in the Iranian Code, the way *sadaq* is practised in Morocco makes it essentially a different payment from the Iranian *mahr*.

In Moroccan practice, *sadaq* consists of two parts: *naqd* (cash) and *kali'* (remainder).[18] *Naqd* comprises the bulk of the *sadaq* money which is paid prior to marriage to the father of the girl; he supplements it with an equal or larger amount to provide her with a dowry (*shura* or *shawar*) consisting of domestic furnishings and clothing. This furniture is usually a set of traditional Moroccan saloon divans (with elaborate Moroccan needlework) and/or a set of bedroom furniture that the bride brings with her to her new home. The traditional clothing that she receives is elaborate and expensive, some of which might be displayed in the wedding ceremony when she changes her dress a number of times. In some cases, instead of paying the *sadaq* money to the bride's father, the groom buys the clothing or material for preparing it and undertakes to provide the furnishing himself; the value of such an undertaking is always recorded in the marriage contract.

The value and composition of the *sadaq* vary according to social class and regional customs. Some regions such as Oujda in the north and Fes in the centre are renowned for their traditions of high *sadaq*. Everywhere in Morocco, among the wealthy, *sadaq* always includes jewellery, namely a gold belt.[19] Yet, irrespective of its value and its composition, it is not the *sadaq* written in the marriage contract which is indicative of the social status of the bride. It is the scale of the wedding celebration, the jewellery that the bride receives (especially the gold belt) and the dowry that she brings to the marriage which are of primary focus. For instance, Hildred Geertz remarks, 'Status competition centres not on the actual sum of *sadaq*, but on the value of the *shura* and the expenses of the wedding feast that follows it.'[20] Further, it must be pointed out that the amount written in

Figure 3.4 *Value of Remainder of Dower* (Kali' al-Sadaq)
in Dirham, as Written in the Marriage
Contracts, Rabat 1987

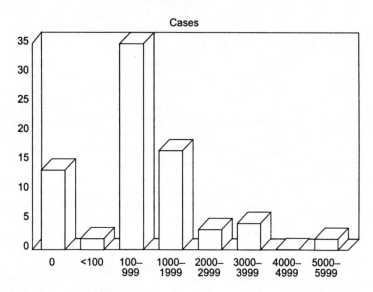

Mean: 856 dirham
Minimum: 0 dirham
Maximum: 5500 dirham

the marriage contract should not be taken at its face value; the arrangement and processes of transferring *sadaq* money are often very complicated. In some cases, although the value of the gold belt and jewellery is written in the marriage contract and it is said that the woman has received it, in practice she comes into the possession of it much later. In three cases that I know it was five years after the marriage before the husband could buy the gold belt that was included as part of the *sadaq* in the marriage contract.

In Morocco, therefore, unlike in Iran, a woman comes into possession of her dower upon marriage, in the form of the *shawar* or *shura*.[21] The deferred portion has nominal importance and often consists of a small sum; in some cases it amounts to nothing. All these details are entered in the marriage contract: both the value of the cash portion of the *sadaq* and its remainder (*kali'*). In Figure 3.4, statistics on *kali' al-sadaq*, inferred from marriage contracts found in these files, reveal its insignificance, especially when placed in the context of marriage expenses. A gold belt costs from 50,000 to 1 million dirham, depending on the quality of gems used; and the average cost of wedding expenses is estimated as up to 100,000 dirham.[22]

In some cases *kali' al-sadaq* is entered as *lashai'* (i.e., nothing); when there is an amount written it is often a round number: in 38 per cent of cases it was recorded as 500 or 1000 dirham. Only two, out of 164 cases of revision of divorce dues, involve a dispute over *kali' al-sadaq*. In both cases, the dispute arose because the agreement reached was not clearly recorded at the time of marriage. In the first case the husband, a government employee, demanded the reduction of the *kali' al-sadaq* of 17,000 dirham. He argued that the wife had already received this amount as he had bought bedroom furnishing which was now in her possession. This argument was rejected by the court on the basis that *kali' al-sadaq* is that which is written in the marriage contract and is fixed. In the second case, the wife demanded 5000 dirham for her *kali' al-sadaq*, arguing that although in her marriage contract *kali' al-sadaq* was recorded as 'nothing', her husband owed her 5000 dirham. Their agreement was for him to provide furnishing to the value of 5000 dirham and he had not done so. This case was also rejected by the court on the same grounds as the previous one. These two cases represent those instances in which the husband did not pay anything at the time of marriage but undertook to provide furniture up to a certain value. It appears that the court does not concern itself to establish whether he did or did not fulfil his promise. I have come across no other disputes involving either the payment or the value of *sadaq*.[23] While 4 per cent of all disputes initiated by women are those in which the main claim is for the return of what she brought to the marriage, they come under *irja' al-hawa'ij* (literally, return of goods); some of them pertain to recent divorces.[24]

Divorce Initiated by Women: *Tatliq*

Chapter 2 of Book 2 of the Mudawwana, under the title of *tatliq*, lists grounds entitling women to a judicial divorce. In this area, the Moroccan Code has not introduced any reform; it reflects the Maliki position, which is the most liberal among the schools of Islamic law. The code empowers the judge to effect a divorce on a woman's demand, upon the establishment of the following grounds.

1. The husband's failure to provide maintenance (Article 53). The article requires the court first to order the husband to comply with his duty and provide maintenance. If he possesses apparent wealth, the court's judgment entitles the wife to a portion of his wealth in lieu of her maintenance. If he neither possesses

apparent wealth nor discloses his financial circumstances, yet persists (in the presence of the judge) in his refusal to pay maintenance, then the judge will be authorized to pronounce divorce on his behalf. However, if he can prove that he is indigent, the court gives him a delay of three months, at the end of which, if he still fails to supply maintenance, the judge will pronounce the divorce. The divorce effected as a result of non-payment of *nafaqa* is revocable and the husband has the right to resume marital relations during the ensuing waiting period, provided that he can satisfy the court that he is willing and has the means to provide the maintenance henceforth.

2.   The husband's affliction with an incurable disease injurious to the wife (Article 54). The code makes a distinction between genital deformities and other illness. In the first case, she is entitled to a divorce if recovery is not expected. In the second case, she is entitled to a divorce if the disease is not curable within a period of one year and if cohabitation would incur harm. The cited examples of the second case are insanity, leprosy, tuberculosis and elephantiasis. However, in both cases she can only demand a divorce if she was not aware of these deformities prior to the marriage. The court can seek medical opinion; divorce granted under this section is irrevocable.

3.   The husband's ill-treatment of the wife to an extent that the continuation of marital life becomes impossible for a woman of her status (Article 56). The article requires the court first to attempt a reconciliation and appoint two arbiters. If the arbiters fail to reconcile the couple, then the court will decide on the matter, taking into account the arbiters' assessment of the causes of the marital conflict.[25]

4.   The husband's absence for a period of at least one year, causing the wife harm (Article 57). The husband's absence, even if he has made arrangements for her maintenance, entitles the wife to a court divorce provided that she can prove that his absence causes her harm. If his address is known, the court gives him a certain time within which he is required either to come and reside with the wife or to divorce her. It is only after his non-compliance with the court order that the judge will pronounce the divorce. If his address is unknown, the judge will appoint a courier to find him and deliver the court order. If he is not found or fails to appear within a certain time, then the judge will pronounce the divorce.

5.   The husband's abandonment of marital relations due to taking an oath of continence (Article 58). Different from both the husband's absence and his failure to maintain the wife, this involves his abstention from sexual intercourse with his wife.

The article requires the judge to give the husband a period of four months to break his oath. If he insists on keeping his oath and fails to resume marital intercourse within this period, then the judge will pronounce the divorce. Such a divorce is revocable.

Unlike its Iranian counterpart, the Moroccan court follows a formal procedure and there is a great emphasis on providing written proofs, which vary according to the ground upon which the divorce is based. In the order of their validity, the evidence required by the court is as follows.

1. Official documents, such as marriage, divorce, and birth certificates. These documents, valid on their own account, are required for all cases; the court will entertain only those where there is a marriage certificate.
2. Legal orders and previous court judgments. These are used as supplementary proofs that the dispute has been judged previously, and the court order was not complied with. They often pertain to orders requiring the husband to pay *nafaqa*; as well as an official document indicating that the husband received the order but did not comply with it.
3. Notarized affidavits, whose validity is derived from being prepared by notaries. These are known as *lafif* in which twelve witnesses testify in the presence of two *'udul* to the truth of a certain fact. There is also another form of notarized affidavit known as *lafif al-mustasfar*. This is a double attestation; twelve witnesses testify in the presence of two *'udul* that they confirm what they had attested to in a previous *lafif*. A *lafif* can sometimes replace an official document, for instance *lafif al-thubut al-zawijyya*, attesting to the existence of marital links between a couple, is equivalent to a marriage certificate if issued by the Court of Notaries.
4. Other forms of written document providing evidence for a claim, such as medical certificates, police reports, bank statements, salary slips, attestations of unemployment and similar types of written documents.
5. The oral testimony of witnesses during the Inquiry Session which take place in the judge's room.
6. The oath (*yamin*), which is only resorted to if no other forms of proof are available, and is used as a final resort in certain types of dispute. There are two types of oath. First, the 'Complementary Oath' (*yamin al-mukamala*), used when the judge has other evidence and resorts to it as means of reinforcing the existing proofs, as suggested by its name: it complements the evidence.[26] Secondly, the 'Deciding Oath' (*yamin al-hasima*), used to

Table 3.7   Tatliq *According to Grounds, Rabat and Salé 1987*

Grounds	Rabat		Salé		Total	
	no	*%*	*no*	*%*	*no*	*%*
Absence (*ghaiba*)	51	43	22	58	73	47
Harm (*darar*)	25	21	7	18	32	21
Non-support (*'adam al-infaq*)	9	8	4	10.5	13	8
Harm and Non-support	24	20	4	10.5	28	18
Absence and Non-support	5	4	1	3	6	4
Absence and Harm	4	4	–	–	4	2
Totals	118	100	38	100	156	100

conclude a case. The judge resorts to this type of oath when there is no other way of reaching a judgment due to the lack of evidence.

Tatliq in practice: grounds and court procedures

Divorce by court action is indeed exceptional: a large majority of divorces take place without the intervention of the court. It comprises those instances in which divorce is sought by the wife but opposed by the husband, where the interplay between law and social reality is most pronounced. I have recorded details of all the *tatliq* cases filed in 1987 in Rabat and Salé, which are summarized in Table 3.7.[27]

As the table suggests, the husband's absence or *ghaiba* is the most frequent ground for divorce sought by women (comprising 53 per cent of all cases). Its procedure is the most straightforward, although it involves a great deal of documentation. Two types of evidence are required: proof of marriage and proof of the husband's absence. The documents that are accepted by the court are the marriage certificate and *lafif al-ghaiba* (absence affidavit). The latter is a written testimony, drafted by two *'uduls* in whose presence 12 witnesses attest to the fact that the husband has been absent for at least a year. Then the court appoints a courier (*qa'im*) to trace the husband and deliver a summons requiring him to appear in the court within a month. The court also issues a summons to the Moroccan National Radio

Services, requiring the details of the case to be broadcast nationally, the husband being informed of his wife's action for a court divorce and required to present himself at the court within a month.[28]

In conformity with the procedure set by Article 57, it is only after receiving a report from the court courier (indicating that all his efforts at locating the husband have failed), and a reply from the National Radio Services (confirming that the details of the case were broadcast), that the court issues the divorce. This is done in a court order in which the husband's absence is recognized and the registration of a revocable divorce is authorized. The content of this order needs to be announced in a national newspaper and the divorce can be registered only a month after its announcement. In some cases the judge requires the wife to take the oath. This is done in the judge's room and the court clerk documents the process in which the woman repeats the following formula: 'I swear to God Almighty that my husband . . . has been absent for more than a year, without leaving any trace and for no specific reasons; he has not given me any *nafaqa*, or has not authorized anyone else to give me *nafaqa*; and he has not given me permission to travel for over a year.'

Out of 73 cases of divorce sought on the ground of *ghaiba* (on its own or combined with others), 48 were accepted by the court, of which 32 were argued by lawyers. All the 48 successful cases contained the following documents: a marriage certificate, a *lafif al-ghaiba*, a report from the court courier, and a report from the radio. All the 25 cases dismissed by the court lacked one of the above documents; only eight of them were represented by a lawyer. In three cases the husband appeared in the court and undertook to return to the marital home, offsetting the wife's claim; in five cases the couple made peace and thus the case was withdrawn.

In terms of their outcome, *ghaiba* cases can be divided into the successful and the unsuccessful, reflecting to some extent the internal dynamics of this type of marital dispute and the way that the legal machinery is used.

In all those cases which are successful the marriage has already broken down and the husband has left some time before. These successful cases are of two kinds. First, there are those relating to long-standing marriages, in which the husband's absence has usually lasted from one to 15 years. In some of these cases, although the wife knows the address of the husband, she does not reveal it; and the husband on his part does not contest the divorce since that would entail expenses, such as maintenance for children, or, if he takes the initiative, divorce dues. In some cases, one gets the impression that there is a kind of tacit agreement between the couple. In others, the husband has genuinely disappeared and the wife is unaware of his whereabouts. Here women are motivated by practical reasons and are not concerned with negotiating the terms of their marriage or divorce. They apply for a divorce either because they intend to remarry or because of the legal problems that they are facing *vis-à-vis* their children. In one case a woman demanded divorce after 12 years only because her son had a car accident. In order to claim insurance money, she needed to prove that her husband, the legal guardian of the child, had disappeared. Otherwise, she said that she would have never gone through the complicated procedure of obtaining a court divorce. She found a lawyer who agreed to take his fee when she received the insurance money.

In the second type of successful cases, the husband has left shortly after the consummation of marriage. The majority of these involve recent marriages of Moroccan men working abroad, or Moroccan women marrying foreigners who later return home.[29] In some cases, the marital home was never established, and in others the marriage broke down because of the reluctance of the woman to live abroad or to accompany her husband. The motivation of women in these cases is also clear and practical: to be released in order to be able to remarry.

Unsuccessful cases are termed by judges 'false absence'; their number is relatively small, and most of them end in dismissal by the court or abandonment by the women. Sometimes the husband is traced, or he comes to the court after hearing the radio announcement, or he sends a relative to inform the court that he is still around and to give a new address for him (a delaying ploy). Some include other demands such as maintenance and a claim of harm. They involve both recent and long-standing marriages. Women's motivations are complex, unlike in the first category; in these cases resorting to the court must be seen as a stage in the development of the marital conflict. Of the ten cases (Table 3.7) in which the stated ground for divorce in addition to disappearance included harm or non-support, eight belong to this category. In some of these cases the husband has actually abandoned the wife but is still unwilling to release her; thus he will do his best to offset her attempts to secure a divorce. If this is the case, the only option open to the wife is to abandon the case and file a new petition, basing her case on another ground.[30]

The internal dynamics of disputes in which women are led to seek a divorce on the grounds of non-support (*'adam al-infaq*) are basically the same as those in *ghaiba* cases. The following case illustrates both the court procedure and the personal motives involved in such cases, crossing the boundaries between the grounds set by the code.

Case No. 7: Rabat, Divorce on the Grounds of Non-support

Latifa was born in 1960 in a small village near Salé. Her father, a low-ranking military officer, later moved to Rabat. There she was married off at the age of 15 to a divorced man, a mason in his forties. He was violent, maltreated her and used to beat her regularly. She became pregnant in the first year of her marriage; and as soon as her child was born she left her husband, returning to her father's house. She then refused to go back to her husband and he in turn refused to release her. She wanted a divorce and her father supported her. A year after she left, her father made a petition to the court, hired a lawyer and conducted the entire process of negotiating her divorce. Finally, three years later, the husband agreed to a *khul'* divorce; in return she renounced her right to receive maintenance for the son. Her father assumed the upkeep of the child.[31]

In 1981 she married another divorced mason, aged 34. Her father had died a year before and her brother was 'busy with his own family' and unwilling to 'keep her'. The new marriage offered the prospect of financial security and a comfortable life; the would-be husband appeared prosperous and was generous. It was later that she found out that he was a fraud, unwilling to work and earn decent money. He had cheated his first wife, a rich older woman: having made her put her house in his name he divorced her, sold the house and started courting Latifa. Their daughter was born a year after the marriage and shortly after that, having exhausted the proceeds of the house sale, he stopped providing for her. She had to make ends meet by working as a maid. She appealed for help to her brother, who gave the husband an ultimatum: 'Start work and provide for my sister, or I shall take her away.'

As the husband did not change his ways, after two years of marriage she left him and returned to her parental home, which consisted of two rooms. One room was occupied by her brother and his family and the other by her aged mother, who was also taking care of Latifa's son from her first marriage.[32] She joined her mother, living on her father's pension. She filed a petition for *nafaqa* and the court ordered the husband to pay 200 dirham per month for her and 150 for the daughter. He did not comply with this order and she did not pursue the matter further. She knew that her husband had no property and thus there was no prospect of extracting any money from him.

As long as her mother was alive they could make ends meet, and it was after her death, when her father's pension stopped, that Latifa faced the task of feeding her two children. She started to work as a washerwoman; but her income was not enough. To educate her 12-year-old son, she had to find a home for him. The husband of one of her employers, a trader in the *souk*, accepted the boy; he went to school, helped out around the house and ran errands in the *souk*.[33]

Three years after leaving her husband, she decided to take action to free herself from a marriage which offered her nothing but had the potential of restricting her. She said that staying married meant to be under his control; he could create problems, scandals, and stop her from working. Although she wanted a divorce she was not willing to give up her rights. She said that she knew that he would agree to a *khul'* divorce if she forfeited the claim to maintenance for the daughter. She was not willing to do so as she felt that she had made a serious mistake by giving up this claim for her son in the course of her first divorce. Despite the fact that the present husband might never be in a position to be able to pay for the daughter, she was determined to retain the claim. For this reason she demanded a divorce on the grounds of non-support as opposed to disappearance. Meanwhile, she heard that her husband had married another woman and abandoned her after a year, and that she had also filed a *nafaqa* suit. He then disappeared, and Latifa suspected that he might be in prison.

She made her first petition for divorce to the court in October 1986, three years after she left her husband. This petition was dismissed by the court; she had failed to provide the necessary documentation. Having learned from her first court experience, she applied for legal assistance (*al-musa'ada al-qada'iyya*), which was granted, and then she was assigned a lawyer. The lawyer started the procedure by filing a petition for *nafaqa* for her and her daughter from the date she 'was ousted' from the marital home.[34] The court accepted the petition and summoned the husband. As he did not appear in the court, and as there was a previous court order immediately after she had left the marital home, the court found for her; and issued its decision requiring him to pay *nafaqa* of 350 dirham from March 1987 (the date of her second petition). The new order was obviously ignored by the husband and the lawyer arranged for the defiance order (*hukm imtina'*). On the basis of the husband's second defiance of the court order, the lawyer proceeded to file the final petition, demanding divorce on the ground of non-support.

This petition was accepted by the court, which issued an order authorizing the Court of Notaries to register a revocable divorce.

The entire process took almost three years and she obtained her divorce in November 1989.

Although the reason underlying Latifa's decision to free herself from a defunct marriage is the same as those in a *ghaiba* case, both the court procedure and the implications of such a divorce are different. Latifa now retains a claim to the maintenance for her daughter until the latter marries.[35] As we shall see in Chapter 5, this claim proves to be useful under certain circumstances.

As regards the procedure, here again the court issued the divorce order only after it was satisfied that attempts to persuade the husband to comply with his duty (providing maintenance) had failed. Even though he did not appear in court, the court issued an order and fixed the amount of maintenance. His absence was taken as the proof of his defiance of the court order, which was presented in a document known as *hukm al-imtina'*, that is, a legal order indicating that the court order was not complied with. In some cases, the court takes an additional precaution and requires the wife to take an oath to the effect that she has not received any *nafaqa* from the date when she was abandoned.

Out of 13 cases of divorce sought on the ground of the husband's non-support, six were successful and the wife obtained a court divorce. All contained these documents: a previous court order (or orders) requiring the husband to pay *nafaqa*, and proof that the husband had received this order but declined to comply with it.[36] In three cases the court rejected the demand for divorce, instead issuing a *nafaqa* order. Two cases were abandoned by the women and their cases dismissed. In the remaining two cases, the couple reached a settlement out of court: one ended in reconciliation and the other in the husband divorcing the wife.

Unlike the above two grounds, cases based on the ground of harm are often those in which the husband is contesting the divorce requested by the wife, for whom it is the last resort. Here again the court requires the wife to prove harm. The type and nature of proofs provided and accepted by the court vary from one case to another; they might involve a combination of the husband's abandonment of marital life, non-support, and maltreatment.

In some cases, proving harm is straightforward. In one, the husband's habitual violence towards his wife and the children led to the death of his 11-year-old son after the boy had been beaten with an electric cable. The husband was subsequently convicted of manslaughter and imprisoned; the wife's demand for divorce was accepted. In another successful case, the husband had been convicted of sexually assaulting his step-daughter. In three other cases, the file contained both medical and police reports that the husband had caused physical injury (such as broken bones, etc) to the wife. Two other cases were accepted on the grounds of the husband's imprisonment for other offences such as embezzlement or theft. It appears that, similar to the Iranian case, in defining 'harm', the court puts emphasis on physical manifestations; if convinced of these, it will issue a divorce without much ado.

The instances that women give as evidence of harm are varied. A majority of cases involve a combination of grievances. They can be roughly classified as follows: physical violence (36 cases); irresponsibility, not providing for the family (28 cases); husband's remarriage and abandonment of the wife (11 cases); husband's sexual manners (sodomy) and ensuing physical violence when women refuse (eight cases); and, finally, husband's criminal record combined with violence (six cases).[37] While violence appears to be a common element in most, the boundaries between the grievances are hazy, a fact which is reflected in the grounds upon which a divorce case is based: 39 out of 60 cases of divorce sought on the grounds of harm could have come under either non-support or husband's absence.

Proof of harm is difficult; and obtaining a divorce on this ground is a lengthy process where much depends on the perseverance of both wife and husband in pursuing the dispute to its bitter end. Cases of extreme violence and cruelty indeed constitute a very small percentage; in most, harm does not necessarily take a physical form; or, if it does, it is not such as to leave semi-permanent physical traces.[38] A significant number of harm cases (47 per cent) also include maintenance claims by the wife, and a counter-petition by the husband for the return of the wife to the marital home. The issues and the legal processes involved can be best examined through the analysis of an actual case.

Case No. 8: Rabat, Divorce on the Grounds of Harm

Huria, a government employee, was born in 1956 in Salé.[39] She comes from a respectable family of Fassi origins who wanted her to marry someone with a similar background.[40] In 1980 she made such a marriage, to Salim from a respectable Salawi family. His mother saw Huria at a wedding and suggested her as a potential wife to her son, who later asked her out twice and then proposed marriage. Her family welcomed the proposal; and Huria, despite some doubts (he was twelve years older and lived with his aged mother) finally allowed herself to be influenced by her family.[41]

Her *sadaq* was 10,000 dirham, of which she received only half, in addition to a gold bracelet and a ring. The *shawar* that she brought, higher in value than the *sadaq*, consisted of Moroccan saloon furnishings (cushions, mattress, and embroidery work); and the bridegroom furnished the bedroom with the other half of the *sadaq* he had promised at the time of the marriage contract. Huria was unhappy from the very first year of marriage: she disliked living with her mother-in-law in an old house with an elderly maid; and Salim was mean. He was trying to control her salary and she found herself paying the bills. She left him several times, returning to her parents' house; and each time he would come after her and her family would persuade her to go back.

In February 1983, following a bitter quarrel, she left again and this time she made a petition for divorce to the Court of First Instance in Salé. She hired a lawyer to follow her case. Her demand for divorce was rejected but the court set a *nafaqa* of 300 dirham per month. His family interceded, and, with the help of hers, again reconciled the couple. She agreed to return only if they lived separately from his mother. Salim made many promises; he was willing to accept any condition. He rented an apartment and paid for two months' rent; but they never moved there and eventually under pressure from both families she gave up the idea of a separate dwelling, withdrew her petition, and returned to her marriage for two years, during which she left him once more, but took no court action and was persuaded to return. She had two abortions during that time, both with Salim's implicit consent.

In March 1985 she left again, and this time filed a petition in the Rabat branch of the Court of First Instance. After her experience of the Salé court she knew that she had no valid ground for divorce. She was advised to demand maintenance and then she would have a trump card to negotiate with her husband for a divorce. She did so and the court order set a *nafaqa* at 300 dirham per month from March 1985 until the date of the order, October 1986. Salim also made a counter-petition, demanding her return to the marital home; this was rejected by her lawyer, who argued that there was no marital home to return to and requested the setting up of a separate home. She took steps to execute the *nafaqa* order; he was not willing to pay and at first ignored the judgment. She then took legal action, made a petition to the Prosecutor-General (*al-na'ib al-'amm*), acquired an execution order and went to his house with a policeman to arrest him. Faced with this action Salim eventually paid the sum of 4000 dirham in three instalments.

All the while she was aiming to spur a *khul'* divorce; she made it clear to him that she was willing to forgo her dowry and renounce her *nafaqa* claim. But he remained adamant and refused a *khul'* settlement.

A year later, she made another petition, demanding *nafaqa* and a separate home. She also complained to the Prosecutor-General, demanding Salim's conviction on the grounds of Neglect of Family (*ihmal al-'usra*). This was ignored by the court, which issued another order requiring Salim to pay *nafaqa* of 300 dirham per month from March 1986 until April 1987, a total of 4284 dirham, and requiring him to set up a separate dwelling for her. She took the necessary legal steps to have the *nafaqa* order executed but did not take any action as regards the separate housing, fearing Salim might actually rent a room, and then by law she would have to live there in order to keep her claim to *nafaqa*.[42]

In August 1987 Huria made another petition, this time asking for a divorce on the grounds of harm and non-support. In the Inquiry Session, the judge asked her why she was unwilling to live with her husband and in what ways the marriage was causing her harm. She replied that he was irresponsible, did not provide her with separate lodging, and did not pay *nafaqa* regularly. Salim interrupted her and said that he bought her jewellery, took her on holidays and so on. The judge told him that these were beside the point, and asked him whether he could prove that he paid *nafaqa*. He produced the receipts of the *nafaqa* that he had paid following the two court orders. The judge informed her that as long as he was willing to pay *nafaqa* she had no case. The session ended without a definite conclusion; the couple were urged to reconcile.

By now Huria realized that she had little chance of obtaining a judicial divorce on the ground of harm, which made her more determined to pursue her only other option of *nafaqa*. But a fortuitous event changed the course of the litigation. In October of 1987, while her case was still open, she went to Salim's house with a policeman to execute a new *nafaqa* order. His mother and her maid had gone to Fes and a young woman opened the door. The policeman, prompted by Huria, became suspicious and inquired who she was and whether she was a family member and whether any one else was in the house. The young woman, in panic, said that no one else was in, and that she was a cousin and was waiting for Salim who had just gone to buy a packet of cigarettes. Huria was quick to deny it and accused her of being Salim's mistress. Huria and the policeman, who was convinced by her promise of an attractive reward, waited outside the house until Salim came: he was arrested and later charged with adultery (*khiyanat al-zawjiyya*).[43] He denied having any illicit relationship with the woman, claiming she was an acquaintance. Huria, anxious not to lose this opportunity, pressed the charge and brought the case to court. Salim was sentenced to two months' imprisonment, but the sentence was suspended as she later withdrew the charge. (She told me that in reality there was nothing between her husband and the woman, who had come to his house asking him to find her a job. Because of his work position as head of personnel, he was able to secure jobs, for which he accepted bribes.)

His family intervened again and she finally dropped the case in return for his consent to a divorce. They arranged to meet in the Court of Notaries to register a divorce. Huria waited all day in the court and no one came. By this stage Salim was so infuriated that he would not give in to his family's pressure and said he would rather go to prison than agree to a divorce under such circumstances. She then added this piece of proof to her court case; she wrote another petition in which she demanded a divorce on the ground of harm, providing as proofs the previous *nafaqa* orders and the new one, convicting her husband of adultery.

This time her demand for divorce on the ground of harm was accepted by the court. The decision, issued in November 1988, authorized her to register an irrevocable divorce. Salim's appeal against this decision to the Court of Appeal was rejected.

Huria was able to register her divorce in December 1989, almost six years after her first petition.

This case highlights the complexities of obtaining a divorce if the husband is present and is seemingly willing to comply with his marital duties – that is, to pay the *nafaqa* – and the marriage has not entailed physical harm. As already mentioned, with the exception of cases of extreme violence, the court requires concrete proof which is not easy to supply. Not all women can rely on a fortuitous event or be prepared to act upon it as Huria did. In only a small percentage of these cases is divorce granted. Here the lawyers play an instrumental role in the outcome of cases based on harm, as suggested by Table 3.8.

Women without lawyers stand almost no chance of having their demand for divorce accepted; a lawyer substantially enhances their chance of success, particularly if we include among the successful cases those which were withdrawn, in some of which an agreement was reached out of the court; in a large majority, women obtained a *khul'* divorce. Likewise it must be pointed out that if the man also resorts to the services of a lawyer, there is a greater chance of the woman's case being rejected. Hiring a lawyer gives a different dimension to the conflict and ensures the continuation of the court dialogue. Fewer

Table 3.8   Tatliq *on the ground of Harm* (darar) *According to Outcome and Whether Represented by Lawyers, Rabat and Salé, 1987*

Outcome	Both		Lawyers hired by Woman only		Neither		Total	
	no	%	*no*	%	*no*	%	*no*	%
Accepted	5	19	8	45	–	–	13	20
Rejected	10	38	2	11	4	20	16	25
Withdrawn	7	27	6	33	9	45	22	35
Abandoned	4	16	2	11	7	35	13	20
Totals	26	100	18	100	20	100	64	100
%	41		28		31		100	

cases represented by lawyers were abandoned: two were for tactical reasons; the lawyer deliberately had the case abandoned to avoid the possibility of rejection.

Women, in choosing grounds on which to base their case, and the court, in issuing a divorce, are both influenced by the procedure and the types of proofs provided. The real conflict within marriage is not only tailored to suit the court but also pursued in a manner which will enable a change of tactics if necessary. Table 3.9 shows the relationship between the outcome of cases and grounds available under the Mudawwana.

Four points emerge from the table. First, a number of cases involve a combination of two of three grounds: husband's absence (*ghaiba*), his failure to provide maintenance (*'adam al-infaq*) and harm (*darar*). Secondly, there are no cases based on two other grounds available under the code: the husband's deformity (*'aib*) and his abandonment of the marital duties (*hajr*). Thirdly, one ground predominates: the husband's absence.[44] Fourthly, as in the Iranian case, boundaries between grounds remain fluid and shifting; grounds upon which a woman bases her application are determined by the nature of the evidence that she can produce. The absence of grounds such as *hajr* (non-fulfilment of sexual duties) and *'aib* (deformity) is due to their hazy boundaries with other grounds; they are thus easily merged with others.

The establishment of grounds becomes more complex and difficult when the husband is present and is contesting the divorce. In these cases the court is used as an arena for negotiating the terms of the divorce, using the trump card of *nafaqa*. This explains why a higher percentage of cases based on a combination of harm and

Table 3.9 *Outcome According to Type of Ground, Rabat and Salé, 1987*

Ground	Judicially decided				Not decided				Total	
	Accepted		Rejected		Withdrawn		Dismissed/ abandoned			
	no	%	no	%	no	%	no	%	no	%
Absence	46	69	1	4	4	14	22	61	73	47
Harm	10	15	6	26	9	31	7	19	32	21
Maintenance	6	9	3	13	2	7	2	5	13	8
Harm and maintenance	3	5	10	44	13	45	2	5	28	18
Absence and maintenance	1	1	2	9	1	3	2	5	6	4
Absence and harm	1	1	1	4	–	–	2	5	4	2
Totals	67	100	23	100	29	100	37	100	156	100
%	43		15		18		24		100	

non-support never reach the state of judgment. Yet, as Huria's case illustrates, through perseverance and clever manipulation of legal machinery a woman can obtain her divorce. Her case also suggests some similarities between the roles of *nafaqa* in Morocco and *mahr* in Iran; both, though effective in a majority of cases, have their limitations in inducing a reluctant husband to consent to a divorce. Their ineffectiveness can be compensated by other strategies – or tricks, such as an accusation of adultery – if the woman is willing to pursue the case to its bitter end.

4

Social Anatomy of Divorce: the Law and the Practice

So far we have examined the legal grounds on which court divorces are sought. They represent legal reality, which at best reflects only one side of the story, that of the woman. Men have no need for grounds: in Morocco, they can register a divorce without the intervention of the court; and in Iran, obtaining the court's permission to register a divorce is not contingent upon the establishment of grounds. We have also seen that demands made in the course of court hearings have a dual meaning. Explicitly, they are tailored to fit the legal rules and argued in accordance with the legal ideology. Implicitly, they are the product of individual circumstances, which are expressed, if at all, in accordance with social norms.

This chapter is concerned with the second, implicit level which seldom finds any expression in the courts. It brings the data from Iran and Morocco together and relies on the judges' assessment of cases and on litigants' accounts of their marital conflict. The chapter offers a different reading of court cases: it attempts to look beyond legal practice in order to locate some common themes or patterns in the internal dynamics of court divorces. My aim is to identify the areas of tension within the marital unit, causing its breakdown. These are of two kinds: first, the institutional tensions stemming from the legal model of marriage and what it entails in terms of marital harmony; secondly, the less structured and more varied personal/individual tensions stemming from the dynamics of conjugal relations. These two types and areas of tension are intertwined; and it is indeed difficult to separate them. Petitions are written with the aim of convincing the court, thus grievances are merged with grounds. Both those seeking a divorce and the court must, as the law stands, do the

115

job of establishing a divorce on the basis of 'grounds'. Yet a closer reading of court files allows us to make a distinction, however crude, between the causes of the marital breakdown and the grounds upon which a divorce is sought.

The reasons given by men and women in their petitions are a window to the nature of the tensions that lead to the breakdown of marriage. There is a sharp contrast between men's and women's accounts. Men do not volunteer details of the marital conflict, and when they do mention them it is always to refute a claim made by the wife. They are vague, brief and non-descriptive, which reflects both their rights in law and the cultural norms: it is both immaterial and inappropriate for men to discuss their marital problems in public. By contrast, women are expressive and provide graphic details of

Table 4.1   *Iran: Stated Reasons for Seeking a Court Divorce*

	Men		Women		Total	
	no	*%*	*no*	*%*	*no*	*%*
Disobedience and lack of cooperation	54	82	–	–	54	32
Incompatibility and problems with extended families	4	6	5	5	9	5
Non-support and irresponsibility	–	–	25	24	25	15
Non-support and addiction/gambling	–	–	19	18	19	11
Non-support and abandonment of marital home	4	6	10	10	14	8
Maltreatment and violence/insult	–	–	29	27	29	17
Addiction and imprisonment	1	1	11	10	12	7
Illness and infertility	3	5	6	6	9	5
Total	66	100	105	100	171	100

the events that led to their seeking a court divorce. After all, they need to make a case: to convince the court of the hardship that they suffer.

Table 4.1 presents a summary of the reasons given for seeking divorce in Iran, where as many men as women resort to the court to secure a divorce.

For Morocco, where the legal machinery and procedures for effecting a divorce are different, such data are not always available in divorce files. But a similar table can be constructed by juxtaposing reasons given by women in their demands for a judicial divorce with reasons given by men in their petitions for reduction in the divorce dues. Table 4.2 presents a summary of the reasons given by men and women, taken from two different types of court files: Revision of the Order of the Notary Judge (mostly initiated by men); and Demand for Court Divorce (exclusively petitioned by women).

Table 4.2   *Morocco: Stated Reasons for Divorce*

	Men		Women		Total	
	no	%	*no*	%	*no*	%
Disobedience and bad behaviour/ temper	38	79	–	–	38	19
Incompatibility and problems with extended family	5	10	10	6	15	7
Dishonour	6	11	–	–	6	3
Non-support and irresponsibility	–	–	23	15	23	11
Non-support and abandoning of marital home	–	–	61	39	61	30
Non-support and polygyny	–	–	22	14	22	11
Maltreatment and violence/sodomy	–	–	40	26	40	19
Total	49	100	156	100	205	100

These tables reveal the strong hold of legal ideology, which is inevitable. By the time that a marital conflict reaches the court it has already been legally defined, irrespective of the issues involved. The salient features of this legal definition, as discussed in Chapter 1, rest on a man's ability to provide and a woman's willingness to submit. Accordingly, for men their wives' insubordination becomes the main cause of marital breakdown: 82 per cent and 79 per cent of men in Iran and Morocco respectively cited their wives' disobedience as the reason for their action to exercise their right to *talaq*. The actual term used in Iran is *'adam sazish* or *nasazigari* (literally, lack of cooperation); and in Morocco, it is *su' al-akhlaq* or *si'at al-akhlaq* (literally, bad temper). This is a list of what men cited in their applications as evidence of disobedience; all are deviations from the expected female role model:

Her bad temper
Her abrasive language
Her habit of answering back
Her leaving the house without his permission
Her insistence on working without his approval
Her excessive economic autonomy (buying, lending things without his permission)
Her periodic visits to her parents' house
Her being influenced by her family (not to obey him)
Her taking possessions out of the house
Her bad cooking and housekeeping
Her dishonesty
Her lack of respect for his family
Her threats to commit suicide (blackmailing him)
Her unjustified jealousy.

Likewise, for women, their husband's failure to provide becomes one of the main causes of marital breakdown. This is a list of what women complained about:

His selling the household furniture
His selling her jewellery
His spending the rent money on drinking/gambling
His failure to provide a separate dwelling
His drinking and gambling habits
His spending money on his natal family
His being under the influence of his mother and sisters
His idleness, being out of work
His contracting a new marriage

His seeing another woman
His taking a temporary wife (in Iran)
His excessive violence, beating her and the children.

Though seemingly diametrically different, when we probe behind the façade of legality we find that men's and women's complaints share a common denominator. They reveal that the breakdown of marriage is dominated by two unresolved types of conjugal conflict: those involving the matrimonial regime and those involving polygyny. Both stem from the contrast between the Shari'a model of marital harmony, based on male domination and viewed as static, and the actual dynamics of marital relations found in practice.

The Legal Matrimonial Regime: Double Rules and Double Standards

In both Iran and Morocco, judges were unanimous that the principal cause of divorce is economic. Court reports certainly convey the impression that everything in the domain of marriage is reduced to its financial aspects, with very little indication of other elements that could have contributed to the breakdown of a human relationship. Each party presents itself as a victim, mainly in financial terms. There is nothing peculiar about this. Divorce is the crux of a process of disinvestment in which each party attempts to get back what he or she brought into marriage, or to hold on to that which was acquired. At the point of divorce what remains from the relationship is often reduced to pecuniary issues. But what is peculiar to Muslim divorces is the sharp contrast that exists between the legal and social conceptions of these issues.

The legal model does not conceive of a shared matrimonial regime: marriage creates no common area of ownership. The husband, as the head of the household, is the sole owner and the sole provider. It is his duty to provide for his wife and children, for which they owe him obedience. The woman is a mere consumer; her property and her income remain hers, and her husband has neither control over nor any share in them.

This regime of total separation of wealth within marriage – an ideal advocated by the Shari'a and enforced by modern law – is negated in social practice. The negation takes different forms according to the socio-economic context, and creates tensions that lie at the roots of marital breakdown. These tensions manifest themselves in three distinct ways: the man's inadequacy as a sole provider; conflict over control of the wife's income; and the attempt by each spouse to keep the other's income within the marital unit, an expression of the conflicting loyalties of spouses to the conjugal unit and to the extended natal family.

The first form of these tensions – man's inadequacy as a provider – is most pronounced among the lower socio-economic groups, who constitute the majority of court customers (especially in Morocco). In an economic climate permeated by unemployment and insecurity (which is the case for a majority of the urban poor in the Third World), men fail to be sole providers, and sometimes even to provide at all. Women, although more marginal, are more wanted as maids and washers on either a temporary or a permanent basis. This gives them better access to the informal economic sector, closely tied to patronage systems. Women create and maintain reciprocal networks of support comprising those for whom they work and their relatives. This network has a distinctly female character to it. Most of these women benefactors, who provide informal employment for other women, derive their economic power from men as mothers or wives, yet they enjoy a great deal of autonomy and influence within the domestic sphere. Women of the poorer strata utilize this network effectively to make ends meet: to feed, clothe and even educate their children in return for the services that they render at weddings, funerals, spring cleaning, etc.[1] Their marginality enables them to sustain such interactions without incurring shame or dishonour. For a man, a similar network rarely includes his family as such activities entail loss of face and compromised honour, undermining his position within his household by displaying his inadequacy as a provider.

Court cases involving the poor depict a situation in which, contrary to the legal model, women are economically active and contribute as much as their husbands to the economy of the household. In some of these cases the woman's earning capacity is much superior to that of her husband. This is particularly the case in Morocco, where women's presence is highly visible in the labour market. In Iran, it is indeed rare to see women as vendors of home produce in the bazaar, as bus conductors, as cleaners in offices, and so forth, which are familiar sights in Moroccan towns.[2] Court files in Morocco contain many instances in which the wife is the main breadwinner. In one case in which the wife demanded divorce on the grounds of harm for non-support, she herself was a petty trader who regularly travelled abroad (with the written permission of her husband) while her husband was a low-salaried government messenger who spent most of his salary in cafes. Their case never reached the state of judgment: she withdrew her petition after he agreed to divorce the wife he had taken during one of her absences. It was the first wife who gave him the money for the payment of divorce dues.

These economic realities among the urban poor go against the very foundation of the legal model of a matrimonial regime, constructed on men's ability to be the sole providers. The ideal role expectations require men to be in charge and to be responsible for running the household, whereas in practice women are more in charge. It is this clash between the ideal and the possible that lies at the root of marital disputes among the poor, in particular in Morocco.[3] The resulting tension is expressed in a variety of ways, as varied as types of personalities and conjugal circumstances. Two common ways in which men respond to these tensions are violence and desertion. Through violence and physical domination, men can reassert the authority which the law bestows on them but which has little basis in their own experience of marriage. Physical violence becomes a measure of the erosion of a man's authority in the household: it is more frequent among the poor exactly because of the more acute need for such a reassertion. Violence very rarely produces a lasting balance or the intended results, and men soon find themselves in an impossible situation, feeling increasingly inadequate. Psychologically they cannot cope with the fact of their eroding authority and the consequences of their violence (which leads to more violence and reactions from the woman's family); thus the way out seems to be to leave the house in protest.[4] In time these periods of absence grow longer and eventually they join the number of absent husbands; a phenomenon so common in divorce cases in Morocco.

Women's reaction to both violence and desertion is to make financial demands. In this way, a woman makes the husband pay (both literally and figuratively). The very elements that give men power in marriage are now turned against them. The husband's authority is a function of his economic capability, a double-edged sword. A man unable to pay has little power over his wife, and has little choice but to concede to a divorce she demands. Yet he lets her take the initiative which will free him from further loss of face, and enables him to escape fulfilling his legal obligations: namely that of paying the cost of registration and divorce dues (in Morocco) and the *mahr* (in Iran).

These are, in a nutshell, the underlying reasons for marital breakdown among the poor, regardless of the grounds on which the law entitles women to seek divorce. There are, of course, significant differences between Iran and Morocco in terms of both the frequency of marital breakdown and the consequences for the wife and children; these will be discussed in the next chapter.

Among other groups, the contrast between the religio-legal ideal and social practice takes a different emphasis. In the middle and upper strata of society, where a man is in a position to resist a divorce demanded by his wife, cases brought to the courts can be understood only in the context of power relations. These cases are those which have already defied other sanctions, namely familial and financial. By denying a divorce a man continues to hold on to his power over his wife, even when the marriage has broken down (as in case No. 3 from Tehran and case No. 8 from Rabat).[5] This is the way, and often the only one, in which a man realizes his legal prerogatives, even at a financial cost. By bringing the case to the court, the wife retaliates and thus takes the marital battle to another stage.

Very often what ignites the battle between the spouses in the first instance, and what sustains it, has its roots in a matrimonial regime which not only impedes the growth of shared resources but induces conflicting interests. Two issues are involved: one spouse's resentment of the other's obligation towards his or her family of origin; and the wife's reluctance to invest in a marriage in which she feels very little security. When the couple both work outside the home, the bone of contention is the allocation of each spouse's earnings. In a large majority of these cases, the wife's salary, although often inferior to the husband's, is acknowledged as crucial to the economy of the household in order to keep up a certain standard of living. The processes involved, in particular the emergence of a new model, can be best illustrated through two actual cases. Both cases are in many respects typical of marital conflicts among educated urban couples. These two cases happened to be from Morocco but there are similar ones from Iran in which the couple reached an agreement shortly after their court sessions.

Case No. 9: Rabat, Conflict over Husband's Obligations

Nadia's marriage lasted only nine months. After her first court appeal, Ahmad, her husband, agreed to a *khul'* divorce. She comes from a well-off family, has a university degree, works in the private sector and has a good income. Ahmad comes from a large family and is the eldest brother, with certain responsibilities towards his younger siblings.[6] They met while both were students at university and were together for three years prior to marriage. Her family was aware of this relationship and, though they disapproved of her choice, finally conceded when they decided to get married.

They had lived together happily for about a year prior to marriage.[7] According to Ahmad, Nadia changed after marriage and started to act 'like a traditional woman'. She resented the fact that part of his salary went to educating his siblings, and in response refrained from spending hers in the house. Ahmad found her contradictory and blamed her entirely for their divorce.

He said, 'The problem with women is that they are neither traditional nor modern. They oscillate from one domain to another whenever it suits them. They are modern when it comes to having a premarital relationship and sharing domestic tasks, but traditional when it comes to sharing their salary with their husbands or feeling threatened by their husband's close contact with his family.'

Nadia for her part found Ahmad too 'traditional' and dominating. She objected to the division of labour in the house and his separate social life. She expected him to share household tasks when they came home after work but he was unwilling and preferred to read or spend time with friends. She felt cheated by him; his family was more important for him than his marriage. The main issue for her was that she saw nothing for her in the marriage. 'Why should I invest whatever I have, my youth and my money, in our marriage so that his family benefits?' She felt that the marriage offered her very little in terms of companionship and security.

Another much more common variation of this conflict revolves around control over the wife's salary; here it is the husband who feels resentful and cheated, as revealed by the following case.

Case No. 10: Casablanca, Conflict over Wife's Salary

Rahima's marriage lasted three years. She is a teacher, the only daughter of an urban middle-class family. In 1984, she married a fellow teacher from a rural background, inferior to hers in terms of prestige and cultural finesse. Her parents and her brothers reluctantly agreed to this union when she insisted. Their daughter was born a year after the marriage.

The marriage was stormy from the outset. The husband, Idriss, was violent and used to beat her. Several times her father intervened and took her away, but each time she decided to return. After their last quarrel, which ended in her being badly beaten, her father said 'enough is enough' and swore that he would never let her go back. He made a complaint to the police and also filed a divorce suit on the ground of harm. The case was withdrawn after three hearings; Idriss agreed to a *khul'* divorce and undertook to pay something for maintenance of their daughter.

The main issues in their fights were the control of her salary and the interference of their respective families. Idriss expected her to spend her entire salary in the house, while he spent a part of his on his own family and also saved some to buy a house which would be in his name. He was never truly accepted by her family, who looked with contempt on his rural origins. She was also not well received by his, who resented her for insisting on living separately from them and thus keeping their son away. Both were criticized and influenced by their families, especially his two unmarried sisters (one divorced and the other widowed), who constantly sabotaged the marriage and talked badly of her. They wanted her to come and live with them. She resisted his demands that she hand over her earnings, which often led to bitter arguments and violent fights; instead she invested them by buying jewellery for herself.

Both cases reveal that the conjugal bond is tenuous and fragile while the pull of the natal family is entrenched and strong. They are but examples of tensions stemming from new expectations in a conjugal relationship. The issues involved, although seemingly very different, are the same as those among the poor. They represent two sides of the same coin: the absence of a joint matrimonial regime and the unequal and asymmetrical nature of conjugal rights within marriage. Despite the fact that the law does not recognize a shared area of conjugal resources, in reality marriage entails the existence of such a commonality of material interests. Court cases confirm that the dispute becomes unresolvable when this common space within marriage becomes too strained by the conduct of either spouse. Such a common space is too fragile and narrow when it is not validated by the law, a fact which is well recognized and pointed out by the families of each spouse. As the above two cases illustrate, their families played an important role in adding to the tension by bringing to light the disadvantages of adopting modern roles in a context which is not conducive to them.

At the root of the conflict lies the incongruity between the legal model of marital harmony and the actual expectations and variations of marital roles. The fact that women are now wage-earners has not totally altered conjugal roles and expectations; instead, the new exigencies of the modern context are grafted onto the old model.[8] In the legal model, the husband's control over his wife's activities is the prerequisite for marital harmony. In the modern context, her salary, which is the fruit of her outside activity, must be controlled by the husband and spent in the house, while he remains free to keep his economic autonomy. The traditional model is still valid and dominant, regulating not only the conjugal sphere but also relations with the extended families. Here each spouse is influenced in different direction by the respective families.

While the changing position of women in society, particularly their participation in the wider economy as wage earners, has upset beyond repair the old and delicate balance of marital harmony, as advocated by the Shari'a, no viable alternative model has yet emerged. Traditional attitudes and role expectations are still well entrenched; both men and women are brought up in accordance with them. A girl's early socialization predisposes her to be dependent and have unrealistic views of marriage.[9] As a male Moroccan lawyer put it: 'As a small girl, whenever she wants something she is told to wait until she marries, the assumption being that then her husband will provide it for her. She looks at marriage as a means of fulfilling all her unsatisfied wishes and desires.' The husband is the saviour and the provider. After marriage she realizes that he has limited means and cannot fulfil all her desires, so she becomes disillusioned and dissatisfied with marriage.

On the other hand, men are given the opposite orientation; they are socialized to be providers and to dominate. In the words of a Moroccan female lawyer: 'Their virility is defined in terms of their economic and physical domination over women. By the time they pass the stage of adolescence, they face the fact that not only are they unable to be the sole providers but they need the income of their wives. Their ego and sense of power are then undermined if she shows signs of autonomy.' In one case which I followed in a Tehran court, the husband petitioned for divorce because his wife had written a cheque (from her own account) to a neighbour who was in financial difficulty. He saw it as the ultimate act of betrayal (disobedience, he called it): her action infringed upon what he considered to be their shared marital resources. The judge, obviously caught in a dilemma, had only this to say: 'These problems are inevitable when women work and earn money; it is for this reason that in Islam it is preferable for them to stay at home; their first duty is that of being good wives and mothers.'

This dilemma is not confined to Islamic judges in Iran; my discussion with the judge of the Personal Status Branch of the Court of Appeal (*mahkamat al-'isti'naf*) in Rabat (renowned for his knowledge of Maliki law) echoes the same ambivalence. When I asked how the court deals with the discrepancy between the Shari'a and the actual marital regimes, the judge replied by reiterating the rules: 'The rights and obligations of women are defined in clear terms in *fiqh*. A woman is entitled to maintenance whether she earns money or not. *Nafaqa* is her right; in return she has obligations: to run the household, to see to her husband's needs at home, to bring up the children, and so on. A woman is free to dispose of her own money the way she chooses, and if she spends her money on the marital home, this must be of her own choice and free will, as legally she need not do so. A woman cannot be expected to give birth, to bring up children and work at the same time; the man must provide for her.' There was no way that I could draw him into a discussion of situations in which the woman's contribution is as essential as her husband's. I presented him with a hypothetical case of a teacher who marries another teacher; for them the Shari'a model is out of reach since they would not be able to make ends meet on his salary alone. He gave the same response: 'The law does not oblige her to spend her money in the house but, if she chooses to do so, it shows her understanding and the strength of her conscience.'[10] I found the same attitude among all judges trained in Islamic law, Iranian or Moroccan.

It is not that these judges are unaware of the contradictions between law and actual practices, it is rather that they hold the Shari'a model as divine and immutable; any other existing models are regarded as deviations from the ideal and thus are seen as corruptions (*fasad*), or at best as situations to be accommodated. Not surprisingly, in response to my question, 'What are the real causes of divorce?' all judges (both in Iran and Morocco) referred to changing values and the erosion of the traditional way of life. This is how the tension is defined by judges:

1. Women's employment outside the home and their apparent equality with men have upset the primordial harmony in Muslim marriage.
2. Women's work outside the family results in the neglect of their wifely duties, thus causing tension. Their positive contribution to the household through their work is far outweighed by the negative entailments.
3. The good traditional familial values are disappearing and are being replaced by materialistic ones. Two examples given are that women in the past were patient (*sabur*) and that they kept the family together, but now they have become ambitious and selfish. Women enter marriage with high expectations, especially in material terms which are beyond the means of the husband.

It is clear that, in the eyes of judges (both Iranian and Moroccan) who adjudicate marital disputes, marital harmony is still conceived as women's subordination. They cite a number of maxims to support their view. The Arabic 'if you find a happy couple, be sure that one of them has submitted', and the Persian 'war is the outcome of having two rulers in a domain', are but two examples. It is this conception, more than anything else, that impedes emotional and material investment in marriage. The facts that men have easy access to divorce, and that the law recognizes them as the sole owners of the matrimonial wealth, not only narrow the possibility of the development of shared interests within marriage but in fact make such an investment on the part of women sheer folly.[11] The extent of such folly is implied in a frequently cited female maxim, 'When a man's trousers exceed two, he'll think of getting a second wife', that is, a woman who lets her husband acquire wealth destroys her marriage by enabling him to exercise his right to polygyny.

Polygyny: the Last Straw

Polygyny is the second area in which the conflict between law and social practice results in specific types of tensions causing marital breakdown. Polygyny is permitted by Islamic law provided that the number of wives does not exceed four. In Shi'a law this restriction is confined to permanent marriages; a man can contract as many temporary marriages as he wishes – more precisely, as he can afford. Despite its religious and legal sanction, polygyny in practice is frowned upon and its incidence is indeed low; and when it occurs the number of wives rarely exceeds two. In other words, it is the area where the gap between religio-legal rules and social norms and practices is greatest.[12] Court files suggest that this low incidence may partly be attributed to the inherent tensions that exist in polygamous unions. These tensions are now more acute since they are in open contradiction with current notions of marriage (as perceived by both men and women), which put into question some elements of the Shari'a model of marital harmony.

A wide variety of disputes have polygyny as the cause. Each case has its own peculiar circumstances, but nevertheless there is one element common to them all: the tension in a polygamous union is such that it necessitates the break-up of one of the unions in order to enable the other to survive. Although there is no direct reference in Islamic law defining polygyny as a possible source of 'harm', in modern legal codes this notion is included. In Iran, the husband's second marriage constitutes a ground entitling a woman to a judicial divorce. In Morocco, polygyny does not constitute a ground for divorce on its own unless it is proved that it incurs harm, although, interestingly, the colloquial term for co-wife is *darra*, meaning that which is harmful.[13]

Over 20 per cent of all marital disputes that find their way to the courts, both in Iran and Morocco, involve issues arising from polygyny. This is a significant percentage, given the rarity of polygyny in both countries.[14] One important feature of these disputes is that few end in settlement out of court, and none end in a new state of balance in which both unions continue. They portray extreme bitterness and a resolve, usually on the part of the women, to take the case to its final end. Here, unlike other cases, the court and the law are not used as a means of reaching a solution to a marital impasse, but rather as means of exacting revenge. Polygyny is seen as an impasse to which there is no solution; what is aimed at in bringing the case to the court is the prevention of further harm and a kind of justice. What constitutes 'justice' is a notion that varies. For the judge, it means ensuring that the husband provides for both wives; for the wife it means transforming the union into a monogamous one. Those Iranian women whose demand for the *nafaqa* resulted in their husbands' being flogged saw the punishment as a form of justice; those Moroccan women whose use of the *nafaqa* card forced their husbands either to pay or to divorce the second wife, felt that justice was carried out.

Court files reveal the following facts about the internal dynamics of polygamous marriages, all indicative of the fact that such marriages are not viable when the husband has limited means and the wife another alternative.

1. The high level of deceit reflects the social and logistical complexities involved. In almost all cases, the second marriage is contracted without the knowledge of the first wife. In some, the new wife is also ignorant of the existence of a prior marriage.
2. The extreme bitterness created leads to violence and conflict; thus a majority of these cases involve divorce on grounds of harm.
3. The economic basis of the marriage is disrupted. Very often the husband is incapable of providing for two households, a fact which is manipulated successfully by the wives concerned. Regardless of who initiates the case, the first or the second wife (and sometimes both), *nafaqa* is the main issue. The petitions give the impression that the wife's objection is not to her polygamous marriage, but to not being maintained, showing awareness of the position of the Shari'a on this issue (as in Case No. 2 from Tehran).

Conclusion: Marriage and Divorce, Ideals and Realities

In the preceding chapters, we have explored the theory and practice of marriage in two schools of Islamic law through analysis of marital disputes heard in Iranian and Moroccan courts. In the first chapter, the focus was on the legal structure of marriage and the rights and duties that it creates between spouses. In subsequent chapters, marriage was examined through its dissolution. What has emerged is the gap between law and social practice: the contrast between marriage as perceived and enforced in law and marriage as perceived and practised by people. Such a gap has two related consequences: it creates areas of tension within marriage which foster particular types of marital disputes; and it necessitates the intervention of courts to settle these disputes. Both are the product of the Shari'a conception of marriage as a contract with diffuse boundaries.

Marriage in its legal structure is a mixed institution.[15] At its inception, marriage is regarded as a private contract in which parties are free to stipulate certain conditions. In terms of the rights and duties that it entails, marriage is treated as a public institution: couples can appeal to the courts to enforce the terms of the contract. When it comes to its dissolution, marriage becomes, once again, a private contract in which the husband has the unilateral, and extra-judicial (in the case of Morocco, not Iran), right to its termination.[16] The same right is not given to the wife; she needs either to secure his consent or to appeal to the law. Not only are court cases the by-product of the diffuse legal structure of marriage, but their very *raison d'être* lies in the rules regulating marriage as an institution. Among these are the absence of a matrimonial regime and the asymmetrical nature of the rights and duties of spouses, namely the husband's right to divorce and polygamy.

The codification of Shari'a and its application by a modern legal system has reinforced the mixed legal nature of marriage. The reforms introduced subjected marriage and divorce to secular provisions but did not bring about any fundamental change in their legal conception. This is evidenced in the extent to which courts in both Iran and Morocco, though in different ways, strive to keep to the Islamic legal format. The Iranian judges go to extremes in bringing about a mutually acceptable agreement between the spouses, as in the symbolic transaction by which the husband delegates the right of divorce to the wife. The Moroccan court's complex procedures in issuing a divorce reflect the same concern.

The end-result of all these is that courts become arenas for negotiations to bridge the gap between law and social practice. The scope and boundaries of these negotiations are well defined. The court is bound to enforce the law as reflected in the articles of the modern codes; and litigants are bound to settle their disagreements within this context. In this way, the Shari'a model of marital harmony is perpetuated as an incontestable model. But the fact that this model neither corresponds to the social practice of marriage, nor can be fully enforced, make such negotiations both necessary and possible.

As these chapters have illustrated, there exist substantial differences between Iran and Morocco in terms of both legal practice and the nature and type of marital disputes heard in their courts. Some of these differences have their roots in the diversity of interpretation in Islamic law in its classical form, which became fixed when the provisions of the Shari'a were codified. Others stem from the differences in the court procedures and the structure of the modern legal apparatus in each country. Whatever the roots of these differences, they have a bearing not only on the type of disputes that make their way to court but also on the options available to women. For instance, the high percentage of *nafaqa* cases in Moroccan courts are the corollary of the fact that the Moroccan Code entitles a woman to retain her claim to maintenance as long as she has not overtly defied a court order for her return. This makes separation a viable strategy for women in bringing about a court divorce. The Iranian Code does not offer a similar leeway to women: it makes a linkage between a woman's right to claim maintenance and her physical availability (i.e. remaining in the marital home). This enhances a man's control and power over his wife, which is paradoxical given that it is in Iran that a man's prerogative to divorce is checked, both in law and in practice. Without his wife's consent, a man not only needs the court's permission to register a divorce but remains liable to pay her *mahr*, always beyond his immediate means.

All these factors find expression in the patterns of marital breakdown found in Morocco and Iran. Generally speaking, in Morocco marriage is fragile and its breakdown is more current among the poor strata; whereas in Iran marriage is stable and divorce is more frequent among the middle and upper strata.[17] To understand these differences and trace their roots and present implications, we need to look at other aspects of family law, namely filiation and custody. We need to ask what happens to the family of procreation when marriage breaks down: this is the subject of the next chapter.

PART II

Areas of Tension between Law and Practice:

Strategies of Selection

5

Filiation and Custody in Law and Practice

This chapter extends the examination of the theory and practice of Islamic law to the domain of post-divorce. It focuses on disputes concerning the establishment of paternity and custody arrangements, and examines what happens to the children, and what choices are available to women when marriage ends. This is the area where the codification of the Shari'a has had its greatest impact: it has brought into sharper relief some of the tensions between religio-legal ideals and popular practices. As we shall see, this is also the area where the divergences between Shi'a and Maliki conceptions of family and filiation come to the surface.

The chapter has three aims: to identify the assumptions underlying the notions of filiation and descent in Islamic law; to highlight differences between Maliki and Shi'a interpretations of these notions; and to examine the ways in which these differences, now embodied in their respective legal codes, affect actual practice in Iran and Morocco. Accordingly, it comprises three sections. The first section looks at the Shari'a notions of kinship and descent and explores their social and legal ramifications. The second focuses on Morocco and illustrates how the ambivalence in Maliki custody rules engenders a special type of dispute and a matrifocal familial organization when the marriage breaks down. The third section examines material from Iran: it first explains why paternity disputes are absent in Tehran courts and then illustrates the ways in which the rigidity of Shi'a custody rules is modified in practice.

133

Shari'a, Legal and Social Modes of Filiation

Shari'a legal notions of kinship and filiation are encapsulated in the concept of *nasab*, which translates not only as parentage and kinship, but also as filiation and descent status. While the child takes its *nasab* from both sides, it is the paternal side which has ascendancy over the maternal. In all schools of Islamic law the primary significance of *nasab* is that of paternity, closely tied to legitimacy, through which a child acquires its legal identity and its religion.[1]

Although both Shi'a and Maliki rites recognize paternity as the primary mode of filiation, they differ significantly in their conceptions of maternal filiation, to the extent that they represent two possible extremes of interpretation of the Shari'a notion of filiation. The titles of the chapters dealing with filiation in their modern codes reveal something of the difference. Book 3 of the Moroccan Code of Personal Status (Mudawwana), outlining the Maliki position, is entitled 'Birth and its effects' (*al-walada wa nata'ijuha*). It consists of three chapters: the first deals with *nasab*, the second with rules for its establishment; and the third with custody.[2] The Shi'a position, codified in Book 8 of the ICC, is entitled 'Of progeny' (*dar awlad*); it also consists of three chapters. The first deals with *nasab*, the second with 'The upkeep and education of children' and the third with 'The obligatory guardianship of the father and paternal grandfather'.

As these titles indicate, two sets of rules regulate a child's relationship with its parents. The first defines its legal filiation and the second decides the question of its care. Since the latter depends on the establishment of the former, it is useful to examine the rules of filiation and how they are defined by each school. This can be done best through analysis of two actual disputes involving the establishment of paternity, which arise only when the union is over. Both cases come from Moroccan courts, since paternity disputes, for reasons that will later become clear, are extremely rare in Iranian courts. The first case, initiated by an alleged daughter, involves the proof of paternity; and the second involves the denial of paternity.

Case No. 11: Rabat, Proof of Paternity

Leila, a 24-year-old girl, initiated the dispute against Hassan, whom she alleged to be her father. In her petition, written by a lawyer, Leila stated that she was abandoned by her father, Hassan, when he divorced her mother, Zeinab, in 1964 when Leila was only eight months old. Leila was raised solely by her mother in her maternal grandfather's house; and after his death was provided for by her maternal uncles. She stated that Hassan had not honoured his fatherly obligations towards her, which in actual terms consisted of paying maintenance for her. It was only in 1987 that she learned of his whereabouts and she now wanted to claim that which was her right.[3]

Leila made two demands in her petition: first, the right to Hassan's *nasab*, that is, to be recognized as his legitimate child, which in modern times means to be entered in his *Kinash al-hal al-madaniyya* (Civil Status Booklet)[4]; and, secondly, payment of maintenance for the previous 24 years, amounting to a substantial figure.

In support of her claim, Leila produced two pieces of evidence: the marriage contract of her mother and the order by which the Notary Judge had fixed the divorce dues (*amr qadi al-tawthiq*). In this order an amount of 100 dirham per month was determined as maintenance for a girl by the name of Leila. As we shall see, these two pieces of evidence played a crucial role in changing the course of the litigation.

Hassan, a tall impressive man, with a distinct air of authority, angrily refuted Leila's claim and refused to recognize her as his daughter. He admitted to a marriage with Leila's mother and to having had a daughter by the name of Leila when he divorced her (he had to admit to both in the face of the documents provided). But he claimed that Leila was not the same daughter: his real daughter died shortly after the divorce. He never saw the child; Zeinab, his ex-wife, prevented him from having any access to her and told him that Leila was dead. Several times he went to see Leila but Zeinab threw stones at him, so he gave up.

By producing her mother's marriage contract, Leila left Hassan with no other option than to build his case upon questioning her real identity. The Shari'a principle of legitimacy holds that a child born in a marriage has the right to claim legitimate kinship and descent status (*nasab*) from the husband, unless he explicitly denies the paternity.[5] He can do this through the procedure of *li'an* (imprecation) in which he takes an oath accusing his wife of adultery and disclaiming the paternity of the child born to her. *Li'an* must be made before the judge and it results in termination of marriage and the creation of a permanent bar between the couple, so that they become forbidden to each other.[6]

The marriage contract proved the existence of the marriage and satisfied the court that Leila was the child of the bed (*walad al-firash*); the divorce papers proved that the dissolution of their marriage happened through a normal divorce (*talaq*), not through imprecation (*li'an*). This pre-empted any claim of denial of paternity, since once a man has either implicitly or explicitly acknowledged his paternity he can no longer deny it. Thus Leila's right to *nasab* was established and it became incumbent on Hassan to provide proofs to the contrary.

Case No. 11 (continued)

In support of his claim that Leila was not his daughter, Hassan offered two arguments. First, he pointed out that Leila did not carry his family name but that of her mother; and in addition she had a passport which proved that she had a viable legal identity (an unmarried woman cannot acquire a passport without being represented by her legal guardian: her father if there is one).[7] These, he pleaded, were concrete proofs that she was not of his *nasab*, as she was legally only attached to her mother. Secondly, he claimed that no one, not even members of his own family, knew of his having such a daughter. Here he was appealing to another element of the rules for recognition of paternity, that of independent knowledge that the child belonged to him.[8] His two daughters from his current marriage (he had remarried twice and now had nine other children, five with the current wife) were brought to the court as witnesses and they attested that they had not met Leila, and had never been told of her existence, whereas they knew and had encountered their father's children from his other union.

Both arguments were successfully refuted by Leila's lawyer: her being registered in her mother's name was due to necessity (*darura*), in order to enable her to enter school. Hassan's whereabouts were unknown to Leila's mother until 1987, as she never heard from him after their divorce. She had to register the child in her own name in order to make her education possible. The second argument was refuted on the basis that in this case the presumed paternity was a well-established fact since there existed a valid marriage contract and he had not denied paternity, thus the question of others knowing of it or not was irrelevant.

Thus what remained for the court to establish was whether Leila was the real daughter of Hassan and Zeinab. This was ascertained through an evidence from the district administrative authority (*qa'id*) and twelve witnesses (in the form of a *lafif*). The court reached a decision after six sessions: Leila was recognized to be of Hassan's *nasab*, entitled to carry his name and be maintained by him. She remained in the custody of her mother and continued living with her, and Hassan was required to provide for her henceforth.[9]

The principle upon which the decision was taken was that of *amarat al-firash*, which translates as the 'the rule of the bed'. It is the primary principle of paternity, entitling a child born in a marriage the right to claim *nasab* from the mother's husband.[10] In this respect, there is no difference between Shi'a and Maliki legal rules. In both, the establishment of paternity is possible only in the context of a legal marriage contract (Articles 1158 of ICC and 85 of MCPS). In both, consistent with the patriarchal bias of the law, men are given some latitude in denying or acknowledging paternity of a child who is born outside marriage. The procedure of *li'an* (imprecation), as mentioned above, enables a man to deny the paternity of a child born to his wife. The procedure of *iqrar*, on the other hand, enables him to acknowledge paternity of a child born outside wedlock, provided that there is no definite proof that the child is the issue of *zina* and that the presumption of paternity cannot be rebutted.[11] Although both of these procedures have their own rules and limitations, they do provide a man with the legal means to incorporate or exclude his or her child into his kin group. The modern legal codes of both countries retain the Shari'a legitimating devices. The Mudawwana devotes an entire chapter (Chapter 2 of Book 3) to the question of attachment (*istilhaq*); while the Iranian Civil Code deals in more detail with *shubha* (marriage by error, see below).

The two schools, however, differ as to the second element of the presumption of the paternity. This element holds that only the child born a certain interval after consummation or within a certain period after termination of marriage can be attached to the husband. In other words, there exists a legally recognized duration of pregnancy. Although all schools recognize six months as the minimum period of pregnancy, they differ greatly as to its maximum.[12] The difference is widest between the classical Maliki and Shi'a: according to the former the legal duration of gestation can be as long as five years, according to the latter it can be no longer than ten months. As suggested, it is conceivable that the Maliki jurists extended the gestation period well beyond the medically proved maximum for humanitarian reasons, in order to alleviate the stigma of illegitimacy, not because of ignorance of the biological facts.[13] What is important to note is that here women are the exclusive beneficiaries, as they can demand paternity for a child born well after divorce or the death of the husband and in this way retain an indirect claim, that is via custody payments and inheritance.

This difference in legal duration of pregnancy, when viewed in conjunction with other rules, reveals a fundamental divergence between the two schools in their conception of legal filiation. This can best be shown through an analysis of a case involving the denial of paternity; such a denial is often made in response to a claim made by a divorced woman for a newly born child; and it is peculiar to the Moroccan context.

Case No. 12: Rabat, Denial of Paternity

The dispute was initiated by Salma, a 21-year-old divorcee, who works in a tailor's shop in Salé and comes from a poor background. In her petition, written by a public scribe, she stated that her husband divorced her while she was pregnant. The divorce took place in her absence and the fact of her pregnancy was indicated in the order which fixed her divorce dues. She made two demands: registration of her five-month-old son in her ex-husband's name and maintenance for him.

In support of her claim, Salma provided the divorce certificate (note, not the marriage contract), dated 7 August 1988, which indirectly proved the fact of her marriage; and the birth certificate of the child, dated 13 October 1988, proving she was pregnant when divorced. Her divorce certificate showed that she had received a total of 6500 dirham as her divorce dues: 2500 dirham as *nafaqat al-haml* (special maintenance that a woman is entitled to during pregnancy); 2500 for *kali' al-sadaq* (remainder of the dower) and another 1500 for *mut'a* (consolation gift).

Her ex-husband Jamil, a 33-year-old civil servant from a prosperous family, made a counter-petition denying paternity on the basis of Article 84 of the Mudawwana, which recognizes the minimum duration of legal pregnancy as six months. In support of his claim he provided the marriage contract, dated 24 June 1988, and birth certificate, issued 13 October 1988, proving that the child was born only three months after the marriage (and that Salma was pregnant at the time of marriage).

His lawyer also demanded the return of what the ex-wife had received as divorce dues, on the grounds that the marriage was irregular and therefore its termination should have taken place through annulment, not divorce. He argued that Salma's pregnancy at the time of marriage in itself rendered the marriage irregular (*fasid*), since one of the Shari'a conditions for its validity was violated: Salma was still in the period of *'idda* (the waiting period which lasts until delivery in case of a pregnancy).[14] To substantiate his reasoning, the lawyer quoted the following from the treatise of a Maliki jurist, Ibn Abi-Zayd: 'A marriage contracted with a woman whose womb is not empty is irregular (*fasid*) and must be annulled (*faskh*).'[15]

Confronted with her ex-husband's counter-petition, Salma

sought legal advice and was told that she had no chance of winning the case: the marriage was indeed irregular and thus had no legal validity. She then abandoned the case in the hope that he would also give up. She ignored the court's summons and did not attend any subsequent sessions, while Jamil pursued the case. On 13 March 1989, after sending her two notices at the request of Jamil's lawyer, the court issued its decision. The demands made by her husband were accepted on the basis of Article 84 of the Mudawwana which sets the minimum period of pregnancy as six months. The evidence provided (marriage and birth certificates) satisfied the court of her pregnancy at the time of marriage. The court, therefore, recognized the marriage as irregular, declared it annulled and required Salma to return the 6500 dirham that she had received as divorce dues. It further stated that since an irregular marriage is of no legal effect, therefore the child cannot be attached to the husband, and only takes the *nasab* of its mother.

Faced with her predicament – not only could she not get any maintenance for the child, but she had to pay back what she had received as her divorce dues – Salma then took a lawyer and made an appeal against the court's decision. In the appeal petition, her lawyer implicitly accepted the court's decision as regards the annulment of marriage but challenged it as to non-attachment of the child to Jamil and as to return of the remainder of *sadaq*.

As regards the attachment of the child to Jamil, the lawyer built his argument on the basis that certain essential facts were withheld from the court. Not only was Jamil aware of the pregnancy at the time of marriage but it could be proved that he was responsible for it. The lawyer provided details of a penal court record in which Salma's father had filed a suit against Jamil, accusing him of dishonouring his daughter, destroying her virginity and making her pregnant.[16] The petition was withdrawn only after Jamil agreed to make a legal marriage contract, which amounted to his acknowledging having had sexual relations with Salma and fathering the foetus. This proved, the lawyer argued, that the child was of his blood, thus of his *nasab* and entitled to carry his name and to be maintained by him. The lawyer begged the court to consider the interest of the child, suggesting that Salma's pregnancy could be construed as an incident that occurred during the period of their courtship, which is not that uncommon these days.

As regards the return of the 6500 dirham, the lawyer pointed out that the first court's decision was contrary to the dominant opinions of the Maliki jurists. He quoted another passage from the same jurist, Ibn Abi-Zayd, that a woman's right to *sadaq* is linked to the act of consummation, not to the validity of marriage.[17] He also invoked Article 37 of the Mudawwana, which makes a similar kind of linkage.

The court of appeal dismissed the lawyer's argument on the question of paternity and affirmed the ruling of the first court. The judgment stated that on the basis of Articles 83 and 84 of the Mudawwana, the child could not be legally attached to the husband, but only to its mother, because it was born outside the recognized periods. The court took the date of the marriage contract as the beginning of the legitimate relationship, not the courtship, as the lawyer suggested. But in considering the return of the *sadaq*, the court accepted the lawyer's argument and overruled the earlier decision. On the basis of Article 37, Salma was allowed to keep 2500 dirham of the amount that she had received as her divorce dues, that is, the entire value of her *sadaq*. She remained liable to return the remaining 4000 dirham (in fact she never did, as Jamil did not follow the case any further).

This case clearly illustrates that the court defines paternal and maternal filiation differently and has two sets of rules for their establishment. The child was denied paternal filiation, despite the evidence which proved Jamil to be its genitor. Here the court's decision stems from a rigid conception of paternity which is common to all schools of Islamic law. Blood paternity creates legal effects only if it is proved that conception occurred in the course of a marriage, whether real or presumed (*shubha*). The latter, known also as marriage by error, is a Shari'a concept which has also been adopted by the modern codes of both countries. Marriage by *shubha* (literally, uncertainty or doubt) denotes those instances in which one or both partners engaged in the sexual act under the assumption that they were married. In such instances not only are the couple exonerated from the crime of *zina*, but the children born to them are legitimate, provided it is proved that the parties had acted in good faith (Articles 87 of MCPS and 1164 and 1165 of ICC).

But as to maternal filiation, the court did not link it to the act of marriage. It recognized the child to be of Salma's *nasab*, despite the fact that it was the result of an illicit relationship (*zina*) as proved by the penal court record. Here, the court in its judgment was guided by Article 83/2 of the Mudawwana: 'Illegitimate birth does not create *nasab* between the child and its father and is devoid of any effects, but as regards the mother such a birth creates the same effects as a legitimate one.' This article embodies the main gist of the Maliki attitude to maternal filiation, which differs significantly from that of the Shi'a. As we shall see, Shi'a law has the same conception of maternal and paternal filiation and links both to the question of legitimacy. Maliki law does not make such a linkage; not only does it not subordinate maternal filiation to the fact of marriage, but it allows it to provide a child with a legal filiation. All the rights and duties arising from a legitimate parentage are established between the child and the mother to the exclusion of the father; more importantly, the issue of *zina* is totally bypassed.[18]

It is this Maliki conception of filiation that characterizes paternity disputes heard in Moroccan courts. Cases of proof of paternity such as Leila's, and denial of paternity such as that brought by Salma's husband, have no parallel in Iranian courts. To understand the reasons for the occurrence of these cases, and what they reveal about Moroccan practices, we need to place them in their wider legal and social context.

Maliki legal rules and Moroccan practices

Paternity disputes in Morocco comprise a small proportion (4 per cent) of all marital disputes; yet their significance lies not in their frequency but in their mere occurrence. They provide concrete evidence of the negation of the patrilineal principles of Islamic law by popular practices. These disputes are the direct corollary of the existence of three distinct notions of filiation: the Maliki concept, the modern legal definition, and the popular social and cultural construction. As we shall see, some of the underlying discrepancies between law and practice implied in these disputes are exacerbated by the codification of the Maliki rules by modern state regulations such as that requiring all citizens to be registered and have civil status.

Out of 1898 cases of marital disputes that appeared in the Rabat court in 1987, only 82 cases could be classified as paternity disputes. They were registered in the court under the following three headings: 37 cases under 'proof of paternity' (*thubut al-nasab*), 26 cases under 'proof of marriage' (*thubut al-zawjiyya*) and the remaining 19 cases under the general title of 'filiation' (*al-nasab*). These disputes are usually brought by women while the children are still young; cases such as Leila's, in which the child makes the demand, are uncommon, and no cases are brought by men.[19] They have two elements in common: first, in all of them the marriage has already broken down, although divorce might not have been registered; and secondly, the central demand in all is for the registration of the child in the Civil Status Booklet of its father. This registration is the modern means by which a child acquires legitimacy as well as a legal identity. In some cases, a woman's motivation is practical: the child is about to start school and needs an identity in order to be enrolled. In other cases, her motivation is financial: to claim maintenance for the child in her care.

I have details of 43 of these cases, which fall into two categories: those involving unregistered marriages, and those involving registered marriages.[20] This division, as will become clear, is essential: not only does it have a bearing on the outcome of the case but it reveals the differences in nature and dynamics of these disputes. Table 5.1 presents a summary of these cases, derived from the 1987 Rabat court records.

Only those cases where the woman can prove the existence of marriage, always by producing a marriage certificate, stand any chance of success. In all cases where the marriage was still extant, the court ordered the husband to register the child in his Civil Status booklet. This order establishes the child's legitimacy and entitles him to what parentage entails. The two cases in which the registration of the child was demanded after the husband's death involved polygamous marriages; in both, inheritance was the main motive. In one of these cases the child was born in 1969 and the wife was divorced in 1970, without having the child registered. It was only after the father's death, when the child was 18, that the demand for registration was made in order for him to inherit. In the petition, the son claimed that the first wife of his father had thwarted all his previous efforts to

Table 5.1   Nasab *Disputes According to Outcome, Rabat*

Proof of Nasab	*Outcome*					
	Accepted		*Rejected*		*Total*	
	no	*%*	*no*	*%*	*no*	*%*
With marriage certificate:						
Divorced	9	57	6	22	15	35
Widowed	2	12	0	–	2	5
Still married	5	31	0	–	5	11
Without marriage certificate:						
Initiated by women	0	–	18	67	18	42
Initiated by children	0	–	3	11	3	7
Grand total	16	100	27	100	43	100
%	27		63		100	

become legitimate and was now preventing the registration by hiding his father's booklet. The court ordered the first wife to hand over the booklet in order to make the registration possible. In the second case, the child, five months old, was not yet registered at the time of the sudden death of its father (in an accident). The first wife, by confiscating her husband's booklet, was hindering the registration. Again the court ordered her to hand in the booklet.

In other cases, where the marriage was dissolved by divorce, the court based its judgment on Article 84 of the Mudawwana which defines the legal period of pregnancy (minimum six months and maximum a year). In all the nine accepted cases, the child was born less than a year after divorce; in the six rejected cases, the birth was over a year later. Here, the court's judgment is not in accordance with the classical Maliki position but with its revised version in the Mudawwana.

As already mentioned, in classical Maliki law the maximum legal period of pregnancy can be as long as five years. This legal fiction also has popular and cultural expressions, such as the belief in *raqqad*, the 'sleeping foetus', which is still prevalent throughout the Maghreb. According to this belief, an embryo for some unknown reasons goes to sleep in the mother's womb, and remains there dormant for some time until it is awakened, for example by a magical potion or through the intervention of a saint. This is often believed to happen after the disappearance of the husband, after death or divorce.[21] It is probable that Maliki jurists were influenced by the existing belief in *raqqad*; some even attempted to understand and explain it. One of them, El-Wansherisi, explains the phenomenon as follows:

when a woman has not submitted to copulation, the embryo can contract itself inside its mother's womb. When the mother is subjected to copulation, the embryo then will expand and will resume its normal development.

He also explains how pregnancy can coexist with menstruation.

A pregnant woman whose foetus has gone to sleep is likely to continue menstruating, which is due to the fact that the foetus has shrunk itself inside the womb. But when such a pregnant woman stops menstruating, it is the indication that the foetus has awakened and is growing normally.[22]

This text is self-explanatory and shows how even the facts of menstruation, sexual intercourse and their connection with pregnancy could be seen in a different light. Interestingly, it also implicitly admits a connection between the sexual act and awakening the sleeping foetus, without of course relating it to *zina*. The fact that such a connection is not made is paradoxical and merits more attention. It goes against the primary presumption of legitimacy, *walad al-firash*, which limits legitimacy to children conceived in the course of a legal marriage. In the Maliki school (as in other Sunni schools), a woman's children are all legitimate in relation to her; and a man's children are his legitimate children unless the intercourse by which they were conceived amounted to the crime of *zina*. In this sense the rules of *nasab* appear to have no necessary connection with legal marriage.[23] This too has been attributed to the jurists' humanitarian instincts. In devising the rules of *nasab*, great pains were taken to spare individuals from the stigma of illegitimacy and the harsh penalty for *zina* which was fixed and could amount to stoning to death, if the person committing it is *muhsan*: a sane adult who has contracted a legal marriage.[24]

It is said that Malik himself was a sleeping foetus; he was born three years after the death of his father.[25] Once during my fieldwork in the court of Rabat, while I was discussing *raqqad* with the judge – I suppose I must have appeared incredulous – someone present reassured me by saying that he himself was the living proof of the truth of *raqqad*: although he was born two years after his father's death, it was a well-known fact that he was conceived beforehand, as his mother showed all the signs of pregnancy; the midwife and other women attested to it. At this point the judge and I had no other choice than to put aside our discussion of the legal and social implications of this doctrine, otherwise we risked offending the man by doubting his legitimacy and implying that he was a *walad al-zina*, a child of fornication, which is one of the worst forms of insult.[26]

The belief in *raqqad*, in addition to conferring legitimacy, could serve another important purpose: prolonging the *'idda*.[27] As we have seen, this is the waiting period that a woman must observe after dissolution of marriage, through either divorce or the death of her husband, during which she is barred from entering any other union. The purpose of this period is to avoid confusion of paternity by ascertaining that the woman's womb is empty. The duration of *'idda* is three menstrual periods in the case of divorce and four months and ten days in the case of widowhood; but if the woman is pregnant the *'idda* will extend until the delivery, during which she is entitled to a special kind of maintenance, known as *nafaqat al-haml*, literally the maintenance of carrying (the child). By declaring herself pregnant, a woman can retain her claim to maintenance. Given the fact that there is no system of alimony in Islamic law and that until recently few women after divorce had any means of support apart from being maintained by their own family, one can understand the practical motivations for such a claim.

This outlet foreseen by classical Maliki law, affording a significant degree of flexibility in the establishment of paternity, was totally abandoned in 1957 when Maliki law became codified. One of the few reforms that was introduced by the code was to limit the maximum period of pregnancy to one year, although a trace of the *raqqad* belief is retained in Article 76. This requires that, if there is doubt over a woman's pregnancy beyond a year after a divorce or the husband's death, the case must then be brought to the court and the opinion of medical authorities must be sought; upon which the judge decides whether to put an end to the *'idda* or to prolong it. I did not come across any case that involved such a claim, and none of the judges that I talked to knew of such cases. Thus one can say that the belief in *raqqad*, or the sleeping child, although still held, has lost its legal sanction after the codification of Maliki law and its application by a modern legal system.

Similarly, the second category of paternity disputes (Table 5.1), those involving unregistered marriages, also stems from the tension arising from the grafting of classical Maliki law onto a modern legal system. All the 18 cases in which women failed to produce a marriage contract pertain to a special type of marriage known as *fatiha*, which is still prevalent especially in rural areas and among the urban poor. It is a socially valid marriage, and the children born into it are not stigmatized in any way, but it is not recognized by the modern legal system, as it is not registered. Registration is simple and possible if the two parties agree to it, which is the case in a large majority of *fatiha* marriages (see Chapter 6). Cases brought to the court are those in which the husband disowns the union. As the table shows, these cases are doomed to fail; a large majority of them never reach the state of judgment, dismissed by the court on the basis of insufficient documentation (the lack of a marriage contract).

The court's rejection of cases involving *fatiha* marriages is due to an amalgam of the classical Maliki interpretation of the concept of *nasab* and the modern definition of a valid marriage. The classical notion of paternity (defined in terms of legitimacy) has been retained while the code recognizes as valid only those marriages which have been registered. This creates a 'catch 22' for women, who need a court order to have their *fatiha* union recognized, in the face of their partner's reluctance to give legitimate status to their children. The only option remaining to these women is to register the child in their own name, which in effect entails their acquiring an autonomous legal identity. Women do not normally have their own Civil Status

Booklets, which are only possessed by men as household heads. Before marriage, a woman is inscribed in her father's booklet, and after marriage in that of her husband. In order to get a booklet, and pass her family name to her child, she first needs to secure her father's permission and the consent of her brothers. The procedure is lengthy and complicated but many women go through it as the only way of securing a legal identity for their children so as to enrol them at school. In this way a child's maternal filiation becomes the primary mode of filiation, an implicit deviation from the Islamic principle of patrifiliation.

This deviation becomes explicit if we look at Maliki custody rules. These disputes can only be understood in connection with custody arrangements. Rules of filiation and custody, more than anything else, define and regulate a child's relationship with each of its parents, which become relevant when the union breaks up.

Maliki custody rules: extending negotiations

What motivates women to claim legal paternity for their children, and what motivates men to disown their children, must be sought in the ambivalent position of Maliki law over the question of what happens to children after the dissolution of marriage. Maliki legal rules pertaining to the custody of children betray a kind of duality; while they retain their patriarchal nature, in practice they contain a strong potential for matrifocality.[28]

In the Shari'a, custody has two separate yet interrelated components: *hadana* and *wilaya*. *Hadana*, which literally means nurturing, nursing or raising, determines who looks after the children and where they reside. In this respect Maliki law has a distinctly matrifocal bias.[29] It gives priority to the mother and, in case of her absence or disqualification, to the females in her line; this is reflected in Article 99 of the Mudawwana. For instance, if a child's mother is dead or has remarried (which can disqualify her from keeping the child), the *hadana* will pass to her mother; in case of her absence or her refusal, it will pass to the mother of this grandmother; and, in her absence, to the maternal aunt of the child. It is only after all the females on the maternal side are eliminated that *hadana* can pass to the paternal kin of the child; here again, females are given priority, starting with the child's paternal grandmother.

Wilaya, which literally means power, authority and supervision, consists of supervision over the child's upbringing and education, making sure that the child is brought up as Muslim; and at the same time providing maintenance for the child. It has a distinctly patriarchal character: it is the father's right and duty, which in his absence passes to the males on his side, starting with his own father (Article 109 of MCPS).

To reconcile these two elements and, more importantly, to retain the patriarchal bias of the law, the mother's share of custody is subordinated to that of the father. This is clearly reflected in legal terminology and rules. To ensure the father's control, the mother is placed in the same category as a carer, a nurse; the underlying assumption is that the child belongs to the father, its care being only temporarily entrusted to the wife. The legal terms clearly reflect this conception; terms such as *ujrat al-hadana* (Article 103, MCPS) and *ujrat al-rida'* (Article 112, MCPS), which literally mean wages for caring and for suckling the child respectively, imply that women's motherly duties are also in the domain of male control. In addition, to keep the *hadana* of her children, mothers must conform to the rules ensuring the father's control. They must reside in the same town as their ex-husbands, or within their easy access (Article 107, MCPS); and they lose the right to keep their children if they remarry a stranger (Article 105, MCPS).

But these two elements of custody provisions have different legal effects, giving rise to another area of contradiction. In contrast to *hadana*, which is the woman's share of custody rights, *wilaya*, the man's share, entails obligation. A man must provide for the child and pay its mother for taking care of the child. By law, he is required to pay maintenance for the children in her care, known as *nafaqat al-hadana*, as well as her fee, referred to as *ujrat al-hadana* (Articles 103, 116 and 124, MCPS). In practical terms this means that, in order to exercise his right, a father must be willing and able to pay; otherwise his authority can be by-passed and the child remains in the absolute custody of its mother. This is what happens among the poor when, after divorce, the child is totally abandoned by the father, who very often remarries and becomes responsible for a new set of children. It is the mother who brings the child up with the help of her own kin group.[30] The situation is different among the more well-to-do classes, where the father can exercise his authority since he is in a position to pay. Even in these cases, like that of Leila, the child is very often brought up by the maternal kin and even adopts the maternal family name.

Yet the claim to parentage and what it entails is retained on both sides, namely the right to inherit from each other, the child's right to be maintained by the father and his right to *wilaya*. Although the motivations and circumstances in which they are demanded vary, these rights are not mere legal fictions; they can be claimed on either side, as in case No. 11. The case was brought at the instigation of Leila's mother and her maternal uncles; it was a kind of vendetta against her father by her maternal kin, who intended him to pay as well as ensuring her right to inherit. Her case is typical as far as the family organization after divorce is concerned. Leila was brought up by her maternal kin group and even adopted the maternal family name, which is in obvious contradiction to the legal model of filiation. It is exceptional only in two aspects: disputes of this nature usually involve inheritance and thus come to the court after the death of the father; or they are brought to the court much earlier.

Unlike Leila's mother, a majority of women whose marriages break down do not give up their claim for the maintenance of children in their care. For them, this maintenance is necessary in order to ensure the viability of the matrifocal unit; and very often the fact that the marriage has broken down irrevocably is never mentioned in the petition. The following case illustrates the processes involved and the dynamics of such disputes.

Case No. 13: Salé, Child Custody and *Nafaqa*

Malika is 36 and works as a maid for a French family in Rabat. She left her husband in 1978 and now lives with her two daughters in a small rented flat in a crowded and poor quarter of Salé. Malika was born in a village near Salé where her father had small-holdings and cultivated. She left her village at the age of 18 to join her brothers who had already migrated to Casablanca in search of work. Her two elder sisters were living in Salé as they had married there. Her mother also left the village after her husband's death, and stays with her children in turn.

Malika married when she was 20 years old. At the time she was living with her brothers in Casablanca and working as an apprentice in a tailor's shop. She met her husband, Aziz, at a wedding. Aziz was 30 years older than she, rich, and married with four children. He took a fancy to her, kept on pursuing her and finally persuaded her to marry him. He set her up in a new house, separate from his first wife and children. They lived together for three years during which she became increasingly lonely and unhappy. He stopped her working and forbade her to travel to Salé to visit her sisters or to receive them. He used to do all the shopping himself and lock the door whenever he left.

The first time that Malika left Aziz was shortly after the birth of their first daughter in spring 1973, a year after the marriage. She took the baby and went to her sister's in Salé. After ten months she came back when he came to fetch her. Her second child was born a year later. Again she felt lonely and depressed, since he would not allow her to have her mother or sister to stay.

In protest, she took her two daughters and went to her sister's in Salé. This time, he did not come after her. She stayed with her sister for a while, then rented a room and started working as a maid to support her children.

Almost a year after leaving Aziz, Malika made her first court petition, demanding maintenance for herself and her children. Her petition was successful and Aziz was required to pay 150 dirham per month from 6 August 1978, the date that she claimed she was forced out of the marital home. Her husband also made a counter-petition, demanding her return to the marital home, which was accepted and an order for her return was issued. She ignored this order, but Aziz did not take any further action to execute it. Malika believes that he did not pursue the matter because he did not want her back this time; he had another woman. There were three other orders for her return but all were left unexecuted, which allowed her to retain her legal claim to maintenance.

On her part, Malika took a lawyer to have the court judgment executed. She received 2500 dirham, of which 800 dirham went to the lawyer as his fee. Two years later, she made a second petition and received 3500 dirham. Since then she has been making petitions every two years, sometimes without a lawyer, and each time has succeeded in receiving a lump sum as maintenance. Her last petition was made two years ago; and she has a current case which is being presented by a lawyer, as her present employer does not allow her time off to go to the court herself. She says she needs a lawyer in order to follow up her case; otherwise her husband would ignore the court order.

On several occasions, Aziz has tried to negotiate with her, telling her that he will pay regularly if she stops the court action. But she is convinced that he is not sincere and wants to deceive her. He told her that he would agree to a divorce if she renounces her right to the custody of their two daughters. She says that she does not want anything for herself but she will not give up her daughters under any circumstances. They would be miserable with their father, who would lock them up and soon marry them off. Although Malika would prefer to be divorced she does not want to start proceedings for a court divorce, which would not serve her interests and might even make matters worse. Aziz can prove that she was the one who left the marital home since she has ignored four court orders to return, and could lose her entitlement to maintenance for herself. If she negotiates with him to get a *khul'* divorce, she could end up losing her claim for maintenance for her children, as he will certainly make his consent contingent on her renouncing such claims.

She has no intention of remarriage, saying, 'I have no luck, once I tried it and look what happened.' She is happier now than when she lived with her husband in Casablanca, although then she had no financial worries. She says that she prefers to be poor than to live in a golden cage.[31]

Malika's case and her choices reflect the situation of those women in court cases in which the marriage has broken down but they do not take any action to terminate it legally. What matters to them, as Malika's case illustrates, is their children, their family of origin and their network of kin and friends. If marriage takes a woman away and deprives her of some of these primary links, she is unwilling to stay in it even if it brings economic security and safety.[32] At the same time she sees no urgency to initiate a divorce. She leaves the marital home of her own accord or he abandons her; in either case the children remain with her. She stays with her parents or a sibling for a while and then gradually starts to work and support her children. She continues to be close to her parental house, occupying a room there or in the house of one of her siblings. She then makes a petition and demands *nafaqa* but not divorce: it is more advantageous to be married than to be divorced. As long as she stays legally married she keeps her claim to *nafaqa* for herself as well as for her children, while divorce often entails giving up such claims. The husband, on his part, also prefers to keep the *status quo*. If he initiates the divorce he has to pay the divorce dues, often amounting to a substantial sum. He is free to enter other unions and he does not want to keep the children himself. In addition, as the children by law remain in her care, he then becomes legally responsible for paying monthly instalments for their maintenance, whereas now he pays only when she takes further action to execute a judgment.

There are, of course, instances where women choose to terminate such unions. Depending on their socio-economic and marital circumstances, there are two options open to them: a court divorce or a *khul'*. In Chapter 4, we have seen the working of the first option. Court divorces comprise a small proportion of all divorces (less than 3 per cent); the prevalent ground upon which they are issued is *ghaiba*, the husband's real or alleged absence. In these cases, as discussed, a woman comes to the court because she is in a state of limbo, neither married nor released: her absent husband is still recognized by the law as the head of the household. She needs to be divorced in order to become free of a defunct marriage; and, most importantly, in order to remove the husband's legal authority over the children.

However, it is the second option, *khul'*, that prevails: 35 per cent and 37 per cent of all divorces registered in Rabat and Salé respectively in the year 1987 were of the *khul'* type. To obtain it, a woman must either forgo her right to keep her children (the *hadana* component of custody) or assume total responsibility for their upkeep (the *wilaya* component). All the nine cases of 'proof of paternity' which were accepted by the court involved a *khul'* divorce in which the wife had undertaken to provide for the child, releasing the father from his obligation to provide maintenance. These women either enjoy the support of their families or are educated and economically independent. They want a clear-cut situation: to be free from the authority of their husbands. They comprise a very small minority; a large majority of women find themselves in the position of Malika, who cannot afford such an option.

In practice *khul'* compromises the right to maintenance for the children, despite the fact that such a compromise is explicitly forbidden by Article 60 of the MCPS when the woman is poor and unable to maintain the child. I came across a small number of cases (18 out of a total of 1898) in which women were demanding the revision of the agreement made at the time of *khul'*. In these disputes, women had given up their right to claim maintenance for their children at the time of divorce, but later, usually after their father's death, they find that they can no longer support their children (as in case No. 7, Chapter 3). They come to the court in order to obtain a maintenance order for the children, but their petitions are dismissed since the agreements made at the time of *khul'* are binding and cannot be changed.

Thus, even in cases when the rule of patrifiliation is not bluntly negated and the child is registered in its father's name, the familial organization that emerges when the marriage breaks down is centred around the mother and her kin group. Two distinct patterns can be identified: one matrifocal and the other bilateral. The matrifocal pattern is the dominant one among the poor, who not only constitute the bulk of court petitioners but also have a higher rate of marital breakdown. Here it happens because a man is unable to claim his share of custody rights, the *wilaya*, which entails the obligation to provide for the children while they remain in the care of their mothers. The bilateral pattern is more likely to happen when men have the option of keeping their authority, which is the case among those who can afford it. Yet even here, the significant rate of *khul'* divorce suggests that men are only too willing to give it up. Cases in which men resort to the court in order to gain the full custody of their children, even after the remarriage of the mother, are indeed rare.[33] Only 46 (less than 3 per cent) of all marital disputes that appeared in Rabat in 1987 involved a demand by the man for the termination of his ex-wife's custody rights; in 34 of these, the man's motivation was not to have the full custody but to be released from the custody payments; in only eight cases did he actually challenge his wife's rights to custody. This is indeed a low percentage in comparison to claims for custody payments initiated by women, well over 50 per cent of all cases.

Shi'a Legal Rules and Iranian Practices

Paternity disputes of the Moroccan type are absent in Iranian courts: Shi'a law neither tolerates nor encourages them. *Nasab* in the sense of legal filiation, both maternal and paternal, is recognized only in the context of a valid marriage. In cases where the existence of a marriage cannot be established, the child is denied any kind of legal filiation. Such a child is considered to be the issue of *zina* and the law does not allow its legitimation. This is stated in clear terms in Article 1167 of ICC: 'A child who is the issue of *zina* is not attached to the *zani* (fornicator).' Marriage by error (*shubha*) can provide an outlet; but the child can only be attached to the party who engaged in the sexual act in the state of *shubha* (doubt), be it the man or the woman (Article 1165, ICC). This explains, in part, why there are so few paternity disputes in Iranian courts. By bringing such a case to the court, a woman gains nothing but risks being charged with *zina*.

It is not easy to argue for a *shubha* marriage: the procedural rules for registration of marriage and birth rule out the establishment of such claims. Unlike Morocco, where a child's legal identity is established through registration in its father's booklet, in Iran a child acquires a distinct identity as a separate booklet must be obtained for each newly born child. This booklet, referred to as *shinasnama* (identity certificate), remains with the child for its entire life, reflecting major life events. The booklet consists of four pages; the first page contains birth details (date and place, the name of each parent). The second and third pages are reserved for information on other events, such as marriages, divorces, details of children, conscription to or exemption from military service; and the final page is reserved for circumstances of death. After the revolution, its use has been widened to cover other information, such as voting in elections and the number and type of food rations.

There is neither a belief in a sleeping foetus nor a type of marriage similar to the Moroccan *fatiha*. *Mut'a* or temporary marriage, as we shall see in the next chapter, is the opposite in the sense that children born into it have legal but not social legitimacy. They are often stigmatized and do not share the privileges of their siblings born into a permanent marriage. This is because the aim of temporary marriage is seen to be that of enjoyment and not the establishment of a marital unit and procreation, therefore its social acceptability does not extend to offspring.[34]

Out of 249 familial disputes registered in one week at seven Tehran courts, only three could be classified as paternity disputes. One was initiated by a woman who claimed paternity for her child, born after an alleged rape. She abandoned the case when she realized that it could not give legitimacy to her child, but at best could only exonerate her from the crime of illicit sexual relations, which was no use to her as she had not been accused of it. The other two cases were brought to the court after the death of the husband; both involved long-standing but unregistered marriages, in one of which the couple had five children and in the other three. Both cases were accepted by the court, as the existence of marriage was established through the testimony of witnesses. On the other hand, a comparable case to that of Leila's (case No. 11: proof of paternity) is always brought after the death of the father and thus involves an inheritance claim. I did not come across any case of denial of paternity similar to that of Salma (case No. 12).

Paternity disputes in Iranian courts usually comprise those cases in which the child was not inscribed in the identity certificate (*shinasnama*) of one of its parents. They often involve procedural issues such as a name error. For instance, in one case a man demanded the insertion of his mother's name in his identity certificate in place of that of his maternal aunt, who had died prior to his birth. The confusion was due to his mother having been married by the identity certificate of her deceased elder sister (to circumvent the minimum age requirement).[35] The correction of the name became imperative after his mother's death so as to enable him to inherit.

Custody disputes in Iran: negotiating the unnegotiable

Whereas in Morocco a combination of filiation and custody rules enables a couple to extend the negotiation of unresolved issues beyond marriage, in Iran such an extension is not possible. Shi'a custody rules leave little room for such negotiations, despite adhering to the same division of custody rights into *hadana* (care) and *wilaya* (supervision). The duality inherent in such a division of custody rights has been minimized by developing the men's share of custody at the expense of women's. *Wilaya* is not only more emphasized, but encompasses the patrilineal unit by including the paternal grandfather of the child. The Iranian Civil Code devotes an entire chapter to 'incontestability of the guardianship rights' of the father and paternal grandfather (Book 8, Chapter 3). On the other hand, the mother's access to *hadana* is severely restricted: she has the right to keep her son until the age of two (as soon as he is weaned) and her daughter until the age of seven (Article 1170, ICC); after that the *hadana* right passes to the father. In case of the death of either parent, *hadana* passes to the one who is still alive (Article 1171, ICC); and in the case of the father's absence or disqualification, it passes to the paternal grandfather. Under no circumstances is custody transmitted through the maternal line.

This not only restricts the scope of custody negotiations but confines them to the pre-divorce domain. Although in theory a woman can use her *mahr* as a bargaining card to gain the custody of her children, in practice this is possible only if divorce is sought by the husband, as in case No. 5, Chapter 2. There are two related reasons for this, the first of which has to do with the customary and popular conceptions of *mahr*. This is seen as providing a woman with a kind of security in marriage, not a licence to divorce: if she wants to leave the marriage, then she has to leave the children behind.[36] Secondly, a woman's limited right to custody means that she cannot make any legal claims for the maintenance of children in her charge, which leaves her with no leverage. A man can always counter by demanding the exercise of his right to custody. Such negotiations necessarily take a different form and the court plays a different role: a greater part of the negotiations takes place outside the court, whose intervention is sought in order to cement the agreement already reached. The judges are certainly aware of this and see their task as that of legalizing these mutually accepted solutions, without overtly violating the Shi'a custody rules.

In practice, this allows the court to modify the rigidity of the Shi'a custody rules; apart from divorce procedures, this is another legacy of the pre-revolutionary legal reforms. Under the FPL, the courts were given discretionary powers in dealing with questions of child custody at the expense of the Shi'a custody rules. If the couple failed to reach a satisfactory agreement, the court was empowered to grant custody to the parent whom it considered more suitable. It also had the power to determine the arrangement for paying the expenses involved in the maintenance of the child while in the custody of either parent. At present, although the Special Civil Court hears custody cases, the judge's discretionary power is severely limited. He is bound to rule according to the articles of the Civil Code, derived from the Shi'a stance in which the right of women to child custody is decidedly restricted.[37] Despite this restriction, the Islamic judge plays an important role in shaping the couple's agreement and in the process becomes the very agent through whom the law is modified.

This point can be illustrated by a detailed examination of a sample of disputes in which the custody of the children is the main issue.

These cases are of two types: those in which the previous custody arrangements are being renegotiated; and those in which these renegotiations are now complete and only the legal sanction is required. In the first category the court plays a mediatory role, while in the second its intervention is sought to grant a legal dimension to the arrangement, and at times for practical purposes. All 17 cases in the first three columns belong to the first category, with no clear-cut boundaries between them. They involve recent divorces; in some, the same issues which were at the roots of the couple's conflict and led to divorce are now being fought over the custody arrangements. This is particularly true of the cases initiated by women.

A majority of cases classified as 'custody' are, in fact, about using the court as a forum for setting the terms of custody. In two of the four cases brought by men, agreement has already been reached. In one of these, the father agreed to pay a monthly allowance and to leave the children (a son aged 12 and a daughter aged three) in the custody of their mother after her remarriage. In the other, the father after his remarriage consented to transfer the custody of the daughter (aged 12) to her mother. The two remaining cases involved changing a previous agreement. In one of them, two years ago, at the time of divorce, the husband had agreed to give the custody of their seven-year-old daughter to his wife, but changed his mind when he heard that she was about to remarry. He petitioned to regain the custody of his daughter.

In five of the six cases in which women demanded custody, they did not meet any opposition from their husbands; in one, the husband was willing to give the custody to the mother, but was unwilling to pay maintenance.

Case No. 14: Tehran, Negotiating Custody

Banu applied to reverse her previous agreement with Qasim, her ex-husband, by which she had renounced her custody rights. In her mid-forties, Banu earns her livelihood by teaching the Koran and officiating at women's religious ceremonies. She told me, 'After 24 years of marriage and having six children I demanded a divorce because of Qasim's sexual inadequacy.' She was vague and contradictory on the reasons for the breakdown of her marriage. When I probed, it emerged that her main complaint was about Qasim's 'irresponsibility' and spending his money on opium, not his sexual impotence. Being aware of the Shari'a grounds entitling women to divorce, and of the impact on Qasim of demanding a divorce on the grounds of impotence (questioning his virility in public), Banu deliberately resorted to this ground in order to compel him to agree.

Qasim not only agreed to a *khul'* but was willing to give her the custody of the children. Banu wanted him to pay monthly maintenance for the children but he was unwilling to commit himself to contributing to their upkeep. After many discussions Banu declined to accept the children in the hope that Qasim would eventually concede. She said she knew that he wanted to remarry; keeping the children would reduce his chances: 'No sensible woman would agree to marry him with four children in the house.'

Five months later, Qasim was still refusing to commit himself to any kind of payment. Meanwhile the children were unhappy and 'living in the streets', and Banu came to the court to claim custody of the children without demanding any maintenance for them. Qasim accepted her new proposal and the agreement was endorsed by the court. Banu obtained the unlimited and unconditional custody of her children, aged from eight to 15 (the eldest son was killed in the war and one daughter had married).

Where the husband is willing to entrust the full custody of the child to its mother the judge plays an instrumental role in forging a mutually acceptable agreement, as the following case illustrates.

Case No. 15: Tehran, Gaining Full Custody

The case involved a temporary marriage, contracted for a period of six months with the condition that the husband, Mehdi, would maintain the wife during the marriage. A month prior to the lapse of the contract, the wife, Nizhat, a 32-year-old secretary and now pregnant, made her application to the court for the extension of the agreed maintenance until delivery. Her concerns, as she expressed them later, were twofold: to secure payments for the upkeep of the child and to have a guarantee that the child would remain with her. She has two children from her two previous marriages (both permanent) who are in the custody of their fathers. Her aim was to prevent, as she put it, 'a situation in which the father would come after three years and claim the child'.

Her court action resulted in the intervention of Mehdi's family, who were unaware of the marriage. His elder brother entered negotiation with her, while Mehdi, a 27-year-old who works in his father's company, remained in the background. In the course of five sessions, with the help of the judge, a mutually satisfactory agreement was reached. Nizhat acquired the unlimited custody of the unborn child and Mehdi agreed to pay a lump sum every two years for its upkeep. At the court's suggestion, the agreement was written in such a way that if the husband under any circumstances decided to take the child back, then he had to pay a substantial sum as penalty for breaking the conditions of the contract.

In this way, Nizhat achieved her objectives, and the court found a way to reconcile the agreement with the Shi'a custody rules. In theory, Mehdi's right to the custody of his child remained intact and he could claim it whenever he wished, but in practice it was constrained as he would be liable to pay a very high sum in order to exercise it.[38]

Reaching such an agreement depends largely on the good will of the husband, which is not always present. There are cases in which the husband is so bitter over the divorce that he denies the mother access to the children. In such disputes the court can achieve very little in bringing about any kind of lasting compromise, as in the following case.

Case No. 16: Tehran, Denying Custody

The case involved a recent court divorce initiated by Akbar, a jealous and suspicious man. He accused his wife, Zahra, of being of 'loose morals' as she once responded positively to a stranger's telephone calls. In order to test his wife's chastity, Akbar used to call her from the office and pretend to be an admirer. After months of telephone seduction, Zahra agreed to meet the anonymous admirer, who turned out to be Akbar. At the time of divorce, although still entitled to custody of her two children (a three-year-old daughter and a nine-month son), Zahra renounced her rights. She did this in order to pacify him and 'not close all doors' – that is, in the hope of being taken back. But after the failure of all her attempts to see the children, with the implicit aim of maintaining contact with him, she changed her position and demanded to have them in her custody.

In the court, Akbar, still furious, refused to give the children back, saying that under no circumstance would he let his children be brought up by Zahra's family. He had to modify his position when the judge told him that it was her right to keep the children (because of their age) and that he could order its enforcement. He then agreed to her having the children overnight every fortnight and she happily accepted, seeing it as the first step to reconciliation.

I have no more data on this case and an enduring solution seemed improbable; as the judge put it, 'They will be our guests for a while.'

All three 'access' cases involved similar issues to the above case, with a difference that the woman no longer had the right of *hadana* as the children were either over two (in the case of boys) or over seven (girls). In these cases, the husband, aware of his rights, was unwilling to negotiate; and the judge's attempts to facilitate an agreement sometimes failed. The dispute was then settled by adjudication on the basis of Article 1174 of the ICC, which grants visiting rights to the parent with whom the child does not reside. In one of these cases, the father was so uncompromising that the court had to secure the mother's visiting rights through the intervention of the police. In this case, in the course of a long and bitter divorce suit, the woman, a teacher, gave up custody of her one-year-old son in order to minimize future encounters with the husband, knowing that he would take the child away from her as soon as it reached the age of two. To tantalize her, he would take the baby to her school without allowing her any further contact. She found this emotionally disturbing as it awakened in her strong desires to hold her child. The other two cases involved similar issues where fathers were unwilling to allow access to the children. The impression conveyed by all these cases was that the husband was using the child as a way of taking revenge on the divorced wife.

Three of the four cases involving a demand for child maintenance were brought by the wife on the grounds that the husband had failed to pay the agreed monthly amount. Women came to court in order to get an enforcement order. In two of these cases the wife sought to change the original agreement by which she would lose the custody

Table 5.2   *Custody Disputes, Tehran, 1988 Sample*

| Petitioner | Demand | | | | | |
	Custody	Access	Maintenance of children	Certificate of custody	Change of guardian	Total
Woman	6	3	4	4	3	20
Man	4	–	–	–	–	4
Total	10	3	4	4	3	24

of her daughter in the event of her remarriage. In the fourth case, the demand for maintenance was made by the daughter, aged 18. In her petition, she stated that her father refused to pay for her expenses on the grounds that she lived with her mother. She could not leave her mother who was ill and needed her care; in addition, her father had remarried and she found it intolerable to be in the same house with the woman who had replaced her mother. She later withdrew her petition after the judge was successful in persuading the father to pay her a monthly allowance.

Cases of 'certification of custody' belong to the second category of custody disputes in which an enduring agreement has already been reached. All four cases involved *khul'* divorces in the course of which the women had already gained the unconditional custody of the children. They came to the court to obtain an order attesting to the fact that they were responsible for the upkeep of their children. This certificate was required in order to entitle them to the child benefit that their employment offered.

All three cases of 'Change of Guardian' were brought by widows, who complained of the difficulties that they were facing as a result of having their fathers-in-law as the legal guardians of their children. In one case, the woman claimed that after the death of her husband (three months before) the paternal grandfather had taken the children away from her and did not let her receive the ex-husband's pension. Similarly, in the other two cases where women lost their husbands in the Iran–Iraq war, the bone of contention was control of the husband's martyr's pension. In all these cases the court gave the women full control over the disputed pension, without addressing the guardianship issue. The court's decisions reflect the post-revolutionary amendment to the custody and guardianship laws. As already mentioned, in Shi'a law the paternal grandfather stands on the same level as the father (even when he is alive) as far as legal guardianship of the child is concerned (Article 1181, ICC).[39] In other words, the paternal grandfather has a say in the control of a minor's property when the latter's father is still alive; and this control becomes total in the event of the father's death. This Shi'a provision has been modified by a law in July 1985, which allows a widow to keep her children in case of her remarriage. It also grants her the right to receive the deceased husband's pension and thus diminishes the supervision rights of the paternal grandfather.[40]

Concluding Remarks

Paternity and custody disputes brought to the courts in both countries must be seen as part of the continuing negotiation between a disputing couple, in which the children are the main objects. This negotiation is defined and shaped not only by the explicit legal rules but also by the ambiguities inherent in them. Disputes in Morocco are the corollary of the matrifocal tendencies in Maliki law which render the court an arena for negotiations, while the virtual absence of similar types of dispute in Iranian courts is a reflection of the greater degree to which the Shi'a law adheres to the principle of patrilineality.

The discussion in this chapter shows the difference between Iran and Morocco in terms of the family organization that emerges when marriage breaks down. In Morocco, in particular among the urban poor, the post-divorce family has a distinctly matrifocal character, whereas in Iran it remains patrifocal.[41] Whereas in Morocco *khul'* divorce often involves women forgoing their right to child maintenance, in Iran what women forgo is their *mahr*. As we have seen, in Morocco a combination of legal rules and social parameters ensures the viability of a matrifocal unit, especially among the poor. The same is not the case in Iran, where a mother–child unit becomes viable only when women are financially able to support their children. This is clearly evident in the disputes from the Tehran court, where the main issue is not that of obtaining maintenance from the father (as is the case in Morocco) but the decision as to which parent the child will reside with. This means that, in practice, a matrifocal option is a possibility for those who can afford to assume total responsibility for the upkeep of the children. Not many women are in a position to do this; for a large majority, divorce often entails the loss of their children, which may partly explain the lower incidence of divorce in Iran.[42]

Yet it is in Iran, where the law has a greater patrilineal bias, that marriage has a more egalitarian character and women's access to divorce is more or less equal to men's. The implications of this correlation and its accompanying paradoxes will be discussed in the concluding chapter.

6

Validating Marriage and Divorce

This chapter explores the relationship between the Shari'a, the modern legal system and social practice, as reflected in their differing notions of what constitutes a valid marriage. It focuses on disputes in which the Shari'a notion of validity conflicts with those of the modern legal system or society at large. These disputes fall into three categories.

1. *Thubut al-zawjiyya* (proof of marriage) cases amount to less than 5 per cent of all marital dispute cases; the majority of them are initiated by women, demanding legal recognition of an already existing 'marital union'. In Iran, they involve requests for legal recognition of temporary marriages (*mut'a*); in Morocco, requests for legal recognition of non-registered (*fatiha*) unions.
2. *Faskh al-nikah* (annulment of marriage) cases are initiated by either men or women, demanding annulment of a registered marriage. They are even less frequent than those of the previous category, making up less than 2 per cent of cases in both countries. In these cases, the demand is in fact opposite to that of the first category: the aim is to prove that the marriage, although legally correct, is incorrect according to the Shari'a.
3. *Ruju'* cases (return to marriage) are initiated by both men and women after a revocable divorce (*talaq al-raj'i*) in which they request the legal recognition of the resumption of marital bonds. For reasons that will become clear, these cases do not appear in Moroccan courts, and in Iran they make up less than 2 per cent of all marital disputes.

In this chapter both the approach used and the cases analysed are different from previous chapters, as we deal here with cases which are few in number and in some way atypical. The aim is neither to locate patterns nor to identify similarities and difference between Iran and Morocco, but to examine the ways in which legal concepts and rules are perceived and used by the litigants and judges. Through a detailed analysis of four cases, I discuss the ways in which the Shari'a concepts are contextually interpreted and reproduced; and how even obsolete concepts and rules can become relevant if invoked. The chapter consists of two major sections: the first deals with instances in which the Shari'a definition of marriage is negated by legal and/or social practices; and the second shows how a Shari'a provision which is not fully observed can negate the legal notion of validity.

Shari'a Versus Legal Validity

Disputes in which the Shari'a notion of marriage is contested by the legal system arise from the coexistence of two equally valid kinds of marriage contract: a legal contract whose validity is established only through registration and a Shari'a contract whose validity rests upon conformity with Shari'a provisions. Types of tension and conflict stemming from this duality vary with the legal machinery and the social context.

An Iranian case

In Iran, tension manifests itself in disputes involving *mut'a* marriages (temporary unions), which are correct according to the Shi'a law, but were ignored by the modern legal system until the Islamic Revolution of 1979. A *mut'a* union can become a legal marriage (*'aqd-i rasmi*) if there is a court order authorizing its registration.

Cases in which the registration of *mut'a* marriages is the central demand are of two kinds. In the first, the two parties are in agreement and are willing to make their union legal; they come to the court because they need a court order enabling them to do so. Ten out of 18 *mut'a* cases that I followed were of this kind. In eight of them, the union was contracted before 1979 when FPL was still intact; the man was already married and court permission was needed for the registration of a subsequent marriage which required the knowledge and consent of the first wife. In the absence of such permission, the only option open to the couple was to contract the second union as *mut'a*, giving it *shar'i* (recognized by the Shari'a) as opposed to *qanuni* (recognized by secular law) status. In the remaining two, the couples first contracted a *mut'a* and then decided to transform their temporary union to a permanent one.[1] In all of them, the couples had already established a marital home and had children, thus conforming to the two important elements of the social construction of marriage (see below).

In the other kind of *mut'a* case, there is dispute between the couple, and the woman resorts to the court in the hope of compelling the man to register the union. This usually happens after the birth of a child and in some cases the union's social validity is not evident. I have data on six cases of this type; they all share many similarities as regards both the dynamics of the union and the strategies employed to render it legal. The following case from a Tehran court will illustrate the processes involved.

Case No. 17: Tehran, *Mut'a* marriage

Dispute title: *thubut-i zawjiyyat* (proof of marriage)
Petition date: 28 April 1986
Number of sessions: four
Court's decision: 5 January 1987

Plaintiff: Pari, born in 1957, is a high school teacher who is also studying for a Master's degree in Management at the Open University in Tehran. She was a divorcee (non-virgin) at the time she contracted her temporary marriage. She is an articulate woman who, as she put it, is 'self-made', having arrived where she is by hard work and without family support. She is reluctant to talk about her past, especially her first marriage. She is vague and at times contradictory.

Defendant: Mehran, born in 1962, left high school at the age of fifteen; he has worked since with his father who is a trader. He was a bachelor at the time of contracting the marriage. He comes from a prosperous *bazaari* family who never learned of his marriage to Pari.

The petition is written by Pari herself; her style is emotive and rhetorical. In the translation, I have attempted to retain her wording if not the style.

> Two years ago I contracted a temporary marriage (*'aqd munqati'*) with Mehran for a period of five years with defined conditions. Our agreement was that, in the event that I bore a child, first, he would make me his permanent wife, secondly, he would pay our expenses. He swore several times that he would not break his promise. Now that I have given birth to a child by Caesarian section, involving

great expense, he not only refuses to make the permanent contract (*'aqd-i da'im*), but also declines to pay the hospital costs. This has brought a great deal of shame and degradation for me among my family, relatives and acquaintances, as what I had told them (that my marriage was a proper one) proved to be untrue. Hence, with a bed-ridden mother and a meagre salary as a teacher, I am now condemned to a life full of hardship, misery and shame.

In support of her claim, she provided the certificates of her daughter's birth and her temporary marriage, hospital bills, and a bank statement attesting to her indebtedness.

During the first session, held three months after her petition, Pari elaborated on what she declared in her petition and repeated her demand for her union to be changed to a permanent one. Mehran, her temporary husband, stated that he was prepared to pay for child support but would not, under any circumstances, agree to a permanent marriage. Their marriage was a temporary one; they had never established a conjugal home together and he still lived with his parents. At this point, Pari burst into tears, saying that the child support was not the main issue; it was because of her reputation (*abiru*) that she wanted him to fulfil his promise and contract a proper marriage. But Mehran remained adamant and she retaliated by demanding 25,000 tomans for the hospital expenses and past maintenance of the child. The session ended with no definite conclusion. The judge attempted reconciliation, advising them to think the matter over and reach a mutually acceptable position. The court fixed another date to hear the case.

To understand this case and the reasons for Pari's petition, we need to examine further the Shi'a notion of temporary marriage and its adaptation by the modern legal system in Iran.

A note on temporary marriage

Only Shi'a Islam recognizes a temporary marriage as valid.[2] Although this type of marriage existed at the time of the Prophet, it was banned by the second Caliph, and was later abandoned by other schools of Muslim law apart from the Twelvers. In Islamic jurisprudence this type of marriage is referred to as 'Marriage of Pleasure': *mut'a* in Arabic denotes pleasure; it is known as *sigha* in Iran. It is a marriage contract with a defined duration which can be from some minutes to

99 years. It legitimates the sexual union as well as the children born into it.[3]

In discussing its legal structure, Shi'a jurists employ the analogy of rent as opposed to the analogy of sale which they use for permanent marriage. Through this contract a man acquires exclusive access to a woman's sexual faculties for a specified period in exchange for a clear and definite payment of *mahr*.[4] Although children born into the marriage are legitimate, procreation is not the aim; indeed, it is strongly discouraged, if not explicitly prohibited.

A *mut'a* contract differs from a regular marriage in two major aspects: the rules related to its validity, and the rights and duties which it establishes between the couple.

For a *mut'a* contract to be valid, its duration and the amount of *mahr* must be specified in definite terms. Any ambiguity in these areas could render the contract void (Article 1095, ICC). A temporary wife, unlike a permanent one, has no claim to maintenance or sexual intercourse unless these are stipulated at the time of the contract. Even in the event of pregnancy, she is not entitled to *nafaqat al-haml* (maintenance of pregnancy), to which even a divorced woman is entitled. On the other hand, the husband has narrower control over her and she has wider autonomy: she does not require his permission to leave the house nor to take up a job, provided that these actions do not interfere with his right to *istimta'* (sexual enjoyment).

The sphere of her marital obligation (*tamkin*) is narrowed to her sexual submission, regulated and sanctioned through rules governing the payment of *mahr*. She can make her obedience contingent upon receiving her *mahr* in full; the man can claim the whole of the *mahr* back if she denies sexual access from the outset; or a portion of it if she does so later. She is entitled to half of her *mahr*, if he terminates the contract prior to the sexual act (Article 1097, ICC). She forfeits her entire *mahr* if this termination is demanded by her or prompted by her action. In short, *mahr* plays such an important role in this union that any ambiguity surrounding it can render the contract void.

There is no divorce in *mut'a*: the contract expires with the lapse of its duration. To continue the relationship, a new contract must be made. The contract can also be terminated by *bazl-i muddat*, which can be translated as 'making a gift of the remaining time'; it can be done only by the man. A woman does not have this option but she can induce his consent through offering him compensation. Consistent with the logic of rent, a man can contract as many *mut'a* marriages as he wishes (more precisely, can afford), and a woman only one at a time; at the end of it she is required to keep an *'idda* (waiting period) for two months (i.e. two menses) prior to contracting a new one.

The Iranian Civil Code (ICC) recognizes *mut'a* as a legally valid marriage and has retained its Shi'a conceptions and rules. In total, the code devotes six articles to *mut'a*. Two articles (1075 and 1076) deal with the duration, and the rest with *mahr*, mirroring the importance which is attached to these two elements of the *mut'a* union in the Shi'a rite. Apart from these few articles, the Civil Code remains silent on the formalities and legal aspects of this type of marriage. This silence is echoed in subsequent legislations. There is no reference to *mut'a* in the Marriage Law of 1931, which confers legal validity only on registered marriages. Likewise, the FPL of 1967, by both omission and commission, excludes disputes involving *mut'a* from being adjudicated on the basis that they were not registered and were thus devoid of legal validity, while registration was made impossible by the procedural rules set by the same act. Thus, prior to September 1979, although the Shari'a validity of *mut'a* marriage was not directly challenged, its legal validity was seriously curtailed. The aim was to discourage and even ban this type of marriage without offending the clergy and challenging the Shari'a directly. The end-result was that *mut'a* became a mutilated form of marriage with no legal consequences.

This situation changed after the revolution when the Family Protection Act was dismantled and its courts were replaced by Special Civil Courts. The new courts, presided over by Islamic judges, see their main function as the administration of Shari'a rules, including conferring legal validity on *mut'a*. However, as the procedural rules for registering marriages have remained intact, a *mut'a* marriage still cannot be registered. The way out of this impasse is also foreseen: these marriages can acquire legal status and be registered if the new courts issue an order authorizing their registration. The procedure is simple if the two parties are already in agreement and willing to make their union legal; otherwise the existence of a permanent marriage must be proved to the court.

Despite this new legal orientation, *mut'a* has remained a socially defective marriage: its transient nature violates the social construction of marriage. It is seen as a temporary union whose object is gratification of sexual needs, and which rarely results in the establishment of a marital home. A *mut'a* wife is referred to as *sigha*, a term which has derogatory implications.

Case No. 17 continued

This was why Pari came to the court: to transform her temporary union to a permanent one which would enjoy both social and legal validity. But her partner was unwilling to cooperate and she had no legal justification for her demand to register her union as a permanent one. By the second court session, Pari appeared to have found a Shari'a argument for her demand and presented her case in a very different light. These are her words:

> The intention (*niyyat*) in our marriage was for a permanent contract. We made the temporary contract out of necessity (*zarurat*). At the time we could not register our marriage, because Mehran did not have his identity certificate: he was evading military service.[5] Our real marriage was permanent, and took place eight months prior to arranging for the temporary contract. I myself recited the marriage formula (*sigha-i 'aqd*) from the Imam's book [Ayatollah Khomeini's treatise, see below] and Mehran accepted it. I can bring witnesses if necessary. It is not a question of money (referring to her demand for childbirth expenses); it is my reputation which is at stake. To be on the safe side I even repeated the marriage formula after we went to a mullah to draw up our temporary contract. This was done only because of necessity, since without it we risked harassment from the *komita* (a revolutionary organization responsible for observance of morals).

At this stage, the judge asked the defendant, Mehran, whether he admitted her claim that they had recited the formula. He admitted that, eight months prior to arranging for the *mut'a* contract, she had recited a formula from the Imam's treatise, but he stressed that it was only to make them *mahram* (lawful) and there had been no reference to duration.[6] He repeated his position that he was not willing to make the marriage a permanent one, and declared that he had decided to terminate the union. The judge once again attempted reconciliation. But Mehran remained adamant and agreed only to pay for the maintenance of the child according to his means. The judge gave them another chance to settle the matter peacefully and advised them to put the future of the child ahead of their own individual interests. The court clerk set another date for them to appear and, under the instruction of the judge, summarized the proceedings of this session as follows:

> The woman's claim is for a permanent marriage (*zawjiyyat-i da'im*). The man's claim is for a temporary marriage (*zawjiyyat-i muvaqqat*) but the man appears doubtful about

this. Since the presumption (*asl*) in marriage is for permanency, it is the man who must provide evidence to the
contrary.

Mehran's admission of Pari's claim that a prior marriage
formula had been recited previously reversed their roles in the
dispute. It freed her from providing any further proofs, as his
admission proved her claim. He was now required to prove that
the formula recited was for a temporary marriage.[7]

To understand Pari's new assertion, it is necessary to look at the
formalities involved in contracting a marriage in Islam.

As discussed in Chapter 1, in Islamic law, marriage is a civil
contract and, in principle, requires no religious ceremony. It is formed
through offer and acceptance in the presence of two witnesses. Offer
is made by the woman or her legal guardian and acceptance by the
man. In Shi'a law the procedure is much simpler: there is no need
for witnesses and a woman (provided she is a non-virgin, that is,
has already consummated a union) can contract her own marriage.[8]
This is done through the recitation of the marriage formula known
as *sigha-i 'aqd*, preferably in Arabic, though it can be done in
Persian. The formula is found in every Shi'a treatise. In Ayatollah
Khomeini's, the one used by Pari, the whole procedure is explained
in a number of legal clauses.[9] There are two formulae, one for
permanent marriage and the other for temporary marriage; the only
difference between them is that the phrase *fi al-muddat al-ma'luma*
(for a definite period) is added in case of the temporary marriage. The
absence of this phrase in the formula results in creating a permanent
marriage bond.

During the last session, held a week later, Pari showed a
greater awareness of these precepts; her temporary husband's
unfamiliarity with the Shari'a subtleties, on the other hand,
resulted in his testifying to his detriment. These are Mehran's
words:

It true that she recited a *sigha* before we decided to go to
a mullah; but it is so obvious that it was not for a proper
marriage: there was no wedding, no registration, no *jahiz*,
no marital home, even my family did not know about it.
What other proof do you want? Do you call this a marriage,
it was a *sigha* for five years.

The session ended in a bitter quarrel between the couple.
The court rendered its judgment after a week, accepting Pari's

claim and recognizing the union as a permanent marriage. The judgment also authorized the registration of the union and required the husband to pay for child maintenance and hospital expenses due for the delivery.

In reaching the judgment, the judge drew upon three Shari'a principles: the permanency of marriage, the intention (*niyyat*) and the necessity (*darurat*). The first principle holds that a marriage is permanent unless its duration is clearly specified. This principle, peculiar to Shi'a law, applies to cases in which there is doubt over the question of duration in a marriage contract: the duration is either not specified or not clear. As regards the validity of such marriages the Shi'a jurists are divided. The dominant opinion, to which Khomeini adheres, considers such a marriage correct but permanent. The other opinion considers such a marriage as void since it is defective in one of its structural elements, that of definiteness of duration.[10] The court acted in accord with the dominant opinion.

The second and the third principles are interrelated. Intent is an important criterion in evaluating the outcome of an act. Sometimes necessity compels an individual to act contrary to the real intent. In this case, the court accepted Pari's assertion that the real intent was for a permanent marriage but that a temporary contract was the only possibility in the circumstances.

This case is typical of the dynamics of *mut'a* unions in which the woman fails to secure her partner's cooperation in transforming the relationship into a legal one. It is exceptional only with respect to its outcome: it is indeed rare that a *mut'a* wife succeeds in changing the terms of the original contract. It also illustrates the existence of two overlapping areas of ambiguity: between the Shari'a and the modern legal system on the one hand, and between Shari'a and social reality on the other. In today's Iran, for a marriage to be valid it must meet certain conditions. On the legal level, this means registration. By requiring the registration of all marriages, the 1931 Marriage Law created the notion of 'legal' (*rasmi*) marriage in Iran.[11] It also conferred the status of *shar'i* on unregistered ones: they are correct according to the Shari'a but without any legal consequences. To discourage these unions, the same law prescribed the penalty for the parties involved as one to six months of imprisonment, thus adding social stigma to legal ineffectiveness.[12]

In time, at least in urban Iran, legal validity has become an important component of the social construction of marriage. This process has been eased by the way that *mahr* is practised. As already noted in Chapter 2, marriage in Iran involves a substantial *mahr*, an amount which is often beyond the immediate financial capacity of the groom.

No transaction takes place at the time of marriage, but the amount is written in the marriage contract and the bridegroom pledges to pay it upon the bride's request. The stipulation of *mahr* in a registered marriage, which becomes a legal document, grants a legal force to the request.

Despite meeting the definition of marriage in the Shari'a, *mut'a* is a socially defective marriage. *Mut'a* is contracted by men and women for a variety of reasons and considerations. If their motives converge in the course of the union, then either the union ends by the lapse of its time or it is transformed into a permanent one by obtaining court permission to register it. A dispute arises when the partners' motives fail to converge. Court cases involving this type of dispute suggest that there is a wide disparity between men's and women's perceptions and objectives in entering this type of union. In all cases the men involved did not consider the union worthy of a proper marriage, mainly because of the personal and social attributes of their partners; while the women agreed to a *mut'a* union in the hope that in due time they could transform it into a permanent marriage. The right time is usually perceived as coinciding with the birth of a child. This explains why Pari was so shamed by her marriage and why her reputation was tarnished; but to achieve her goal, she needed a Shari'a justification.

She found this justification in another area of ambiguity, that involving the Shari'a concepts and their popular construction.[13] Terms such as *sigha* and *sigha-i 'aqd* have different connotations in colloquial Persian from their Shari'a legal usage. *Sigha* can have several meanings and functions according to the context in which it is employed. It literally means the special formula employed at the time any contract is made. In Shari'a legal terminology, *sigha 'aqd* denotes the recitation of a certain formula which results in the creation of a contract. Colloquially, *sigha* (used both as a verb and a noun) means a temporary wife or a temporary marriage, which is performed by the couple themselves or by a mullah; whereas *'aqd* refers to the contract of permanent marriage, which is always performed by a marriage registry officer. The court's definition of these terms naturally reflects that of the Shari'a which is obscure and unknown to many.[14]

It was through manipulation of these ambiguities that Pari was able to win her case. It is evident that when she contracted her marriage by reciting the formula, her understanding was the same as that of her husband-to-be, and that shared by the populace. Otherwise she would have used it in support of her claim in the first court session. All the facts about their union attest to its temporary nature: they all deviated from the norms and rules constituting a permanent marriage. He was a bachelor and she was both older than he and divorced, two major disadvantages which should, for him, have ruled out the eligibility of a woman from her social class. In addition, it was never intended to establish a marital home, an important element of a proper marriage. He continued to live with his parents and kept the union secret, whereas marriage involves publicity, celebration and announcement.

A Moroccan case

In Morocco, the tension created by the existence of parallel notions of marriage validity are manifested in a type of dispute involving unregistered marriages known as *bil-fatiha wa bil-jma'a*, so named because they are solemnized by recitation of the first *sura* (the *fatiha*) of the Koran and celebrated in a gathering (*jma'a*). Theoretically, this marriage meets all the formal requirements of Maliki law. The woman is given away by her father, or in his absence by his nearest male relative, the amount of dower (*sadaq*) and the manner of its payment are defined, and the relevant marriage formula is uttered. Yet a *fatiha* marriage does not enjoy legal recognition, as it does not fulfil the modern criteria of a valid marriage, set by Article 5 of the Mudawwana (MCPS).

Unlike the Shi'a, Maliki law requires a marriage to take place in the presence of two reliable witnesses.[15] This requirement, in time, has produced a class of professional witnesses (*'udul*) who now function under the supervision of the Ministry of Justice, located in the Court of Notaries. They are specialists in the Shari'a: they act as witnesses, and also draw up marriage, divorce and other contracts. A marriage is recognized as valid only when it is conducted by the *'udul*, who not only ensure the observance of Shari'a rules but give it legality by drawing up the contract, which is referred to as *'aqd*.

Yet the possibility of rendering a *fatiha* marriage valid is not ruled out, as the code includes a procedure for its registration. Article 5/3 empowers the Court of Notaries and its judge to legalize unregistered unions. The procedure is simple, if the two parties acknowledge the existence of marital relations; then, they need only produce twelve witnesses, to support their claim. This is done in a document drawn up by two notaries, known as *lafif*, which is, in effect, the written testimony of twelve witnesses (all male, or two females in place of any male). This *lafif* is known as *thubut al-zawjiyya* (proof of marriage), and is analogous to a marriage contract.

The need to register a *fatiha* marriage usually coincides with the birth of the first child, who in order to become legitimate must be entered in his father's Civil Status booklet. As discussed in Chapter 5, when there is agreement between the parties, the procedure is simple, which is the case for a large majority, registered without further ado in the Court of Notaries. The problem arises when one of the partners, always the man, disavows the union, when it becomes incumbent upon the other to prove the existence of a marital relationship. These cases appear in the Court of First Instance and all of them are initiated by women, usually after the birth of a child and thus involving claims of paternity. They stand very little chance of success, as shown in the previous chapter. A large majority of them are dismissed by the court on the grounds of insufficient documentation, as they lack a marriage contract: the court entertains only legally valid marriages.

Fatiha marriages, although decreasing, are still practised, especially in rural areas and among the urban poor, the majority of whom are recent migrants. In her study of marriage and divorce in Casablanca, Baron reports that 53 per cent of all marriages registered in 1953 were of *fatiha* type, where the marriage was later registered by means of a *lafif*. This percentage rises to 81 among the inhabitants of shanty towns, who are recent rural migrants.[16] In 1987 and 1988, 10 per cent and 11 per cent of all marriages registered in Rabat were respectively of this kind (*thubut al-zawjiyya*).

Marriages are not registered for many different reasons. Sometimes the girl has not attained the minimum age of 15 required by the law; the marriage payment might not be ready; the man might not be in a position to register the marriage; or he might be avoiding commitment by evading the legal consequences of a registered union. Whatever the motive behind such a marriage, the woman's fate and that of her children depend on the good will of the man. The following case, which never reached the state of judgment, illustrates some of the processes involved in disputes of this kind, and why women at times have little choice but to concede to them.

Case No. 18: *Fatiha* marriage, Salé

Dispute title: *thubut al-zawjiyyat* (proof of marriage)
Petition date: 21 April 1989
Number of sessions: one
Case dismissed: 18 October 1989

Fatima, now 38 years old, comes from a poor background. She was born in a small village near Salé, where her father, a peasant, died when she was 13 years old. Shortly afterwards, to reduce the family's burden, she was given as a maid to a family in Salé. When she was 18, she entered her first *fatiha* marriage. The union had been arranged by her master and the father of the groom. The ceremony took place in her master's house and the writing of the contract (*'aqd*) was deferred until the accumulation of the *sadaq*.

Later, the father of her *fatiha* husband asked for her to move in with them, promising that he would arrange for the *'aqd* in a short time. She lived with his family for two years and the promised *'aqd* was gradually forgotten. She became pregnant, then, after a series of bitter fights with her mother-in-law, Fatima left her husband and returned to her mother's house, hoping that they would soon come after her. But no one came to take her back, and there she gave birth to a son in 1972.

Meanwhile the husband contracted a proper marriage with another woman, with a contract and a paid *sadaq*. He no longer wished to continue his union with Fatima, denied paternity and refused to register the child. Fatima threatened to take him to court, but after the intervention of the family Fatima had lived with and worked for prior to her *fatiha* union, he gave in and agreed to register the child. The 'proof of marriage document' was made in October 1974, in which it was noted that they had been living as husband and wife for two years and a child was born into the union. The following day, they registered a *khul'* divorce, ostensibly requested by Fatima, in which she renounced the right to child maintenance. In this way she realized her goal and gained legitimate status for her son. The *khul'* was part of their agreement for giving legality to the union.

Four years later, she entered another *fatiha* union, again without a contract. At the time she was living with her sister, and her new husband was her sister's husband's brother, who had just finished his baccalaureat and was joining the army. He promised marriage but said that he could not do the *'aqd*, since he was a trainee army officer and was not allowed to marry during the first four years of his service.[17] The *fatiha* was recited in a small ceremony.

He rented a room for her in Salé and came to visit her while on leave; after a year she moved with him to his rooms in the military base in another town. The union lasted for four years, and she became pregnant in the final year. He wanted her to have an abortion but Fatima said, 'I fear God and will never commit such a crime.' She gave birth to another son in 1982. In the same year, he contracted a proper marriage with a woman from Marrakech, where he was temporarily stationed, and asked Fatima to leave. At first she refused, but finally she gave in after he promised her that he would rent a room for her in Salé and would register the child.

But he never fulfilled his promises, mainly (according to Fatima) because of his legal wife's objection. In 1989 the boy was seven years old and without a legal identity, which was causing problems in registering him at school. So far all her attempts to resolve the problem had failed: her brother-in-law's intervention, her threats to go to the court. She filed a petition in the Court of First Instance in Salé, in which she requested the registration of her child. She was asked to provide a marriage contract to prove that her child was born into a legal marriage; obviously she failed and then had to abandon the case. Having made more inquiries and having talked to the judge, she realized that she had no case. She needed to prove the prior existence of her marital union in order to demand registration of her son in his father's name. She had no other recourse than registering the child under her paternal name, as discussed in the previous chapter.

An element in Fatima's case which I came to learn later, and which might explain her choice, is that she was not a virgin at the time of her first union. She was pregnant when she was taken as a maid by the family in Salé, who later became her patrons. They arranged for the adoption of her child by a barren woman, as well as for her *fatiha* marriage. She has not traced her first child and never refers to the incident while talking of her misfortunes.

Fatima's case shows something of the dynamics of these unions and the reasons behind women's acceptance of them.[18] A *fatiha* wife in Morocco is in the same precarious situation as a *mut'a* wife in Iran, at the mercy of her partner's good will. To gain some degree of security in these precarious unions, a common strategy adopted by women is to get pregnant, a ruse resorted to by almost every woman who came to the court. In their petitions, they justify and argue their case on the basis of the welfare of the child. But it is difficult to avoid the impression that they purposely manipulate this fact to enhance their chances of winning the case. A child gives a woman the status of a mother; therefore, it gives a procreative dimension to the union, bringing her closer to the position of a proper wife. It can be an effective way of manipulating a reluctant man into a more committed union. If this strategem works, and the union is then transformed into a legal one, the case never reaches the courts. But if the man is not persuaded, the legal recourse otherwise available to women in these unions is very limited, as illustrated by the above case.

Both *fatiha* and *mut'a* marriages, although theoretically correct from the Shari'a perspective, are defective; they satisfy the criteria of only one of the two major elements that comprise a socially proper marriage. In social practice there are two phases to a marriage, both intertwined with the Shari'a rules. The first phase is known, both in Iran and in Morocco, as *'aqd* (literally, contract); it consists of a small ceremony during which the marriage contract is drawn up. The second phase is the wedding celebration, known as *'urs* in Morocco and as *'arusi* in Iran. It marks the social recognition of the contract made during the first stage, allowing the consummation of the marriage and the establishment of a marital home. There is usually a time lapse between these two stages. In Morocco, *'urs* is delayed until all the conditions specified in the marriage contract regarding the payment of the *sadaq* are fulfilled; and, in Iran, *'arusi* is delayed until the bride's *jahiz* is ready.

The distinction between these two stages, especially the time interval, was clear-cut until recently. Now they seem to be in the process of amalgamation, especially among the middle classes. The *'aqd* is often conducted in the afternoon, in the presence of the notaries; and the wedding celebration in the evening. This is more evident in Iran, where the *'aqd* is acquiring more importance at the expense of the *'arusi* stage, whereas in Morocco the *'urs* stage is still associated with the public announcement of the union, giving it social legitimacy. In a socially complete marriage the *'aqd* phase always precedes the consummation. It renders the couple licit (*halal*) to each other but does not establish the conjugal unit. After *'aqd* a girl is expected to save her virginity until the wedding ceremony which marks her transfer to her new home. I know of a case in Morocco where the *'aqd* phase was completed four years ago without any accompanying celebration, because of the financial problems. The couple live together in the same house, again through necessity, but she is still a virgin and is determined to keep her virginity until the *'urs*. She told me: 'I am not a street girl who sleeps with a man without a real marriage.' For her, the *'urs* celebration is the true marker of a marriage, not the contract which is only the legal marker.

The importance of *'urs* is also evidenced in another type of dispute, entitled *talab al-dukhul* (literally, demand for penetration – that is, consummation of marriage) heard in Moroccan courts. These disputes represent the other end of the spectrum of the notion of marriage validity: there exists a legal marriage contract but there is no conjugal unit as the *'urs* ceremony has not yet taken place. They are initiated by both men and women and are less common than cases involving 'proof of marriage' (in 1987 there were 16 *dukhul* cases as opposed to 82 cases of *thubut al-zawjiyya* among 1898 marital dispute cases that appeared in Rabat court). The stated demand in these petitions is the consummation of the marriage, but the hidden agenda is renegotiating the terms of the marriage payment, or dissolving the contract without incurring the payment of *sadaq*. By bringing the case to the court, the woman's family seeks to establish a legal claim over the husband, as a wife becomes entitled to maintenance only after the consummation. If the husband fails to comply with the court order requiring him either to consummate the marriage or to establish a marital home, depending on the circumstances, then the bride's side can apply for a *nafaqa* order. This order can be used as a trump card in negotiating either the transfer or the increase of the agreed *sadaq*. In cases brought by men the aim is preempting these claims, as a woman who refuses consummation cannot claim maintenance.

The Modern Code Versus the Shari'a

So far we have dealt with cases in which a marriage was denied validity because of lack of conformity with the requirements set by the modern legal system. This section examines another area of tension, stemming from non-observance of a Shari'a provision. These cases, initiated by both men and women, come under annulment (*faskh*) disputes. They illustrate the relevance and importance of the Shari'a rules and how they can be used effectively to offset the effects of legal marriage. By way of illustration I have chosen two cases, one from Morocco and one from Iran.

A Moroccan case

Case No. 19: Rabat, Annulment of Marriage

Dispute title: *faskh al-nikah* (annulment of marriage)
Petition date: 24 August 1988
Number of sessions: seven
Court's Decision: 26 June 1989

Plaintiff:	Wafa, born in 1961, comes from an upper-middle-class family. She is a civil servant and has a university degree. This is her first marriage.
Defendant:	Muhammad, born in 1960, comes from a lower-middle-class family. He is an electrician, and left school at the age of fifteen. This is also his first marriage.
Date of Marriage:	13 May 1987

Amount of Sadaq: 3000 dirham, plus 1000 dirham pledged for furnishing a Moroccan saloon. She received a total of 1500 dirhams; the remainder (*kali' al-sadaq*) is 2500.

The petition is by Wafa's father. It is written by a professional lawyer, and the style is succinct and legal. This is an outline of it:

> Muhammad took advantage of Wafa's naïveté and deceived her; he took away her virginity and continued having sexual relations with her until she became pregnant. To avoid a scandal (*iftidah*), their marriage was arranged; the *'aqd* took place on 13 May 1987 and three months later Wafa gave birth to a baby girl. After marriage, the defendant continued to exploit Wafa: she paid for the rent of their apartment, bought him a motorcycle, and so forth.
>
> Above all, the marriage does not conform to the Shari'a rules as Wafa was pregnant at the time of its contract. This renders the marriage *fasid* (irregular) as she was in the state of *'iddat al-istibra'* [see below].
>
> On the basis of the above, I request:
>
> the annulment of the marriage;
>
> to divest him of the paternity of the child (*nafi al-nasab*);
>
> the payment of her *kali' al-sadaq* of 1500 cash plus 1000 pledged for furniture;
>
> reimbursement of a total of 3000 that she paid for the rent of the apartment;
>
> the return of her knitting machine, valued at 3000;
>
> 300 per month as the cost of feeding the child with powdered milk, plus 300 custody wages (*ujrat al-hadana*);
>
> cancellation of the monthly instalments that she pays for his motor cycle.

In response, the husband made a counter-petition dated 25 October 1988 in which he demanded the return of his wife. He emphasized that the marriage was made according to the Shari'a procedure, in the presence of two *'udul*, with a *sadaq* of 3000 dirham, and that there was a marriage contract to this effect. He also accused his father-in-law of plotting and intending to ruin their marriage. He made no allusion to prior sexual relations, but mentioned that they had a child registered in his Civil Status booklet. He expressed his wish to continue the marriage and stressed that his marriage conformed to rules outlined in Chapter 2 of the MCPS, dealing with the formation of marriage.

This case, which appeared in the Court of the First Instance of Rabat, lasted ten months, during which the plaintiff only once came to the court, when her presence was required for an Inquiry session in the judge's room. Her case was represented and followed by her lawyer. The defendant, despite having a lawyer, frequently came to the court and followed the case personally. The court's judgment was rendered after seven sessions; it ruled as follows:

As regards the main petition:

it declared the marriage *fasid* (irregular) and annulled it;

it authorized the Notary Judge to register the annulment on the bottom of the marriage contract;

it declared the child not to be from the legitimate paternity (*nasab al-shari'i*) of the defendant; and

it required the defendant to pay 2500 dirham for the remainder of *sadaq*, as stated in the marriage contract.

As regards the counter petition, it rejected the demand for the return of the wife and required the defendant to pay the cost of the trial.

Before discussing the court's judgment in more detail, we need to examine the Shari'a concepts that this case raises, namely those related to marriage validity.

Of 'iddat al-istibra'

We have already seen that *'idda* is the waiting period that a woman has to observe following the dissolution of her marriage. Originally, *'iddat al-istibra'* was the period of sexual abstinence imposed on a slave woman when she became the property of a new owner. *Istibra'* literally means to ascertain the 'freedom', that is the vacuity of the womb.[19] Later, the term was used to denote the waiting period that a woman has to observe if she has had sexual relations through either rape or *shubha* (intercourse by error).[20] In the case of a pregnant woman, it lasts until her accouchement; otherwise its duration is one menstrual cycle. *Istibra'* is mentioned once in Article 37 of MCPS as a waiting period that a woman must observe in case of an irregular marriage.

Of the Shari'a classification of marriages

Marriages, in terms of validity, are divided into three kinds: correct (*sahih*), void (*batil*) and irregular (*fasid*). A correct marriage is a valid and fully effective union in which conditions of substance (*asl*) and attributes (*wasf*) are fulfilled. It has a total effect in law: sexual intercourse is lawful and it creates rights and obligations between the contracting parties.

A void marriage is no marriage at all. What makes a marriage void is the existence of a permanent irregularity that cannot be removed, such as marrying within prohibited degrees (blood relationship, affinity or fostering).[21] A void marriage does not have any legal effect; it only exonerates the two parties from the act of *zina*, provided that they were unaware that the marriage was void, taking the marriage for a valid one (*shubha*). The issue of such a marriage is illegitimate and there is no process for legalizing the union.

An irregular marriage, similar to a void one, is no marriage at all. The difference is that here the irregularity is of a temporary nature, such as marrying a woman during her *'idda* period. That is, if the parties were to separate and the temporary bar be removed they could then contract a correct marriage. The issue of such a marriage is legitimate provided the parties acted in good faith and were unaware of the legal bar (again *shubha*).

The distinction between void and irregular, which has always been blurred and was not made by all schools, has disappeared in modern codes. All non-correct marriages are referred to as irregular (*fasid*), as in Article 37 of the Moroccan Code, which authorizes the court to annul such marriages without specifying what renders them irregular.[22] Although there is no reference to *batil* marriage in Book I, Chapter 5, the impediments to marriage are divided into two kinds: permanent and temporary. This division corresponds to the Shari'a bars that could render a marriage either void or irregular.

We can now return to case No. 19 and examine it in the light of the foregoing. Wafa and Muhammad's marriage fulfilled all the necessary conditions of formation (it took place in the presence of *'udul*, *sadaq* was specified and there was a marriage contract), but its nullity is, nevertheless, manifest as she was pregnant at the time of the contract: she gave birth only three months later. In other words, there existed a temporary bar; she lacked the capacity to contract a valid marriage. On this point, as seen in the previous chapter, Article 84 is explicit, establishing a minimum and a maximum duration of pregnancy: six months to one year. Having recognized the marriage as irregular, the court dealt with its effects in three parts.

On the separation: it annulled the union and ordered this to be registered by the Notary Judge. This is in conformity with the classical law that requires the Qadi to separate the spouses.[23]

On the payment of *sadaq*: it allowed the wife the *kali' al-sadaq* (remainder of the dower), since the consummation had taken place. This is also in line with the classical position which relates the dower to the act of consummation, regardless of the validity of marriage.

On the issue: it denied the attachment of the child to the father, and only attached it to the mother. This is apparently contrary to the classical law and Article 37 of MCPS, which recognize the issue as legitimate and entitled to a share of inheritance if the two parties acted in good faith and were ignorant of the bar. But it is in accordance with articles 84, 85 and 86, which recognize the issue of any union as legitimate only if it is born within the recognized limits of the period of pregnancy. The court chose to act according to the latter.

Examining the case from the perspective of the actors reveals a different dimension of the dispute. A closer reading of the case suggests that the concern of Wafa's father was not to determine the Shari'a validity of his daughter's marriage, but to find the easiest and most effective way to terminate a union deemed no longer desirable. He was opposed to his daughter's choice from the outset, mainly owing to the humble social origins of her suitor. Yet despite this Wafa went ahead with the relationship, and when she became pregnant her father gave his consent, as he put it, 'to avoid a scandal'. Without his consent the marriage could not have taken place: the consent and presence of a girl's guardian is one of the essential conditions of its formation. A woman herself cannot contract the marriage; she must be represented by a matrimonial guardian (*wali*), her father if she has no adult son.[24]

The marriage took place in May 1987 and the petition for annulment was made more than a year later. This request, it is important to stress, was due to the change in the relationship, not out of concern for a Shari'a principle. Contrasting this case with case No. 12 in Chapter 5 illustrates the extent to which the impact of legal rules is relative and context-bound; they affect different people in different ways. In both cases legal facts are identical, but social facts and circumstances are diametrically opposite.

To recap, Salma came from a poor background and worked in a tailor's shop in Salé where she lived with her married sister; her parents still lived in Fes. She became involved with Jamil, a civil servant from a prosperous family. When she became pregnant, he rejected the idea of marriage and wanted her to abort, but she refused in the hope that he would be persuaded to marry her. This led to the intervention of her parents: they made a police complaint, accusing Jamil of deceiving their daughter. To avoid a scandal, he agreed to marry her. A month later he divorced her, hoping that the whole affair would be soon over. But she was insistent: her petition requesting paternity and maintenance for the child heralded a new course of demands. To eliminate any further demands, Jamil also discovered that the best way out was to prove that there was no marriage in the first place, that the union was *fasid*, thus of no legal consequence. In Wafa's case the scenario is the same, only the roles of the protagonists are reversed: it is the husband who resists the termination of the relationship.

Both cases show how an obsolete concept like *istibra'*, which was meaningful and relevant when concubinage with a slave girl was a possibility, can be invoked and become relevant in a different context. It now serves as a means of offsetting the legal consequences of a union no longer desired by one party. A factual, as opposed to legal, reading of these cases reveals that the present usage of this Shari'a rule is entirely different from that intended by those who devised it. Above all, *istibra'* was about legitimacy and correct paternity; by ensuring the emptiness of the womb when a slave girl was transferred to a new owner, who also acquired the right to her sexuality, the aim was to avoid confusion over paternity. In the above cases, on the other hand, neither the court nor the litigants paid any heed to the issue of blood paternity which underlies the logic and the aim of this rule.

In both cases, the judge was confronted with contradictory rules: Article 37 allows the legitimating of the issue of an irregular marriage, while Articles 84, 85 and 86 recognize a child as legitimate if it is born not less than six months after the marriage. In choosing between them, he had to conform to the rules of procedure and take into account the incontestability of the evidence presented. In both cases, it was the existence of a birth certificate that settled the matter.

Litigants are also concerned with their immediate interests, moulded by gender and power relations in the society. As these two cases suggest, it is the party with more resources, be it the man or the woman, who can avoid the legal duties that marriage entails. To achieve their aims, they have no qualms in invoking a Shari'a principle as a strategy; such strategies are not always successful. For instance, in one case, a man demanded the annulment of his marriage on the grounds that he had sexual relations with his wife for a year prior to marriage. At the time they were both students and he could prove their *khalwa* (sexual intimacy) through witnesses and confession (*iqrar*). His petition, written by him, is a well-argued five-page document on the concept of *istibra'* and validity of marriage, with references from the Koran, *hadith* literature and *fiqh* treatises; he even uses the work of French scholars in support of his claim. He shows a complete and thorough awareness of the issues. The irony of his petition is that it can be used as evidence that he committed *zina*. When I pointed this out to him, he dismissed it by saying, 'This is between me and

Allah, and I have already repented.' This case never reached the state of judgment; he abandoned it after the third session when he realized that he had no evidence (their only child was born two years after the marriage). His wife denied his claims and said that his real intention was to divorce her without having to pay the divorce dues.[25]

An Iranian case: ruju'

The Iranian version of invoking a Shari'a principle is evidenced in *ruju'* disputes, in which one of the parties strives to prove that the marital relation is still extant in spite of a registered divorce. These claims are pertinent only in case of a revocable (*raj'i*) divorce, where the termination of marital ties is suspended until the wife completes three menstrual cycles. During this period (*'idda*) the husband has the right to resume marital relations and revoke the divorce. While the modern legal system recognizes this Shari'a principle, its validity is subordinated to the imperative of registration.

These disputes are rare in Moroccan courts, whereas they have become increasingly common in Iran since the revolution. The reason for this is related to procedural rules, not to textual differences between the Maliki and Shi'a schools. In Morocco, the court does not entertain claims of resumption of marital bonds when the *ruju'* is not registered (Article 5, MCPS). This was the situation in Iran prior to 1979. The Family Protection Courts not only rejected claims of unregistered *ruju'* but required all divorces, with the exception of those arranged by mutual consent, to be registered as irrevocable. The procedure of *ruju'* in irrevocable divorces preempts such claims, as it requires both the consent and the active participation of the wife. For instance, in case of *khul'* where the divorce is effected by the husband's acceptance of compensation from his wife, *ruju'* is only possible when she claims back what she has forfeited (*ruju' bi al-'awad*). The establishment of the Special Civil Courts has changed the situation.

Here again, if the two parties admit to the resumption of marital relations during the period of *'idda*, the procedure is simple and the court grants permission to legalize the union by registration of the *ruju'*. The conflict arises when one party denies the claim of the other. Out of 11 cases of *ruju'* from Tehran courts, four involved mutual consent; three were initiated by women (two of them after the death of the husband, where the dispute involved inheritance); the remaining four were initiated by men. Interestingly the latter claims were made after the remarriage of the divorced woman.

The following case illustrates the legal and social dynamics of this type of dispute.

Case No. 20: Tehran, Return to Marriage

Dispute title: ruju' (resumption of marital links) and *faskh-i nikah-i jadid* (annulment of the new marriage)

Petition date: 28 November 1986

Number of sessions: four

Court's decision: 18 December 1986

Plaintiff: Javad, born in 1928, is a retired university professor of physics. He comes from a landed and wealthy family, with a PhD from an American university. This is his first marriage.

Defendant: Mitra, born in 1952, is a housewife. She has never worked and has a high school diploma. She married Javad when she was fifteen. She comes from a middle-class family.

Date of marriage: 1967

Date of divorce: 16 October 1985

Date of Mitra's second marriage: 6 November 1986

Javad agreed to his wife's insistent demands for a divorce and registered a divorce *raj'i* in one of the registry offices in Tehran. A year later, when he found out that his ex-wife had remarried and was planning to leave the country, he took action against her. He impeded her departure on the grounds that she was still his Shari'a wife and could not leave the country without his consent.[26] She was arrested at the airport and the case was referred to the Special Civil Court, as it involved a marital dispute.

Javad submitted his petition, written by him, two days after the airport episode. It was a long document covering the events that led to the break-up of their marriage and his decision to register a divorce; this is a summary of it.

I married Mitra 18 years ago; due to her fragile health we could not have children until ten years ago when God gave us a son and then four years ago a daughter. We were happy and our marriage was perfect. It was after our daughter's birth that my wife started *nasazigari* (uncooperativeness) and persisted in her demand for a divorce.[27] Her mother and sisters attributed her changed behaviour to post-natal depression and suggested a temporary separation might help. Despite my wish to keep my marriage, I finally gave in and agreed to a divorce as her condition was getting worse. I went with her to register the divorce with reluctance (*ikrah*), and with the clear intent (*niyyat*) of making the *ruju'*.

However, I refrained from registering the *ruju'*, as she was still in a nervous state and I feared that it would have aggravated her condition. I talked of my intention with friends but I kept this from her, waiting for her to recover and come to her senses. She was gradually improving and her comportment was indicative of her implicit willingness to resume marital life. She would come home to visit the children and often would cook for us; we even went together to the holy city of Qum. I was intending to tell her of the *ruju'* at an appropriate time, when I was informed (via an anonymous phone call) of her imminent departure.

I made some inquiries and I learned, only ten days ago, that she had remarried and intended to leave the country. This has obliged me to act in the interest of my children and prevent her departure. She is still my *shar'i* wife and I now wish to demand the permission to register my *ruju'*. I also request the annulment of her subsequent marriage, as she is still my wife. I have ten witnesses who are willing to submit their testimony, and I am willing to take the oath.

A note on ruju'

Ruju' literally means return, that is, to return to the marriage by revoking the divorce, which is only possible when the divorce is of the revocable (*raj'i*) type. In its legal structure, *ruju'*, like *talaq*, is an act of *iqa'*, a unilateral act by the husband. Its exercise is possible in the case of a revocable divorce and only during the period of *'idda*, which is three menstrual cycles after the divorce, unless the wife is pregnant. He can exercise his right to return to the marriage in two ways: *lafzi* (verbal), by stating his intention explicitly or implicitly; or *fi'li* (by action), through an act, a gesture that implies marital intimacy, such as kissing, touching, or being alone with the divorced woman in one room. In sum, any interaction with the divorced wife which is forbidden (*haram*) to anyone but the husband can be taken as his intent to make the *ruju'*.

The important factor in proving *ruju'* is the establishment of intent; actions or sayings can be interpreted as an indication of *ruju'* only if the husband performed them with the intent of taking the wife back. This of course can only be verified by him, a factor which grants a wide latitude to men claiming the resumption of marital relations or denying such claims made by their wives. In Shi'a *fiqh*, however, a

line is drawn, on a saying from the sixth imam: 'Sexual intercourse
is the proof of *ruju'* even if the husband denies the intent.'[28] The
absolute right of men to effect a *ruju'* and the facility with which
it can be proved is manifest in Clause 2525 of Khomeini's treatise,
which reads:

> To effect a *ruju'*, a man does not need to have witnesses nor to
> inform his wife. If a man, unknown to anyone, says to himself,
> 'I made *ruju'* to my wife,' that *ruju'* is correct.[29]

Thus Javad's *ruju'* was correct from the Shari'a perspective,
provided that he indeed had the intent, as he claimed in his
petition. In support of his claim he produced ten witnesses; six
of them submitted their testimony in writing, the rest in person.
They all testified either that Javad had spoken of having made
the *ruju'* (some said that he mentioned this during the period
of *'idda* while some said it was later); or that they had seen the
couple together since their divorce (all said since the termination
of the *'idda*), and they had interpreted this as the resumption
of marital relations. To ascertain marital intimacy, the judge
questioned each witness as to whether Mitra was observing the
rules of *hijab* (covering herself) while in the presence of Javad,
whether she served tea when they went to Javad's home, and
so on.[30]

Mitra's lawyer, in a long defence that he read out in the court,
attempted to refute Javad's claim.[31] The essential points of his
refutation were as follows.

1. The alleged *ruju'* lacked legal validity, as it was not registered during the period of *'idda*; its Shari'a validity was also
   doubtful and must be proved.
2. Javad never communicated his intent of *ruju'* to Mitra, who
   considered herself a free woman and thus contracted another
   marriage, which was perfectly valid.
3. His claim of *ruju'* was fictitious and was motivated by
   jealousy aroused by the remarriage of his ex-wife. Why had
   he not taken action to legalize the *ruju'* earlier?
4. He never paid any maintenance to Mitra after the registered
   divorce, a proof of the termination of the marriage. Why had
   he not provided for her if, as he claimed, he believed that she
   was his *shar'i* wife?
5. Testimony of witnesses could not be taken as the proof of
   ruju' since their *'adalat* (justness, capacity to act as witness)
   had not been proved;[32] one of the witnesses was once in

      Javad's pay, as gardener (now a revolutionary guard); and the others were his friends.

6. The *ruju'* could not be established by his taking the oath, since the Shari'a rules of procedure place the oath on the wife; therefore he must prove his case by other means.[33]

7. Mitra was a young divorced woman and in need of male support and protection, so it was her religious duty to marry.

8. Her subsequent marriage was correct (*sahih*), all the conditions of formation were observed and there was no legal obstacle to it.

      The first four points were refuted by Javad: he did not register the *ruju'* because of her nervous state; he was not required to inform her of his intention to take her back; she was not entitled to *nafaqa* since she was in a state of disobedience (*nushuz*); and her subsequent marriage was void as she was still his *shar'i* wife. Then he proceeded to establish his case by arguing that his *ruju'* was by action (*fi'li*). As evidence of the continued marital intimacy, he presented the following: once, while his wife was bathing their daughter, he handed her a towel; twice they travelled together to the holy city of Qum; and twice she spent the night in his house.

      Mitra denied having any kind of marital intimacy with Javad after the divorce and dismissed his evidence as 'totally irrelevant and inconsequent'. As regards the *hijab*, the judge's question whether she appeared uncovered in Javad's presence, she said 'It proves nothing, I have never covered myself in front of men, so why should I have done it only with him?' As for going to visit the children in his house, she said, 'I had no other choice since he wouldn't allow me to see them anywhere else, and I spent two nights there because my daughter was ill.' She admitted that once he handed her a towel while she was in the bathroom; and said 'It proves nothing, I was not totally naked, it is like being seen in a swimming costume.' She also admitted that she went to Qum with him, but dismissed it as inconsequential, saying, 'So what? it was an outing with my children.'

      Throughout the trial, Mitra appeared unconcerned with the Shari'a rules, emphasizing the fact that her divorce was legal and there was no registered *ruju'* to prove the claims made by her ex-husband. She continually stressed that she always feared that he might use his right to revoke the divorce and made him swear that he would not do such a thing. To preempt a *ruju'*, she avoided him during the period of *'idda*; it was only after her *'idda* was terminated that she went to his house to see her children (see below). Her entire defence was based on the fact that he could not have made the *ruju'* as she saw him well after her *'idda* was over. She considered herself a divorcee, and therefore free to remarry. His motive was revenge and he wanted to ruin her life since she had married a young man and he was jealous.

On the other hand, Javad argued in accordance with the rules of Shari'a. He succeeded in convincing the court that he was a deeply religious man, that he would never commit an act in contradiction of the Shari'a. He divorced her with reluctance (*ikrah*), out of necessity (*zarurat*) and out of consideration for his wife's state of mind. He made the *ruju'* according to the Shari'a and did not register (i.e. legalize) it again out of consideration for her. He considered her as his *shar'i* wife, otherwise he would never have allowed himself to be alone with her in the house, gone to the bathroom where she was semi-naked, or travelled with her to Qum, all actions in contradiction to the Shari'a (*khilaf-i shar'*), something that he would never do. The testimony of the witnesses confirmed the strength of his religiosity. For example, during the seven years that he lived in America, he would not touch meat unless he was convinced that it was *halal*. His religious conviction was also underlined inadvertently by Mitra, who called him a religious bigot (*khusk-i madhabi*), someone who would stay up all night and pray but would lie through his teeth about his marital life. He also succeeded in showing to the court that Mitra was not mindful but dismissive of the Shari'a, a fact which was confirmed by her conduct throughout the trial.

After three sessions, the court declared its judgment; it recognized the *ruju'* as correct and ordered its registration; recognized Mitra's second marriage as irregular and ordered its annulment. The judgment was based on two factors. The witnesses' accounts convinced the court of the truth of Javad's claim, as they revealed his fear of God and his religiosity (*taqva va dianat*). Mitra's admission of having travelled to Qum with him and the bathroom episode were taken as sufficient evidence of the continuation of marital intimacy. Mitra's lawyer appealed, but on 28 January 1987 the appeal court confirmed the decision of the first court.

This case is the only successful one among *ruju'* cases in which there was no agreement between the spouses. Its success was partly due to Javad's ability to convince the court of his religiosity, and his good contacts expedited the whole process (the speed at which the case was dealt with is exceptional). Above all, what enabled him to win his case was his skilful manipulation of differing notions of permissible spheres of male–female interaction. His notion of what was permissible was shared by the court but not by his wife. He proved the *ruju'* by convincing the court that his interactions with Mitra after the divorce were of the sort that are only permissible in a marital relation. These were regarded by Mitra as 'normal interactions' not amounting to anything more than social intercourse. Her view is shared by a certain class of urban Iranians, but is in contrast to the court's ideology.

The case also reveals the existence of a popular body of knowledge of the Shari'a regulations. Popular belief holds that a man can exercise his power to make *ruju'* only if he sees his divorced wife during the period of *'idda*. For this reason, traditionally families who did not wish the resumption of the marital bond sent away their divorced daughter or did not allow her to leave home until the *'idda* was over. Mitra acted on the basis of this popular belief, which explains why she was so convinced that there could be no *ruju'*: she abstained from going to his home to see the children for over three months after they went to register the divorce.

The judgment indicates that the judge, despite sharing Javad's notion of spheres of permissible male–female interaction, took into consideration the popular belief and accepted that Mitra was genuinely unaware of the authentic rules of *ruju'*.[34] It only ordered the annulment of the second marriage without subjecting the two parties to the *fiqh* penalty, which is the creation of a permanent marital bar. Contracting a marriage with a married woman or with a woman who is in the *'idda* of another man creates a permanent bar (*hurmat-i abadi*) unless the good faith of the parties is established, namely that they were ignorant that the woman was not free. This could have been one of the objectives of Javad: to make it impossible for her to remarry the man she chose.

It is difficult to ascertain the real intention and motives of Javad; throughout the trial, he was calculating and manipulative, constantly aiming to impress the judge. For instance he would bring their daughter to the court, which made the sessions emotionally charged. The little girl would cry and would refuse to leave the court without her mother, a scene which immensely moved the judge who each time would remark on the selfishness and cruelty of some mothers, and the dangers of giving women a free hand in divorce. Javad also successfully manipulated Mitra's ignorance of the Shari'a principles and manoeuvred her to testify to her detriment.

Perhaps the subsequent development of the case can give us a clue. Shortly after the judgment, Mitra filed a petition for a divorce, to which Javad reacted by demanding her return to the marital home. It is in these court documents that the dynamic of their dispute is revealed and that one can gain some insight into the reality of this case. The marriage was arranged and imposed on her; she was only fifteen, too young to resist. She never liked him and found him sexually repulsive; she left him many times and asked for divorce; but each time her family persuaded her to go back. She finally became so ill with depression that her family came to support her demand for a divorce. Javad's account reveals that he knew very well their marriage was over; but he was angry and felt betrayed by her remarriage, so wanted to keep her in a state of limbo.

A year later he finally agreed to a divorce and they registered a *khul'* divorce on 30 September 1987 in which she agreed to forgo her *mahr* (a piece of land) and her right to the custody of their daughter (aged five).

Concluding Remarks

The grafting of the Shari'a on to a modern legal system has given rise to the existence of two parallel but distinct notions of legitimacy. At the same time there are overlapping areas of ambiguity, namely between the Shari'a and the modern legal system on the one hand, and between the Shari'a and social practices on the other. The ambiguity is at times successfully manipulated by the petitioners to negotiate the terms of their relationship. These cases also illustrate the existence of different systems of values, each with its own respective concepts, rules and resulting areas of tension.

The ways in which these value systems are reconciled and the tensions managed at the legal level differ in each country. In Morocco the court's concern is to apply the articles of the code derived from the Shari'a in accordance with the civil rules of procedure, not to trace these rules to their origins and adjudicate in accordance with their essence. The situation itself is the by-product of the eclectic codification of the Shari'a and its application by a court bound by civil rules of procedure derived from the French legal system. Not only are the Shari'a concepts trapped in articles of the code but the modern judge has very little discretionary power: he is bound to the interpretation adopted by those who wrote the code.

In Iran the court, free from the civil rules of procedure, sees its prime function as upholding religious values and administering the Shari'a rules. The Iranian judge is caught between the legal logic of the Shari'a rules and their popular constructions. This creates a situation in which he becomes not only the final arbiter but the interpreter of the Shari'a rules in the modern context, using his own notion of justice. The judge, in selecting a particular aspect of a Shari'a injunction, appears to be taking into account the social interpretations of these rules and the best interests of those involved. The two cases from the Tehran court (cases Nos 17 and 20) clearly illustrate how flexible the decision-making process can be and how selective can be the ways in which certain facts are given legal weight. In the first case involving *mut'a*, the judge was prepared to accept the petitioner's assertion of permanency of the marriage, despite the evidence to the contrary. In the second case, the petitioner's religiosity and his history of living in accordance with the Shari'a convinced the judge of the truth of his claim of *ruju'*. In both cases, his main concern, articulated several times, was to keep the couple together in the interest of the children.

Yet, setting aside the differences between Iran and Morocco in the role of the judge and the court procedure, these cases suggest that, in both countries, the Shari'a rules have come to acquire a legal logic and force sometimes at variance with their original spirit.

Conclusion

In the course of this study, in analysing different types of marital disputes heard in courts of Iran and Morocco, I have attempted to elucidate two interrelated sets of problems. The first pertains to the relationship between Islamic law and family structures; and the second to the ways in which individuals relate to a body of legal rules rooted in divine revelation, but now codified and implemented by a judicial bureaucracy. In conclusion, let us return to the beginning and paraphrase the questions posed in the Introduction, for which, I hope, the preceding chapters will have provided some answers. What is the relationship between the model of the family advocated by the Shari'a and the existing family patterns in contemporary Muslim societies? To what extent does the Shari'a direct or reflect the social practices? What are the differences between Shi'a and Maliki schools? Do they mirror the prevalent patterns of familial organization found in contemporary Moroccan and Iranian societies? What is the impact of the patriarchal bias of the law on marriage and marital stability? How do women come to terms and deal with their subordinate position in law? In what ways is the Shari'a relevant to today's Muslim society? Finally, what does all this tell us about Muslim societies in general and marriage in particular?

The Shari'a Model and Family Patterns

The existence of parallel but distinct patterns of marriage and family structures in both societies suggests that the hold of the Shari'a is far from absolute: the model sanctioned by the Shari'a is one among others. The patterns found can be summarized under three broad

191

analytical categories: patrifocal, matrifocal, and bifocal, each with its own source of legitimacy derived from a set of implicit or explicit values and norms. These three models are not mutually exclusive, although at times they can be identified as distinct entities. The actual situation is, of course, more complex than these models imply. While the first model corresponds to the Shari'a, the second represents its negation and the third its modification.

The Shari'a model is based on an ideology of male dominance, expressed and sustained through the rules regulating marriage and its dissolution. Neither the codification nor the reforms of the Shari'a in this century have tempered this ideology, although they have subjected marriage to secular provisions and thus resulted in its appropriation by the modern state. As discussed in Chapter 1, marriage occupies a special place in the Shari'a schema, with shifting boundaries between the religious and the legal. Though not a sacrament, marriage is imbued with a wealth of religious symbolism; yet, in its legal structure, marriage is a civil contract with defined terms and consequences, patterned after the contract of sale. The blurring of boundaries between the religious and legal dimensions of rules regulating marriage serves a double purpose: sustaining the patriarchal ideology that informs these rules, and at the same time allowing for their modification.

Yet this ideology is not free from inconsistencies and inner contradictions; and it is through the manipulation of these that men and women renegotiate their relationships. In previous chapters we explored the processes through which this negotiation takes place without either compromising the sanctity of the Shari'a or directly questioning the theoretical immutability of its rules. We have seen in Chapters 1 to 4 how, through a combination of legal rules and social practices, a man's Shari'a prerogatives are restricted; and how the very rules granting men power in marriage are effectively manipulated by women to offset that power. We have also seen how couples use the courts for rewriting the terms of their marriage contracts; and how courts become instruments for modifying the very rules that they are bound to uphold. While the peculiar role played by the courts is a function of the theoretical immutability of the Shari'a, which assigns the courts the uneasy task of perpetuating the Shari'a model while accommodating social practice, the disputes themselves are the corollary of a legal conception of marriage which relegates women to a subordinate position. As Ronald Cohen remarks of marriage in a different Islamic context:

> All superior–subordinate relations are governed by two opposing forces: legitimacy and entropy. Legitimacy describes those

forces, values, customs, and supports which maintain the authority of the superior over the subordinate and bind the subordinate
to his inferior position with respect to the power his superior
wields over him. Contrarily, entropy is the resentment, and
striving for equal or more power, on the part of subordinates.
Thus all situations of social inequality have inherent in them the
potentiality for change in a direction of more equality or even a
reversal of the inequality.[1]

The Shari'a marriage is an example of a relationship with inbuilt
asymmetry of rights and duties, sanctioned by a body of religious law,
and thus seen as divinely ordained and not to be openly challenged.
This fosters a special type of tension within marriage, which comes to
the surface when the relationship is too strained. Chapters 2, 3 and 4
explored some of the myriad ways in which this tension is expressed in
different socio-economic contexts. Two salient origins of this tension
are to be found in the absence of shared marital resources, and in the
husband's prerogatives of repudiation and polygamy. It is this tension
that provides the impetus for change, which often entails either the
negation or the modification of the religio-legal model.

Marital dispute cases in Morocco reveal a matrifocal alternative
model of the family that persists in a system dominated by a patriarchal
ideology.[2] Ironically, this ideology, embodied in the legal rules, is the
only means for resolving familial disputes. The very foundation of the
Shari'a model is based on the assumption of a man's ability to be the
sole provider; such an assumption is negated by social reality. Court
cases involving the poor, who comprise the majority of both court
petitioners and the urban population, depict a situation in which not
only are men not the sole providers but their wives often have better
access to the informal sector of the economy. Although more marginal,
women are often in a better position to utilize the patronage system
and earn a livelihood by working as maids and washerwomen.[3]

For masses of people the religio-legal model is an ideal which
remains out of reach, no matter how hard they strive to achieve it.
It can neither be adhered to nor enforced by law; there is no way
that a patriarchal model of the family can be enforced and maintained
when it is in contradiction with what is possible. There is little that
any system of law, even if it is rooted in religious precepts, can do to
ensure the authority of a man as the head of the household if he is
out of work and incapable of providing his own maintenance.[4]

Among a small and relatively better-off section of society, where the
material conditions for realizing the Shari'a ideal are present, we are
witnessing the emergence of a family structure that is based on a more
egalitarian ideology of relations between sexes. The process itself is

fostered by changes in the wider society, namely women's access to education and the job market; and above all the integration of Muslim countries into the global economy. In both Iran and Morocco, in particular among the middle strata, women's contribution to the household economy is often essential in order to achieve and sustain a certain standard of living. In a consumer-orientated economy a conjugal unit in which the husband is the sole wage earner is no longer viable. Here the Shari'a model is modified for two related reasons: to create a community of resources within the marital unit and to ensure its stability. Yet the fact that the concept of a shared matrimonial regime is absent in law has a far-reaching impact on the actual dynamics of marital relations.

However, it is important to remember that the significance of the familial model inherent in the Shari'a does not lie in the degree to which it corresponds to actual social practices. Its power lies in providing the only frame of reference which can be used in justifying demands and expressing grievances in the course of a marital dispute. In this sense, the Shari'a is an ideology which serves to legitimate certain power relations within the family: like other ideologies, it is neither uniform nor stagnant. Its different levels and shades are both moulded and expressed in interaction with other socio-historical factors. The diversity of legal rules and social practices in Iran and Morocco is best understood in this light.

The Shari'a and Patriarchy: Different Constructions in Iran and Morocco

Both Shi'a and Maliki schools of law support the Shari'a ethos of patriarchy, yet the ways in which this ethos is interpreted, translated into legal rules and expressed in practice vary significantly in contemporary Iran and Morocco. This is borne out by divorce patterns in the two countries, and is also reflected in marital dispute cases heard in their courts. Whereas in Morocco marriage is fragile and its breakdown is more frequent among the poor, in Iran marriage is stable and its breakdown is more likely to happen among the middle and upper strata. There is a sharp contrast between Moroccan and Iranian dispute cases, in terms of both the nature of the dispute and the socio-economic origins of those who resort to the court to resolve a marital impasse. In Morocco, the bulk of those who resort to the court are women of the lower classes and most disputes revolve around maintenance claims; while, in Iran, there is no significant difference in terms of class or sex among those who use the court, and most disputes concern divorce. Likewise, as illustrated in Chapter 5, family patterns that emerge when marriage breaks down differ in the two countries:

the strong patrilineal and patrifocal bias in Iran contrasts with the matrifocal tendency in Morocco.

It is difficult, and probably futile, to calculate how far the fragility of marriage and the matrifocal alternative of family organization in Morocco are products of Maliki law, or how far the ambiguities inherent in Maliki law mirror the *de facto* dominant practices. Equally, it is unclear whether Shi'a law reflects or shapes the prevalent practices in Iran. Such speculation needs both a greater historical depth and a wider comparative dimension than are within the scope of this study.[5] What can be said with some certainty is that there is a strong correlation between stability of marriage, on the one hand, and family patterns and the rules regulating marriage, divorce and the custody of children, on the other.

In Chapter 5, I traced the differences between Iranian and Moroccan family patterns to the differing notions of filiation in Shi'a and Maliki law, which have endured until today and are embodied in their respective modern codes. In both, paternity is the primary mode of filiation and is linked to legitimacy, which can be established only through the existence of a marriage contract. Nevertheless the Maliki position is ambivalent: not only is the issue of *zina* bypassed, but the theory of the 'sleeping foetus' enables a women to remain legally pregnant for up to five years.[6] Although the Moroccan Code has done away with this concept, the code still entitles a child born outside marriage to legal maternal filiation and in child custody favours the mother and females in her line at the expense of the father. The same does not hold true for Shi'a law where, in both its classical and modern forms, such a child is deprived of legal filiation, and where, in the event of divorce, the care of children is entrusted to the father and the paternal side.

Such a difference questions two prevalent assumptions: first, that Islamic law sustains a uniform concept of family, characterized as strictly patrilineal, patriarchal and virilocal.[7] Secondly, that Islamic law is either the cause or the cure for the subjugation of women in Muslim countries, an assumption which lies at the root of the family law debate, to which I shall return later. As to the first assumption, differences between the Shi'a and the Sunni have generally been seen as confined to the rules of succession, and as superficial in other areas of family law.[8] But, as Coulson argued, these differences are too fundamental to be dismissed as 'superficial modifications'. He suggests that they must be seen as a reflection of a deeper divergence in political theory between the Shi'a and Sunni rites, which are reflected in their conceptions of the family.[9] In contrast to Sunni law, which rests on the concept of the patrilineal extended family,

Shi'a law rests on the notion of the immediate family, consisting of parents and lineal descendants.

While concurring with Coulson's thesis, the findings of this study have extended it by demonstrating that these differences are not confined to rules of succession and that they have significant repercussions on other areas of family: they define choices available to men and women when marriage ends, which in turn inhibit or facilitate the break-up of the conjugal unit. In Maliki law, where the emphasis is on the patrilineally extended unit, a child's attachment to the family is a function of its paternal filiation and maternal filiation is of little consequence. This explains why rules for its establishment can be lax and why the issue of *zina* can be bypassed with impunity. In Shi'a law, on the other hand, where the emphasis is on the nuclear family formed through bilateral filiation, maternal filiation acquires the same importance as paternal. Thus, neither can the rules for its establishment be relaxed, nor can *zina* be overlooked. If we accept this premise then we have to deal with two intriguing paradoxes.

First, why does paternal filiation lose its importance in Morocco when marriage breaks down? And why does it gain importance in the case of Iran? The answer lies in the ways in which legal concepts and rules interact with socio-economic factors and parameters. In the previous chapters we have explored the workings and specificities of some of these parameters in the Iranian and Moroccan contexts, namely marriage and what it entails in terms of transfer of wealth and loyalties, the degree of the merger of each spouse into the conjugal unit and the possibility of creating shared marital resources, the economic insecurity faced by families in the lower strata, and, finally, the involvement of women in economic activities outside the home.

A host of legal and social factors in Morocco create a situation in which, when marriage breaks down, it is the husband who becomes alienated from the family of procreation. To retain his link with his children, he must be in a position to provide for them and pay their mother a 'custody wage'. This is not possible if he is poor. Men often remarry and become responsible for a new set of children as well as remaining accountable to their natal family. The wife goes back to her natal family where she is accepted with her children. For her, remarriage does not necessarily entail the loss of custody since this is passed on to her mother, and in her absence to her sister.

In Iran, on the other hand, a different situation is created in which, when marriage breaks down, it is the wife who is excluded from the family of procreation. Her natal family rarely welcomes her with her children; even if she manages to get their custody, she is bound to lose them if she remarries. It is only among the middle and upper strata, where divorce is less stigmatized and her options are wider, that a woman might keep her children, a choice which she makes at the risk of diminishing her chances of remarriage.

In other words, a combination of Shi'a custody rules and Iranian family structure make it impossible for the mother/child unit to be viable in Iran, whereas Maliki law and Moroccan family structure ensure the viability of such a unit in Morocco. It must also be stressed that Moroccan women in the poorer strata play a more active role in the outside economy than Iranian women do. It is rare to see Iranian women as vendors of home produce in the bazaar, as bus conductors, as cleaners in offices, and so forth; but these are familiar sights in Morocco.

The second paradox, which touches on assumptions underlying the family law debate, is why the matrifocal tendencies of Maliki law are not accompanied by a better position for women in marriage. In Shi'a Iran, by contrast, where there is more consistency with patriarchal principles and where the patrifocal bias extends beyond marriage, not only is marriage more stable but it has a more egalitarian structure. I suggest that in order to understand this paradox we need to return to the Shari'a conception of marriage; the definitions given by the mediaeval jurists clearly indicate what marriage is about. It is, as they defined and regulated it, a contract based on inequality and domination, through which a man acquires exclusive access to the sexual and reproductive faculties of a woman and consequently to the issue of such a contract: the children. It seems that Moroccan women's experience of greater male control, a lesser say in marriage and yet a greater dependence on it than Iranian women, is in part due to the matrifocal tendencies of Maliki law. These tendencies, which are allowed within the patriarchal framework of the family, in practice affect women in two major ways. First, they leave women of the poorer strata with the task of maintaining the children while freeing their husbands to enter other unions; secondly, they necessitate tighter control over women's sphere of action in order to retain the children within the patrilineal unit and to ensure the power of the husband within the marriage. Relaxation of such control, by giving women a freer hand in contracting marriage and an equal access to divorce, would contribute to the further alienation of the children from the paternal side.

On the other hand, in the case of Shi'a law, the extension of patriarchal control beyond marriage not only diminishes the need for controlling women, as the children remain within the patrilineal unit, but ironically makes it easier for them to escape an unwanted marriage. It is this configuration of legal rules and practice that affords Iranian women a greater degree of legal and social protection than their Moroccan counterparts. This fact suggests that neither secularization nor a return to a Shari'a-based society in themselves ameliorate or worsen women's lot. Paradoxically, it is in Iran, where the Shari'a is now enforced, that women enjoy better status, both in law and in marriage. Not only do women have a freer hand in contracting marriage, as evidenced in the absence of the concept of *jabr*, a guardian's constraining power, but they have more or less the same say as their husbands in bringing about a divorce, made possible by the way in which *mahr*, an element of the Shari'a contract of marriage, is interpreted and practised. On the other hand, the grafting of Maliki law onto a modern legal system in Morocco has created a situation in which the patriarchal elements of the Shari'a are reinforced, while the classical leeways are reduced. This has brought to the surface some of the dormant tensions and has resulted in widening the gap between the religio-legal model and popular practices, as evidenced in the new requirement for legal identity and redefinition of marriage validity. The main casualties of this situation are poorer women whose unregistered marriages leave them with no mode of redress before the law.

The Shari'a and Individuals

The ways in which men and women relate to the sacred in the Shari'a are evinced in the very nature of marital disputes and the strategies deployed in the court. Strategies, which are an integral part of court processes, serve two main purposes: to reconcile the law with the actual dynamics of marriage and its breakdown, and to help redress some of the inequalities inherent in the religio-legal model of marriage. The first is necessitated by the distance between law and practice, the contrast between marriage as perceived in law and marriage as practised by people; and the second by what Ronald Cohen calls the working of entropy: a constant seeking to equalize the relationship.[10] Both are corollaries of the very nature of the Shari'a: the need to maintain its theoretical immutability even at the expense of its distortion.

The selectivity that both men and women exercise in conforming to the Shari'a suggests that the main motivation stems not from a desire to conform to religious precepts but rather from a need to circumvent the law in order to achieve a different purpose. To individuals, certainly to those who use the court, the sacred in the Shari'a is irrelevant; and, if it matters, it is subordinated to the conflicting interests that marriage creates. This places the Shari'a on the same level as other systems of law and challenges prevalent assumptions regarding popular belief in its sanctity.

If, as the findings of this study suggest, the Shari'a model of family and marital relations is negated or modified with impunity, and if Muslims in their adherence to Islamic legal precepts are motivated by the exigencies of social reality rather than religious ideals, then how can we account for the seemingly popular demand for its application and its central place in the contemporary Muslim scene? In other words, why has family law become such a sensitive issue and why does its reform stir up such strong emotions? One apparent answer is that the sacred and the legal are so closely intertwined in Shari'a family law that any reform can be construed as tampering with the divine elements, thus the potential of a religious backlash is always present. But to understand why this has remained the case, as argued in the Introduction, we need to look at the place and role of the Shari'a and its relevance to the family in contemporary Muslim social life. This takes us to the domain of politics; the issues involved and the ensuing dilemmas have been explored from different angles in a number of studies.[11]

At the macro level, a host of factors both internal and external to Muslim societies – some reflecting the changed balance of power between the state and religion, others the workings of world capitalism – have resulted in a form of distorted change which Sharabi calls 'neopatriarchy'.[12] In this peculiar duality, where modern and patriarchal orders coexist, often in a contradictory union, the Shari'a has come to acquire a special place. It symbolizes a golden past and vindicates a present soured by ties of dependency, given the overwhelming superiority of the West; it acts as a buffer against rapid erosion of the traditional way of life and the aggressive invasion of Western values; it provides a refuge in a world permeated by uncertainty and chronic economic crisis; it is an innate answer to the crisis of identity; and, above all, it is an ideology which is used to justify unequal relations, of which gender relations are only one facet. An ideology which can claim divine roots is thereby more persuasive. Its relevance to today's Muslim society must be seen in this light, not solely in the light of the degree of its application and adherence to it.

At the micro level of this study, the Shari'a can be understood and studied only in its complex double image, as both expressing and moulding social practice; it can neither be divorced from the social context in which it operates nor understood merely by textual analysis. Here again, the Shari'a is an ideology whose present function is that of perpetuating a certain type of relations within the family by restraining women's sphere of action. Not surprisingly, it is only at the level of theory that change is resisted, while at the level of practice change is both accommodated and encouraged, as evidenced in the post-revolutionary situation in Iran.[13] As long as the Shari'a is recognized as the incontestable law of the land, as long as its guardians, the ulema, are in a position to interpret it, it can be modified with impunity.

Those who use the courts are well aware of all this: they might not adhere to the Shari'a model of family relations, but they certainly fight their marital battles armed with its discourse. In so doing, litigants, who are largely women, succeed in changing the terms of their Shari'a marriage contracts. For every ideology carries both the seeds and the means of its own mutation.

Notes

Introduction

1. Islamic resurgence, with its social and political implications, has dominated the recent literature on Muslim societies. For some insightful collections of articles, see Ayoob (1981); Hillal Dessouki (1982); Stowasser (1987); and Hunter (1988).

2. For two recent collections of papers, see Dwyer (1990), especially articles by Fischer on Iran and Mayer on Libya; and Hillal Dessouki (1987).

3. For an account of Libya and Qadafi's attempts, see Mayer (1990); for Iran, see Amin (1985) and Arjomand (1989); for attempts in the Sudan, see Fluehr-Lobban (1987); for Egypt, see Hussein (1985).

4. For two excellent comprehensive accounts, see Schacht (1964) and Coulson (1964).

5. Recent studies in legal anthropology have argued for placing law and legal processes in their proper historical context; see Starr and Collier (1987 and 1989).

6. Schacht (1964: 199).

7. This tendency is particularly evident in the genre of literature on Islamic law written by Muslim lawyers trained in the West, in which the accounts of historical development of the Shari'a in the works of Western scholars are discredited as orientalist projections. They believe in and argue for the eternal validity and relevance of Islamic law, which governs the choice of their facts and sources. For two lucid and well argued examples see Ramadan (1961) and El-Awa (1991).

8. See the chapter 'Islam in Practice' in Eickelman (1989), for a discussion of this issue. For the need to contextualize the recent Islamic movements, see Tibi (1987 and 1988); Hillal Dessouki (1982).

9. Montgomery Watt (1953 and 1957); Levy (1957); and Rodinson (1961).

10. The Muslim calendar (*hijri*) starts with the year 622 AD, the year

201

in which the Prophet migrated from Mecca to Medina, where he succeeded in gaining political power. He had received his mission in 610 AD, twelve years prior to the *hijra* (migration), at the age of forty in Mecca, his home town. The fact that the Islamic era starts with the year of the establishment of the Muslim state, not the year that the Prophet received his first revelation, is a clear indication that Islam is perceived as coming into existence with a political order.

11. The Shi'a are in turn divided into several groups; the most numerous is that of the Imami or Twelvers (Ithna 'Ashari) who believe in a line of twelve Imams.

12. Coulson (1969: 2).

13. See Coulson (1964: 17–20) and Vesey-Fitzgerald (1955: 87–91).

14. Anderson (1959: 12).

15. Anderson (1951: 245).

16. Schacht (1960: 101 and 1964: 209).

17. Among devices used was *istihsan*, juristic preference, applied to cases where strict analogical deduction produced rigid results. Its use was justified on the basis of two Koranic verses. Another method was *istislah*, public interest, by which public interest or human welfare became a source of law. Another method was *istishab*, permanence, which refers to a presumption in the law that conditions known to exist in the past continue to exist unless the contrary is proven. For a brief but clear summary of these, see Esposito (1982: 7–10).

18. The Imami school of Shi'a law is also known as Ja'fari, named after its founder Ja'far al-Sadiq, the sixth Imam of the Shi'as. For an introduction to this school, see Modaressi Tabataba'i (1984).

19. Schacht (1964: 57); Coulson (1964: 224) and Anderson (1959: 15).

20. Schacht holds that 'closing the gate of ijtihad' served the purpose of sanctioning a state of things which had come to prevail in fact (1964: 69–71).

21. Schacht (1964: 71).

22. Among the Sunni schools it was only the Hanbalis, most prominently led by Ibn Taymiyya (d. 1328), who objected to the rule of *taqlid* and argued for the validity of *ijtihad* (independent reasoning).

23. There is a wide literature on this; for a recent contribution, see Al-Azmeh (1988).

24. Schacht (1964: 72).

25. Schacht (1964: 75).

26. Coulson (1969: 20).

27. Coulson (1969: 75–6).

28. The methods employed in the reform, and the degree to which the Shari'a was subjected to change, have been discussed extensively. See Schacht (1960); Anderson (1959 and 1976); Mahmood (1972); and Esposito (1982).

29. Amin (1985) and Dwyer (1990).

30. See Schacht (1964: Chapter 26); Coulson (1969: Chapter 4).

31. Legal fiction, *hiyal*, was widely used and perfected by the jurists (Schacht 1964: 79–80). Also see Powers (1990b: 11–31) for an interesting study

of how the inheritance rules of the Shari'a were circumvented and how the means by which these circumventions were achieved become incorporated in *waqf* (endowment) laws.

32. Schacht (1964: 77–85); Anderson (1959: 20); Coulson (1964: 135–9).
33. Bohannan (1967: 49).
34. As Vesey-Fitzgerald (1955: 89) commented, existing laws can be understood only by reference to those which have become obsolete. Many parts of the Shari'a are obsolete, either for reasons internal to Islam or owing to the impact of the West. I shall deal with an instance in which an obsolete law can become relevant again in Chapter 6.
35. Schacht sees this classification of acts into five categories as a central feature that helped to preserve the unity of the Islamic law, despite its diversity, since 'law proper has been thoroughly incorporated in the system of religious duties' (1964: 200).
36. It is important not to overlook this. A great part of the misconceptions about the Shari'a has its roots here, as reflected in the debate between Muslim traditionalists who see the Shari'a as both honouring and protecting to women, and modernists who see it as degrading and suppressing women. Both are right, but argue on different grounds. The first appeals to the moral and the second to the legal elements of the Shari'a laws.
37. Anderson (1968: 221).
38. While some of these states, such as Iraq, Syria and Lebanon, came into being with the break-up of the Ottoman Empire in 1918, others, such as Iran, have a long history of sovereignty.
39. In practice, the situation was rather different. For an interesting discussion of this, see Schacht (1960).
40. For a general account, see Hourani (1962). For a specific account of the impact of the state ideology on women in different Muslim societies, see Kandiyoti (1991 and 1992); on pre- and post-revolutionary Iran state ideology, see Najmabadi (1991) and Higgins (1985).
41. Only in the countries of the Arabian Peninsula and Northern Nigeria is Shari'a family law applied more or less in the traditional manner. Otherwise, elsewhere in the Muslim world it is now generally expressed in codes, and it is only in the absence of a specific code that recourse is made to the classical manuals.
42. I owe this point to Geoffrey Hawthorn.
43. In Turkey the reformist government went as far as abolishing the Islamic law and replacing it with Western codes.
44. Schacht (1964: 210).
45. Schacht (1964: 5).
46. Anderson (1959: 15).
47. On this issue see, for instance, Hillal Dessouki (1987), Sharabi (1988), Tibi (1988), and, for a general treatment, Rosenthal (1965).
48. See Anderson (1959), Coulson (1964: 160–4) and Layish (1978).
49. Esposito (1982); Azari (1983); Mernissi (1985 and 1991); Hijab (1988); Haeri (1989) and Ahmed (1992).
50. See, for instance, recent works of Fatima Mernissi (1991) in which she

studies the *hadith* literature in order to refute the Islamic construction of gender relations developed by the Muslim jurists.

51. As Kandiyoti says, 'the terms of the "women question" were forged in the process of search for identity and legitimacy' (1991: 4).
52. Moore (1978: 244).
53. See Moore (1978: 48) for a discussion on this; she says, 'An adequate study of what is negotiable in situations cannot be made without attention to what is not negotiable in the same situation.' This is in fact what needs to be addressed in an analysis of Islamic law, but has been so far ignored.
54. Rosen (1989: 79).
55. Moore (1978: 238–9); see also Collier (1975).
56. This is even the case in recent studies such as Esposito (1982); Nasir (1990); Mallat and Connors (1990).
57. Among studies in which court cases are the main source of data are the following: Djamour (1966); Layish (1975 and 1982); Fluehr-Lobban (1987); Hill (1979); Rosen (1989) and Antoun (1980 and 1990).
58. Among those whose work examines Islamic law as part of the culture are: Hoebel (1965); Dwyer (1977); Hill (1979); Starr (1978); Mundy (1988); Antoun (1980 and 1990); and Rosen (1989).
59. Among the above studies it is only Antoun's (1990) that deals with litigants' strategies, but in a rural context. Mundy's work is not based on the court attendance; Rosen's focus is on the judge and the court rather than the litigants.
60. There is a strong anthropological argument in support of the study of law cases as a standard field technique; see Gluckman (1965), Epstein (1967) and Hamnett (1977). Epstein demonstrates the various ways in which the case method is preferable to informants' accounts in determining rules, concepts and categories. One reason for the paucity of such studies in the case of Islamic law is the difficulties involved in fieldwork, such as language competence and access to court files.
61. See Mir-Hosseini (1986 and 1993).
62. Both Iranian and Moroccan law, and the extent to which they conform to or depart from the Shi'a or Maliki principles respectively, are treated in the context of court cases in the course of the following chapters.
63. Contrary to the widespread assumption, some elements of the Family Protection Law have been retained; this and the extent of actual implementation of Shi'a principles are discussed in the relevant chapters.

Chapter 1

1. For the pre-revolutionary situation see Banani (1961), Hinchcliffe (1968a and 1968b) and Haeri (1980). For a general account of legal changes after the revolution, see Amin (1985: 101–44); and for changes in family law see Higgins (1985) and Mir-Hosseini (1986).
2. Banani (1961: 71); Mahmood (1972: 154).
3. Banani (1961: 81).

4. Hinchcliffe (1968a: 304–5) and Anderson (1976: 128).
5. In a speech delivered in 1967 and in two legal rulings (*fatwas*), Ayatollah Khomeini strongly opposed the Family Protection Law. In *fatwa* 2836, he said: 'The law designated the "family law", which has as its purpose the destruction of the Muslim family unit, is contrary to the ordinances of Islam. Those who have imposed [this law] and those who voted [for it] are criminals from the standpoint of both the Shari'a and the law.' In *fatwa* 2837, he said, 'It is the duty of the ulema (may God Almighty support them) to protest forcefully against laws such as this that are void from the standpoint of both Islam and the law; they should not seek to gain the favour of the true criminals by pretending that lower-ranking officials are responsible for executing the orders of the opponents of Islam.' For a translation of these two rulings see Algar (1981: 441–2).
6. The Civil Court Act was legislated 1358/7/1 which corresponds to 21 September 1979, not to 20 October as Amin (1985: 133) has it. The latest version of this act and other post-revolutionary legislations are to be found in Qurbani (1991: 181–7).
7. Article 1 of the Special Civil Court Act requires the court to be presided over by a *mujtahid jami' ul-sharayit* (a religious judge qualified to exercise *ijtihad*, that is, independent interpretation of the religious law; a person so qualified is termed *mujtahid*) or his appointee.
8. As we shall see in the following chapters, the legacy of the pre-revolutionary reform remains in the form of procedural rules and, more importantly, in its impact on women's awareness.
9. Friday is the day of rest in Iran, thus the week starts on Saturday and on Thursday the majority of offices close at mid-day.
10. For the codification of family law in Morocco see Anderson (1958), Decroux (1962), and Colomer (1963); for more detailed accounts, see Borrmans (1977) and Moulay Rchid (1986).
11. For attempts at reform and proposals for change, see Khamlichi and Moulay Rchid (1981) and Moulay Rchid (1985).
12. This is not the case among the judges of *Mahkama al-tawthiq* (the Notary Court) where registration of marriages and divorces take place. It seems those who are trained exclusively in *fiqh* become *'udul* (notaries) and later reach the position of *qadi al-tawthiq* (notary judge).
13. Mi'adi (1988), who studied all files for the year 1981 in Casablanca, made the same observation.
14. The fee charged in Tehran in 1988 was 40 tomans (equivalent to £2 at the official exchange rate); in Morocco in 1989, it was 30 dirham, also about £2.
15. It costs an average of 500 dirham to hire a lawyer for an entire case, which is high considering the average amount set by the court as maintenance payment is 300 dirham monthly. In maintenance cases, the lawyers operate on a percentage basis, that is, the litigant pays nothing in advance but pays an agreed percentage after receiving the maintenance.
16. Such a critique encompasses a vast literature, which can be divided into two categories: works by Muslim feminists, seeing the Shari'a rules as

both cause and manifestation of women's oppression; and works with an apologetic tone, defending the Shari'a rules in the light of perceived attacks. For examples of the first kind, see Sabah (1984), Mernissi (1985 and 1991), Azari (1983) and Afshar (1987); for the second kind, see Mutahhari (1981), Maudoodi (1986), 'Abd Al'Ati (1977) and A. Rahman (1986). For specific studies on the position of women in Shi'a Islam, see Nashat (1980 and 1983), Mahdavi (1985), Ferdows (1985 and 1986) and Madelung (1985).

17. The Special Civil Court in Iran was established in order to ensure that Shi'a law is applied; Article 82 of the Moroccan Mudawwana authorizes the judge to base the judgment on the dominant opinions within Maliki law in case of deficiency of the Code.

18. For English translations of these works, see Russell and al-Suhrawardy (1906) and Ruxton (1916). For French translations, see Bercher (1960). There are several French translations of Khalil: Bousquet (1947), Fagnan (1909) and Perron (1848). I also used the following works, based on Maliki texts dealing with aspects of marriage and sexual mores: Pesle (1936, 1937 and 1946), Milliot (1953), Bousquet (1948, 1950 and 1966) and Malik (1982). For judicial practice, see Berque (1944) and Toledano (1981).

19. Hilli (1364/1985); Shahid-i Awwal (1368/1989); Mazandarani-Haeri (1985); Meshkini (1987); Khomeini (1366/1987). The last three are contemporary sources.

20. Its name, *'aqd al-nikah*, literally means the contract of coitus, see Schacht (1932b: 912).

21. With the exception of the concubinage of slave girls, which is now obsolete. *Zina* has a much wider connotation than 'fornication'; it includes incest and adultery. It appears that *zina* in early Islam covered other types of accepted sexual unions that were later banned by the Koran. It also appears that what defined *nikah* was that which was not *zina*, which could have had important implications in forming the early jurists' conception of marriage; see Schacht (1929a); Stern (1939); Bousquet (1966) and Ahmed (1992).

22. For a contemporary discussion, see Maudoodi (1983: 6–7) and 'Abd al'Ati (1977: 50–62).

23. On the concept of marriage as a contract in Islamic law, see Liebesny (1975: 129), Bousquet (1948: 63–74) and Milliot (1953: 263–73); and for a recent study, see Haeri (1989: 23–32).

24. Because it is a contract, both parties at the time of marriage can stipulate certain conditions provided that they are not in opposition to the essence of marriage, as defined by the jurists. For instance, a condition can give a woman the right to divorce but a condition which takes away the husband's right to divorce is void. For a list of valid and void conditions see Verma (1971: 97–104).

25. Bercher (1960: 177); Bousquet (1950: 94 and 107); Sebti Larichi (1985: 44).

26. Ruxton (1916: 106). Khalil's conception is shared by other Maliki jurists; for instance Jorjani defines marriage in the following terms: 'a

contract through which the husband acquires exclusive rights over the sexual organs of a woman', quoted in Pesle (1936: 20).

27. Hilli, (1364/1985: 428).
28. On the concept of marriage in Islam, see Bousquet (1948: 63–74).
29. For a list of legal distinctions between marriage and the contract of sale, see Verma (1971: 16).
30. There are several sayings attributed to the Prophet enjoining marriage; for instance: 'Marriage is my *sunna* (practice or order) and those who do not obey it are not my followers,' or: 'One prayer of a married man is equal to seventy prayers of a single man.' See Meshkini (1987) and Mazandarani-Haeri (1985).
31. Marriage is considered to be a *sunnat muvakida*, that is, if one complies, one will be rewarded after death, and the failure to comply can be a sin (Verma 1971: 17).
32. This is partly due to the very nature of *fiqh* treatises: they are not analogous to legal codes; they are to be seen as an ongoing dialogue on Muslim institutions.
33. For a modern discussion, see Mutahhari (1981), 'Abd Al'Ati (1977) and Rahman (1986). See Haeri (1989) for the implications of such a conception.
34. On the legal confusion created by this, see Amirian (1938), who compares marriage in French and Islamic law and argues that marriage in the modern legal systems of Muslim countries has a mixed legal nature.
35. See Chapter 6.
36. Imami (1984: 268).
37. Muhaqqiq-Damad (1986: 22).
38. The Moroccan code does away with the provision of classical Maliki law, which restricted a woman's freedom to a third of her property. See Milliot (1953: 341) and Borrmans (1977: 22).
39. While the ICC is silent on the issue of polygamy and a man's right to control his wife's movements, the MCPS, again in the spirit of incorporating moral injunctions, alludes to them in article 35, which delineates woman's rights in marriage.
40. There is no direct reference to polygamy, either in the ICC or in MCPS, but it is implied in the above articles; see Chapter 6 for Iran.
41. Again, there is no allusion in the ICC to these wifely duties in order to accommodate temporary marriage.
42. For this line of argument, see sources mentioned above in note 16.
43. It is neither the aim nor relevant here to provide an exhaustive account of divorce rules in the different schools within the Shari'a; there is a wide literature on this in both English and French. For example, see the following: Ameer Ali (1925), Fyzee (1964), Anderson (1970), Pearl (1987), Nasir (1990), Layish (1982 and 1991), Pesle (1937), Milliot (1953) and Linant de Bellefonds 1964).
44. For an interesting comparison of divorce in French and Islamic law, see Amirian (1938).
45. For a general introduction to *talaq*, see Schacht (1929b: 636–40) and Gibb and Kramers (1953: 564–71).

46. There are 11 acts which come under *iqa'at* in the Shari'a. Two of them relate to the dissolution of marital lines: *talaq* (divorce) and *ruju'* (return to the marital status after a revocable divorce). In both, the right of exercise is given to men and the consent of the woman is not required. See Muhaqqiq-Damad (1986: 379) and Ja'fari-Langarudi (1989a: 100).
47. For a clear summary of these procedures, see Pearl (1987: 100–4).
48. Schacht (1929b: 638).
49. Milliot (1953: 351).
50. Fyzee (1964: 143).
51. Apart from *talaq*, the Shari'a includes two other modes of unilateral repudiation known as *ila'* and *zihar*. In *ila'* the husband takes an oath to cease marital intercourse with the wife, and if he keeps his oath and does abstain for four months, it will bring about a revocable divorce. *Zihar* is another form of oath of continence taken by the husband in which he pronounces the following formula: 'Thou art to me (as untouchable) as the back (*zahr*) of my mother.' The utterance of this formula has the effect of making marital intercourse between the husband and wife forbidden (*haram*) until the husband has made a special atonement through expiation (see Gibb and Kramers, 1953: 570). Both *ila'* and *zihar* are obsolete in practice. There is no mention of *zihar* in either code. In the Moroccan Code, *ila'* is recognized as a ground for divorce upon which a woman can initiate court proceedings, but, as we shall see, it is obsolete in practice.
52. See Haeri (1989: 44).
53. This has been the area in which most reforms of family law in the Muslim world have been concentrated in order to give women easier access to divorce: see Esposito (1982), Anderson (1976) and Mahmood (1972). The specific reforms in Iran and Morocco are discussed in the next two chapters.
54. Although the husband can give the wife unconditional right of *talaq*, this rarely happens in practice, as we shall see.
55. There is another form of separation by judicial practice which has now become obsolete, although it is mentioned in both Iranian and Moroccan codes. This is known as *li'an* (imprecation) in which the husband accuses the wife of adultery and denies the paternity of a child born by the wife. In itself *li'an* is not a divorce proper but results in the dissolution of marriage if the Islamic judge intervenes.
56. See Chehata (1965).
57. See Lapanne-Joinville (1952b: 431–50).
58. See Chapters 5 and 6 for cases.
59. See Katouzian (1368/1989: 277–9); and Muhaqqiq-Damad (1365/ 1986: 376).
60. See Rosen (1984).
61. This table and others throughout the book are used primarily to summarize data; they do not pretend to make either statistical statements or inferences.
62. Only marital disputes are taken into account; other disputes heard relating to matters such as inheritance and proof of identity are excluded.

Data from Tehran come from the seven central Special Civil Courts; and data from Casablanca come from Anfa Prefecture exclusively.

63. These are discussed in greater detail in the following chapters.

64. One of the legal devices used for reform in the process of codification of the Shari'a was the eclectic selection of certain opinions at the expense of the others. This factor, combined with the different structures of modern legal apparatus of the two countries, has added a new dimension to the classical differences between the schools of law within the Shari'a. I shall highlight these differences when analysing each category of disputes in the course of the following chapters.

65. Cf. Mi'adi (1988: 61–98).

66. The term *nafaqa* has a wider connotation than implied in its English translation 'maintenance'.

67. For a discussion on *nafaqa* in Maliki law, see Milliot (1953: 326–30) and Lapanne-Joinville (1951b: 102–14); in Shi'a law, see Muhaqqiq-Damad (1365/1986: 290–309), Imami (1363/1984: 433–46) and Ja'fari-Langarudi (1368b/1989b: 171–6).

68. Imami (1363/1984: 34).

69. Despite differences of opinion among the schools on details, all relate woman's right to maintenance to the sexual act; see Verma (1971: 94).

70. The mandate for obedience has only one exception: she can disobey her husband only if obedience entails her committing an act which results in violation of her religious duties (e.g., not doing her prayers). For a contemporary discussion of obedience, see Maudoodi (1983: 23–4), and 'Abd Al'Ati (1977: 170–83).

71. 'Abd Al'Ati (1977: 169); Imami (1363/1984: 435); Lapanne-Joinville (1951b: 100) and Khomeini (1366/1987: 362–3).

72. For a discussion of these positions, see 'Abd Al'Ati (1977: 157–9) and Muhaqqiq-Damad (1365/1986: 296–9).

73. Article 1115 of the Iranian Civil Code sets out the Shari'a reasons, consisting of situations in which there is a fear that her stay in the marital home would cause her physical, financial or moral harm.

74. Similar data for Iran were not available. As explained above, this was because I found no easy way of monitoring the outcome of cases; I only had access to the records of the disputes as they were registered.

75. Forty-one cases involving non-marital disputes, over matters such as inheritance and attainment of majority, were excluded.

76. Cf. Mi'adi (1988), who reached similar conclusions in her study of the 1981 files at the Court of First Instance in Casablanca.

Chapter 2

1. For a translation of the text of the Family Protection Law of 1967, see Naqavi (1967); for an analysis of this law in the context of legal reforms in the Muslim world, see Hinchcliffe (1968a and 1968b), Anderson (1976), and Coulson and Hinchcliffe (1980).

2. For a translation of this ruling, see Algar (1981: 441). The section pertaining to divorce reads as follows: 'The divorce of women divorced

by court order is invalid; they are still married women, and if they marry again, they become adulteresses. Likewise, anyone who knowingly marries a woman so divorced becomes an adulterer, deserving the penalty laid down by the Shari'a. The issue of such union will be illegitimate, unable to inherit, and subject to all other regulations concerning illegitimate offspring. All of the foregoing applies equally whether the court itself awards the divorce directly, orders the divorce to take place, or compels the husband to divorce his wife.' Nevertheless the divorces issued by FPL courts remained valid after the revolution: in the courts I came across no case of their validity being challenged, and none of the judges whom I talked to knew of such cases.

3. The translation of the article is my own; that of the Koranic verse is Arberry's (1983: 78); for the text of the article see Qurbani (1991: 183).

4. Article 11 of the FPL of 1967 and Article 8 of the 1975 version list the grounds for divorce.

5. This stipulation is new and did not exist under the FPL. Although it is too early to assess its practical implications in restricting a man's easy access to divorce, in theory it can provide women a degree of material security in case of an arbitrary divorce.

6. This punishment comes under *ta'zirat* in Islamic law which is a discretionary form of punishment awarded by the Shari'a judge (*Hakim-i shar'*). Article 105 of a post-revolutionary enactment regarding 'offences related to Public and Moral Chastity and Familial Obligations' gave it legal force. This article sets the maximum penalty at 74 lashes. For the text of this article see Vatani (1366/1987: 295).

7. The grounds upon which women can apply for a divorce are basically the same as those which were available to them in the pre-revolutionary period. The present grounds differ only in matters of detail, such as a lapse of six months before a woman can be entitled to a divorce in the event of her husband's failure to pay maintenance or his desertion of the marital home, and of five years in the case of her husband's sterility.

8. This article was amended on 8 Dey 1361 (29 December 1982), see Qurbani (1991: 100). In the original version there was no reference to *'asr va haraj*, it merely authorized the judge to issue a divorce if a woman could prove one of the following: her husband's failure to comply with his marital duties; his ill-conduct to the extent that marital life is intolerable to her; or his affliction with any incurable disease endangering her health.

9. Veiling became compulsory in Iran in the early 1980s. To appear in public without a headcover is an offence which can incur up to 74 lashes (Note to Article 102 of Offences Related to Public and Moral Chastity and Familial Obligations); see Vatani (1366/1987: 293).

10. For a commentary, see Mazandarani-Haeri (1364/1985: 80).

11. This was one of the very few cases in which a divorce was issued in the husband's absence.

12. This is a modern view, and has an apologetic tone to it, for example see Maudoodi (1983), Mutahhari (1981) and Rahman (1986).

13. It is essential to stress that the Shi'a position is not different from that of other schools; therefore the rules described below are valid for all schools.
14. Article 15 of Regulations for Marriage and Divorce Registries, which came into effect at the same time as the Marriage Law of 1931. See Qurbani (1370/1991: 141).
15. For a general account of marriage ceremonies in Iran, see Betteridge (1987: 666–70), Betteridge and Javadi (1987: 189–91); in Chapter 6, I shall deal with two stages of marriage as reflected in the ceremonies that surround it.
16. For changes in marriage prestations and the new importance of *mahr* in one region of Iran, see Mir-Hosseini (1989).
17. The 1974 and 1977 data are from the Iranian Statistical Centre; the rest were provided by the Ministry of Justice.
18. In 1974, one dollar was equivalent to 7 tomans, and there was only one rate of exchange. After 1979, although the value of the dollar at the official rate of exchange remained unchanged, as the Iranian currency started to depreciate, an unofficial rate came into existence. The unofficial rate for one dollar in 1979, shortly after the Revolution, was 15 tomans; by 1981 it had increased to 70 tomans. At present (1992) one dollar is unofficially equivalent to 140 tomans.
19. In Shi'a jurisprudence the opinion of an ayatollah *'uzma* on legal matters has the power of the law – thus, in theory, the replies to these three judicial inquiries are binding on the court and can take precedence even over the provisions of the Civil Code.
20. See Chapter 5 for custody provisions in Shi'a law and their impact on divorce.
21. See Chapter 6 for disputes involving temporary marriages.
22. Given her reputation as a former entertainer, she felt that she needed to make such overt gestures to prove her ideological correctness.
23. Apparently, she was not aware that as a temporary wife she was not entitled to *nafaqa*; her permanent marriage was only one year old, reflecting another misconception of the Shari'a rules (see Chapter 5).
24. There is also a black market rate for gold coins; banks sell a limited number of coins at an official rate which are then resold at a much higher price.
25. Both cases owe their *raison d'être* to the procedural changes effected after the revolution, making the registration of polygynous unions possible; for these changes, see Chapter 6.
26. According to statistics provided by the Ministry of Justice, in 1980, 1981, 1982, 1983, 1984, 1985 and 1986 respectively, 53, 54, 52, 52, 53, 54 and 55 per cent of all divorces registered in Tehran were of *khul'* type.

Chapter 3

1. These are from the French text of the Mudawwana. Although they do not render the accurate meaning of the Arabic words, they reveal the ways in which these terms were viewed by the European jurists.

2. These modifications aimed to realign the procedure of *talaq* with that of *talaq al-sunna*, or the 'regular forms of *talaq*', discussed in Chapter 1. For the reforms introduced in this area by the Moroccan Code of Personal Status, see Borrmans (1977: 209–13).

3. These relate to *ila'* and *zihar*, as mentioned in note 51, Chapter 1.

4. *'Udul* (plural of *'adl*, literally, a just man) are a body of professional witnesses, and in Morocco they act as notaries. See Coulson (1964: 146) and Rosen (1989: 23).

5. Article 67 of the code requires every repudiation to be revocable unless it is a *thalath* (third consecutive), a *khul'*, or is pronounced prior to consummation of marriage.

6. For marriage and divorce in Maliki law, see Pesle (1936 and 1937); and for rules of *mumalik*, Toledano (1981: 128).

7. That religious functionaries such as *'udul* are reluctant to insert conditions in the marriage contract, and that they regard such stipulations as harmful to marriage, is not peculiar to Morocco. The same attitude exists among the Iranian mullahs. Their reluctance often stems from their narrow knowledge of the rules and their incompetence to work out the formula in a correct way to meet the *fiqh* requirements and accommodate agreements between the spouses. I know of a number of cases in which the bride's request to have an insertion giving her equal rights to terminate marriage was not met, since marriage notaries (both in Iran and Morocco) argued that it is not possible to do so. There is also a great use of the double standard. A deputy head of Court of Notaries in Morocco told me that his daughter, who is the first woman pilot in Morocco, will not contract a marriage without having the option of divorce. He found this appropriate for her, while holding to his view that the fate of a marriage cannot be left to the whims of women.

8. I could not obtain similar data for Casablanca, as the Judge of Court of Notaries in Casablanca refused access.

9. This is a by-product of the reforms made by the last president of the Courts in Salé.

10. *Mut'a* also denotes 'gratification or pleasure', as in the case of *mut'a* marriage (marriage of pleasure) but here it is the abbreviated form of *mut'at al-talaq*, which denotes the compensation that a divorced woman receives.

11. Compare with Table 1.2 in Chapter 1.

12. Compare with Table 1.4 in Chapter 1.

13. The payment of such a gift was commended in the Koran itself but there is a great deal of disagreement among the jurists on the question of when this gift acquires an obligatory character. See Pesle (1936: 12) and Borrmans (1977: 211).

14. In that sense it has somehow a similar function to the Iranian *mahr*; it provides a woman with a form of compensation, although it cannot act as a deterrent to an unwanted divorce.

15. It is assumed that if the husband repudiates her in her presence, then she has implicitly consented to it.

16. These arguments were given by lawyers on the basis that *kali' al-sadaq* is regarded by the Maliki jurists as a form of compensation for women. The name of Sidi Khalil and the section on dower in his treatise were mentioned but the references were vague. I did not follow them, as the court did not take any notice of them.

17. Chapter 5 deals with custody rights and related disputes.

18. There are, of course, regional differences but this division of *sadaq* into two parts holds true, especially when marriage is registered. For marriage payments, see the following sources: Bousser and Khelladi (1942), Westermarck (1914) and A. Cohen (1974 and 1975). Marriage customs and payments are also discussed in the following studies: Hildred Geertz (1979), Maher (1974) and Mernissi (1985).

19. Having a gold belt is an important asset for women, a kind of insurance against a rainy day and also a sign of wealth. A woman who wears a gold belt is displaying not only her wealth but also the extent that she is valued and appreciated by her husband.

20. H. Geertz (1979: 367).

21. This is in fact what has been called indirect dowry; Goody and Tambiah (1973) and Comaroff (1980).

22. For an idea of costs, see A. Cohen (1974 and 1975), H. Geertz (1979).

23. It is clear that *sadaq* does not play the same role as *mahr* does in Iran: my early enquiries about *sadaq* surprised both officials and women who saw it as irrelevant to the question of divorce.

24. See Table 1.1 in Chapter 1.

25. As we shall see, this is not observed in practice. Moroccan courts have no arbitration procedures similar to those of Iranian courts.

26. For oath in Maliki law, see Kellul (1958).

27. Cases from Casablanca are not included; although I was able to examine the court register for 1987, I was not able to study the files for that year. The Court of First Instance of Casablanca was then going through the process of being divided into three branches; and as a result the files were dispersed and I was permitted only to attend the sessions, read the current cases and examine the court registers.

28. In 1989, these announcements were made in the afternoon (between 2 and 3 p.m.).

29. The majority of these cases involve marriage with students from Tunisia and Algeria who left after their studies.

30. If the case is judged and rejected by the court the petitioner cannot file a new suit within a year.

31. Article 65 of the code clearly specifies that a woman need not forgo her children's right to maintenance in order to obtain a *khul'* divorce. But in practice it is often the one compromise that men insist on (see Chapter 5).

32. This is a common pattern; women who remarry leave their children from the previous marriage with their mothers (see Chapter 5).

33. For comparative material, see H. Geertz (1979), Maher (1974 and 1976), Crapanzano (1980) and Rassam (1980).

34. The lawyer wrote '*tardha*': that is, she was forced out of the marital home, which is a standard term used in all petitions. Although women leave the home of their own accord it is necessary to say that they were forced out in order not to lose their rights to claim *nafaqa* (see Chapter 1).

35. See Chapter 5: a father is responsible for the *nafaqa* of his daughter until her marriage transfers this duty to her husband.

36. According to the Penal Code, abandonment of marital unit becomes an offence only when children are involved. In that case, if one of the parents abandons the conjugal unit without any valid reason for more than two months, he or she can be sentenced to a term of imprisonment of one month to one year. See Sebti Lahrichi (1985: 11–2).

37. This form of sexual intercourse is forbidden (*haram*) under Islamic law (Alayli 1980). Women are aware of this and thus it is very likely that they use it as a means of saying that their husbands are making illegitimate demands on them.

38. Moroccan judges share the same concept of 'harm' as their Iranian counterparts.

39. I came across this case among the 1987 files in the Court of Appeal of Rabat; later I met Huria who happened to be my assistant's neighbour in Salé. I have reconstructed her case in the light of the information that the file contained and her own account of it.

40. There is a great deal of snobbery among the Salawi and Fassi families towards outsiders. Intermarriage is disapproved unless involving families with these two origins. When Huria first started work, a colleague proposed marriage; she was very willing to accept it but it was opposed by her family because he did not come from Salé or Fes.

41. Respectability and financial security are two valued criteria of any would-be husbands: he came from a good family and was a government employee.

42. As discussed in Chapter 1, Article 123 of the Mudawwana entitles a woman to *nafaqa* even if she has left the marital home, unless there is a court order demanding her return.

43. Adultery is defined by Moroccan law as sexual relations with a married person. It is a moral offence and the charge can be brought only by the spouse, who can also withdraw it after the conviction. The maximum penalty is two years of imprisonment, but if it is committed by the wife, and if her husband reacts to it by murdering her, he can be exonerated (Article 418 of Penal Code). See Sebti Lahrichi (1985: 19–22). Women sometimes press a charge to induce a divorce, as Huria did; in some cases the aim is to exact revenge when the husband abandons them for another woman. In one such case, the wife refused to withdraw the charge and the husband was sentenced to three months of imprisonment. He later abandoned her for good but refused to register a divorce. She initiated a divorce procedure eight years later on the ground of his disappearance.

44. The paucity of cases based on these two types of ground was also pointed out to me by judges. I came across only one case in current

files (1989) in which the wife demanded divorce on the ground of her husband's skin condition. This case was rejected as the husband proved to the court that she was aware of his condition prior to marriage and was using it as a pretext in order to obtain a divorce.

Chapter 4

1. For instance, in Case No. 7 from Rabat, Latifa entrusted the education of her son to her patroness; for other examples see H. Geertz (1979), Crapanzano (1980). On female networks in Morocco, see in particular Maher (1976), Rassam (1980) and Dwyer (1987b). Although not as well documented, similar networks exist in urban Iran, see Bauer (1983). I know many cases in which women benefit from connections with wealthy patronesses who often provide them with financial help.

2. In Iran this was the case even before the revolution in 1979; but since then the exclusion of women from the public sector has been more pronounced.

3. Differences in divorce patterns between Iran and Morocco are discussed in Chapter 5.

4. For a discussion of these issues see Ben Miled (1988) and Allami (1989).

5. There are many instances in which the husband is so offended by his wife's court action that, even at great personal expense, he refuses to agree to a divorce. In one case, the husband was so annoyed by his wife's temerity that he swore he would not let her, as he termed it, 'have her way'; see also Case No. 20, Chapter 6.

6. It is indeed a very common phenomenon, both in Iran and in Morocco, that an elder son to some extent shares the responsibility of the head of the household, even if his father is still alive. He is expected to contribute towards the education of his younger siblings. In Morocco, young professional women increasingly assume the same role.

7. This is particularly common when young women move out of their home town and study or work in metropolitan centres such as Rabat or Casablanca. For a study in Casablanca, see Naamane-Guessous (1988).

8. For a study of salaried women and sexual division of labour in the household in Morocco, see Belarbi (1988); and for a study of working mothers in Iran, see Weiskopf-Bock (1985).

9. These issues have been the subject of recent studies; for some contributions, see Akesbi Msefer (1985), Allami (1989) and Khayat-Bennai (n.d.). See also Adam (1968: 752–63) and Pascon and Bentahar (1971: 253–66), for two surveys of the attitudes of youth to marriage.

10. At one point the judge inquired about divorce laws in England. When I explained, he immediately drew parallels between the English payment of maintenance and the Islamic consolation gift (*mut'a*). He suggested that the difference is that, in Islam, a man upon divorce pays the amount once and for all.

11. Women's attachment to jewellery must be seen in this light; it is a form

of investment which can provide them with security. Little attention has been given to the role that jewellery, especially gold, plays in a woman's life in the Middle East.

12. There exists a genre of literature on the issue of polygyny and why it is permitted in Islamic law. It is argued that polygyny, if practised according to its rules, is in fact in the interest of women. The reasons given range from psychological to economic, the most important being that it gives some women the only chance of having a family life, due to the fact that in every society the number of marriageable men is far less than that of marriageable women. For some modern interpretations, see 'Abd Al'Ati (1977), Sharrif (1977), Mutahhari (1981), Maudoodi (1983) and Rahman (1986).

13. For an interesting article on the psychological impact of polygyny see Ben Miled (1988), who argues that polygyny in itself is a form of violence that a man imposes on a number of women.

14. For figures on polygamy, see Payman (1970: 52) for Iran, and Baron and Pirot (1955: 34–7) for Morocco. Examining the 1966 national census in Iran, Payman found less than 1 per cent of men to have more than one wife. In her study of 1000 households in Casablanca, Baron found 2 per cent to be 'polygamous'. These figures are imprecise and non-comparable, but they serve to demonstrate the rarity of polygamy in both cases.

15. See Amirian (1938: 18–21).

16. Note that, in divorce by court action, it is the judge who pronounces *talaq* on behalf of the husband; in *khul'*, it is the husband who pronounces the divorce, in return for a compensation from the wife.

17. Other studies lend support to the pattern revealed by court cases; for Morocco, see Adam (1968: Chapter 6), Baron (1953), Baron and Pirot (1955), Maher (1974) and Mernissi (1980 and 1986); for Iran, see Nassehi-Behnam (1985) and Fathi (1985).

Chapter 5

1. Coulson (1971: 22). This is one of the underlying reasons for the Shari'a prohibition of marriage between a Muslim woman and a non-Muslim; whereas a Muslim man can marry a non-Muslim woman since the issue of such a union will be Muslim by definition.

2. Rendered as '*De la filiation*' in the French translation of the code.

3. Parentage is the child's first right, which is followed by the right of upbringing; see Nasir (1990: 140). This notion is also reflected in Articles 116 and 126, MCPS.

4. The Civil Status booklet is the property of the household head and also serves as an identity card for children, enabling them to be registered at school, etc, as well as serving as a proof of their legal filiation (*nasab*). See also Sebti Lahrichi (1985: 70).

5. Nasir (1990: 140–2); Pearl (1987: 85).

6. *Li'an*, although mentioned in the modern legal codes of Iran and Morocco, is an obsolete concept. I did not come across any cases (either

in current or closed files) in which paternity was denied through using this option.

7. To obtain a passport or any other legal document, an unmarried woman needs to be represented by her guardian (*wali*), who is always her father unless she has none.

8. Lapanne-Joinville (1956); Fyzee (1964: 180–7).

9. Her demand for past maintenance was not accepted, on the grounds that maintenance is due only from the date of the demand.

10. This is based on a tradition from the Prophet which states that '*al-walad al-firash wa al-ahir al-hajr*', literally, 'the child is of the bed [i.e. the husband's] and the adulterer's share is stone'. For two variations in interpretation of this *hadith*, see Ait-Zai (1990: 287–301).

11. Fyzee (1964: 181); Pearl (1987: 90); Coulson (1971: 26).

12. The notion of six months as the minimum period of gestation is derived from two Koranic verses, which makes it invariable in all schools. These two verses are: (1) 'And we have commended unto man kindness to his parents: in pain did his mother bear him, and in pain did she give him birth, and bearing him and the weaning of him is 30 months'; (2) 'And we have commended upon man concerning his parents: his mother beareth him in weakness upon weakness, and his weaning is two years.' The jurists arrived at six months as the (minimum) period of pregnancy by subtracting from 30 the 24 months for weaning. See Nasir (1986: 141), Pearl (1987: 85) and Jahir and Bousquet (1946: 10–1).

13. Jahir and Bousquet (1946: 12); Milliot (1953: 405–6); Pearl (1987: 85).

14. This waiting period is referred to as '*iddat al-istibra*'; see Chapter 6.

15. The lawyer did not give a reference to the text itself; but he must have been referring to Chapter 33 of the treatise which deals with '*iddat al-istibra*'. For the text and its translation see Al-Qayrawani (1960: 195–8).

16. These cases very often end in withdrawal; the charge is made in order to force a reluctant man to contract a legal marriage and save the girl's reputation. Men who concede, in order to avoid a prison term, shortly afterwards exercise their right to divorce.

17. For the relevant text see Al-Qayrawani (1960: 176–7).

18. While the Moroccan Code makes no reference to *zina* in the context of *nasab* rules, the Iranian Code does.

19. I came across two cases among current files in which the dispute was initiated by men; both cases involved unregistered marriages, and later were withdrawn as an agreement was reached outside. In both, the real motivation was to gain control over the estranged wife, who had left the marital home with the child and was unwilling to return.

20. These marriages will be discussed in Chapter 6.

21. For a medical explanation of the phenomenon of the sleeping foetus, see Champagne (1955) and Lalu (1954); and for a legal and social analysis see Jahir and Bousquet (1946).

22. As quoted in Jahir and Bousquet (1946: 17).

23. Vesey-Fitzgerald (1955: 89–90).

24. Gibb and Kramers (1953: 658); Bousquet (1966: 60).
25. Champagne (1955: 20).
26. In her novel *L'enfant endormi*, Sbai (1987) relates how a young divorced woman, who later becomes pregnant, attempts to gain respectability and employment as a maid by claiming that she is carrying a *raqqad*.
27. Here I am concerned with this myth only in the context of dissolution of marriage. It certainly can serve other purposes when the marriage is extant. Given the important value attached to fertility and having children, it gives women a breathing space if they fail to get pregnant, i.e. by delaying a divorce.
28. I use the term matrifocality in the sense that it is the mother who is the focus of the parent/child relationship. This is similar to Smith's (1973: 125) usage: 'Women in their role as mothers come to be the focus of relationships, rather than heads of the household as such.'
29. In all schools of Sunni law, the right of *hadana* is given to the mother and in her absence to females in her line. But unlike the Maliki, others impose some limitations. For instance in the case of Hanafi law, the mother (or another female in her line) retains the right of custody until age seven for boys and nine for girls; in Hanbali it is seven for both boys and girls; and in Shafi'i law, on the attainment of discretion, the child is allowed to choose which parent to live with. See Pearl (1987: 97).
30. Cf. Adam (1968: 748).
31. Before I met Malika, she was described to me as 'pretty and fair-skinned; she does not have to wait a day to find a suitable husband if she chooses to free herself'. This makes her choice all the more significant.
32. Cf. Maher (1974).
33. In the course of my fieldwork in Morocco, I came across two cases in which the husband took the child away from the mother on the pretext that she was seeing another man; both cases involved upper-class families and neither reached the court.
34. See Chapter 6 for cases involving *mut'a* marriages; it is usually after the birth of the first child that the wife demands the transformation of her marriage into a permanent one.
35. This used to be a common practice, especially in rural areas where a newly born baby usually inherited the identity card of a deceased sibling.
36. Witness cases Nos 5 and 6 in Chapter 2. In case No. 5, the wife was successful in using her *mahr* to obtain custody, first because divorce was initiated by the husband, and secondly because she had the sympathy of the judge: she was willing, even in the face of his remarriage, to keep the family together.
37. A law passed on 15 Mehr 1358 (7 October 1979) cancelled all previous laws conflicting with the Civil Code provisions regarding custody (Vatani 1366/1987: 141).
38. The legal logic behind this is very similar to that of *mahr*, restricting but not abolishing a man's right to *talaq*: in theory his right to exercise

it remains intact but in practice it is restricted as he has to pay a substantial amount if he fails to acquire her consent.

39. In pre-revolutionary Iran, this provision was overruled by the FPL which empowered the court to grant widows legal guardianship of their children.

40. This Law was passed on 13 Mordad 1364 (4 July 1985). Its style is rhetorical, and a first reading leaves the impression that only in cases where children become orphaned as a result of their father's martyrdom does the mother obtain unconditional custody and access to his pension; see Vatani (1366/1987: 141–2).

41. This is borne out by household statistics. According to the 1980 census, 8.2 per cent of all households in Tehran had a female head (see Iran 1981: 44, Table 28); according to the Moroccan 1984 census, 20.9 per cent of all urban households are headed by women (see Morocco, 1989: 137 and 153, Table 4.1).

42. This observation is borne out by other studies; for instance see Haeri (1989: 120, 126, 132, 141). In all cases in her study women lost their children after divorce and in some cases the ex-husband never allowed the wife to see her children again.

Chapter 6

1. For instance, as in case No. 2 in Chapter 2, in which the couple decided to register their union after 17 years.

2. For the most exhaustive study of the theory and practice of this type of marriage in Iran, see Haeri (1989); for a *fiqh* perspective, see Murata (1989); and for a compilation of views of contemporary Shi'a authorities and the text of a relevant sermon delivered in the Friday Prayer (April 1983), see Hussein (n.d.).

3. This is seen by the jurists as the main purpose of this marriage. The separation between the sexual and procreative sides is very distinct. Haeri brings this to light in her book (1989). However, I take issue with her contention that woman play an active role here and that *mut'a* becomes an arena for the expression of their sexuality. On the basis of my data, I suggest that *mut'a* is what a woman has to accept because of her social disabilities, for example her age, not being a virgin, or coming from a lower social class. Women always strive to change the terms of their contract to attain the esteemed and socially accepted status of a permanent wife.

4. Haeri (1989: 51–4).

5. This was at the height of the Iran–Iraq war when some young men were evading their military service. One common trick was to disappear from the records through declaring their identity cards lost or faulty and demanding a new one with the aim of changing certain details including their date of birth, which could exempt them from service. Thus, these men could not register marriages as identity cards are required for their registration.

6. This is known as *sigha-i mahramiat*, which renders the parties lawful

(*mahram*) and allows social intercourse between them and their immediate relatives. Haeri (1989: 89) calls it a non-sexual *sigha* and sees it as a means of circumventing the rigid rules of sexual segregation imposed by the Shari'a. Its purpose is not the same as that of a *mut'a* marriage, although it can lead to a sexual relation if the woman gives her free consent. Evidently, Mehran understood it to permit sexual relations. See also Khatib-Chahidi (1981) for another variation of this practice in which the aim is to create fictive kinship.

7. In cases like this in which the evidence is lacking, the most important thing is to determine which of the two parties carries the burden of the proof. The positions of plaintiff and defendant can be reversed; see Russell and Al-Suhrawardy (1906: 89–103).

8. There is a case reported in the Official Gazette involving a dispute over marriage validity which suggests that the court takes a much more liberal view and allows a non-virgin to contract her marriage, even if she has lost her virginity outside a valid marriage. The full case is to be found in Qurbani (1991: 194–212).

9. *Mas'ala* (clause) 2368 gives instructions for contracting a permanent marriage, *mas'ala* 2369 those for a temporary marriage and *mas'ala* 2370 to 2372 set exact conditions for the validity of these formulas. These are: (1) the formula must be read in correct Arabic; if the couple are unable to do so they can recite the formula in Persian; there is no need for a proxy. (2) The couple must have the intention. (3) The contracting parties must be sane and, preferably, have reached puberty. (4) The woman needs her legal guardian's permission if she is a virgin. (5) Both parties must give their free consent. Khomeini (1366/1987: 356–7).

10. Muhaqqiq-Damad (1365/1986: 216).

11. Article 2 of Marriage Law of 1931.

12. Article 1 of Marriage Law of 1931.

13. Haeri (1989: 50) maintains that these linguistic ambiguities are fostered by the contemporary ulema in Iran as they use *mut'a* and *nikah* interchangeably.

14. For other variations of the usage of *mut'a* in contemporary Iran, see Haeri (1989: 75–102).

15. On the emergence of this class of professional witnesses, see Coulson (1964: 146).

16. Baron (1953: 424–5); also see Adam (1968: 747).

17. This is not true, but women choose to believe it; it is one of the excuses that men give in order to avoid commitment.

18. Here I am referring only to those *fatiha* marriages in which the man can later deny the union and evade legal consequences. Of course *fatiha* marriages in rural settings have totally different dynamics; they enjoy social validity and registration is not the determining factor in safeguarding women's status.

19. Linant de Bellefonds (1965b: 252); Bousquet (1950: 97); Fagnan (1909: 193–201).

20. See previous chapter for intercourse by error (*shubha*).

21. Impediments to marriage are: (i) blood relationship, namely between a man and his female ascendants and descendants, his sister, his brother's female descendants and ascendants, as well as his aunts and great-aunts. (2) Foster-relationship (*rida'i*) is an impediment to marriage in the same degree as blood relationship. (3) Relationship by marriage, namely between a man and his mother-in-law, step-daughter, etc, in the direct line; marriage with two sisters, or with an aunt and her niece at the same time, is forbidden.

22. This distinction has never been clear-cut; apart from Hanafis, other schools of law including the Shi'a recognize no real distinction between *fasid* and *batil* marriage; see Linant de Bellefonds (1965a: 829).

23. Theoretically, the union may also be terminated by either party at any time; neither divorce nor the intervention of the court are necessary.

24. According to Article 11, MCPS, a woman's matrimonial guardians in order of priority are: her son, her father, her brother, the son of her brother, her paternal grandfather, her adopted father and, finally, the judge.

25. The absence of similar cases in Iranian courts can be attributed partly to the fact that *zina* is taken more seriously and those implicated are liable to punishments.

26. A married woman is required by law to have the written permission of her husband for foreign travel.

27. This expression is used when a woman appears reluctant to compromise and make the marriage work; see Chapter 2.

28. Muhaqqiq-Damad (1365/1986: 443) quotes the *hadith* as follows: 'Whoever has intercourse with his ex-wife after the expiry of *'idda* is liable to the punishment for *zina*; intercourse prior to the lapse of *'idda* amounts to *ruju'*.'

29. Khomeini (1987: 378).

30. Strictly speaking, a woman may relax the rules of *hijab* only in the presence of her husband and those men who are *mahram* to her, i.e. with whom she is forbidden to enter a marriage. In practice, however, the rules of *hijab* are much more relaxed and vary according to the degree of religiosity of a woman, which is in turn determined by her social environment. Although the observance of *hijab* has become obligatory in public since the revolution, in private its practice has remained as before.

31. This was one of the rare cases in which one of the parties had a lawyer, and it was looked upon unfavourably by the judge.

32. *'Adalat* literally means justice but here it refers to the capacity to act as a witness. A witness must be *'adil*, that is, he must not have committed a major sin and not have been associated with the minor ones.

33. This point relates to rules of proof in Muslim procedures, one of which is the taking of an oath when there is not sufficient evidence. The oath falls upon the defendant, not the claimant.

34. Article 1050, ICC states, 'Marriage with a married woman or a woman who is in the state of *'idda* is void and the woman becomes eternally forbidden to the man if he was aware of the fact that the woman was

already in a marital bond.' Article 1051 waives the permanent bar if the two parties were unaware of this fact.

Conclusion

1. R. Cohen (1971: 179).
2. For instance, Dwyer (1978a: 588) finds a similar phenomenon when it comes to the domain of informal religion and affiliation to saints. She points out that, despite the overt belief that religious affiliation is patrilineal, in practice 'far from being automatically provided with their father's affiliation children tend to be associated with their mother's group as often.'
3. Cf. Jansen (1987) for a similar phenomenon in Algeria.
4. This is not peculiar to Muslim societies. For instance, see Smith (1973) for a similar phenomenon in the Caribbean context where the discrepancy between the ideal and possible performance of male domestic roles results in the development of a matrifocal family, defying the ideal pattern.
5. The comparison should be extended to include other schools such as Hanafi and Shafi'i. For example, comparatively low rates of divorce are found not only in Shi'a Iran, but also in secular (formally Hanafi) Turkey and in Hanafi Afghanistan. See Gluckman (1951), Barth (1973), Holy (1989) and, for a discussion of Arab and non-Arab models of marriage and divorce in the Muslim world, Tapper and Tapper (1993).
6. Powers, who studied 14th-century court cases in Fes, finds a similar matrifocal bias (personal communication); see also Powers (1990a).
7. This has been a widely held assumption (e.g., Jeffrey, 1959), although questioned by other studies; for instance, Coulson (1971: 125–34) points out that, contrary to what had been assumed by Schacht, Shi'a law differs in more substantial ways from other schools of orthodox Islam. Likewise Antoun (1990: 57) says 'To hold that Islamic law reflects the point of view of the consanguine family is as erroneous as to hold that it reflects the point of view of the conjugal family'.
8. Schacht (1959) 260–2).
9. Coulson (1971: 125–34).
10. R. Cohen (1971: 179).
11. E.g., Hillal Dessouki (1982); Tibi (1988); Hunter (1988); Sharabi (1988); Shayegan (1989); Kandiyoti (1991).
12. Sharabi (1988).
13. Haeri also reports a similar tendency (1989: 200–11).

Glossary

abadī	eternal
ābirū	reputation
ʿadālat	justness, capacity to serve as a witness
ʿadam al-infāq	non-support (in Morocco)
ʿadam-i sāzish	lack of cooperation, incompatibility (in Iran)
ʿadam-i tamkīn	lack of obedience (in Iran)
aḥkām al-zāwaj	effects of marriage
aḥwāl al-shakhsiyya	personal status
amārat al-firāsh	'rule of bed', the primary presumption of paternity
ʿaqd	contract
ʿaqd-i dāʾim	permanent marriage contract (in Iran)
ʿaqd-i munqatiʿ	temporary marriage contract (in Iran)
ʿaqd al-nikāḥ	marriage contract
ʿaqd-i rasmī	legal/registered marriage (in Iran)
amr al-qāḍī al-tawthīq	order of Notary Judge
ʿarūsī	wedding celebration
ʿasar wa ḥaraj	hardship and harm
aṣl	presumption, principle
ʿawaḍ	price, compensation
awlād	progeny
bad-akhlāqī	bad-temper (in Iran)
bad-dahanī	bad-mouthing (in Iran)
bāṭil	void
Dādgāh-i Madanī-yi Khāṣṣ	Special Civil Court (in Iran)
dādkhāst	petition (in Iran)
daftar	secretariat in Tehran court

223

daftar al-ḍabt	secretariat in Moroccan court
dalīl	reason
ḍarra	harmful; co-wife (in Morocco)
ḍarūra	necessity (in Morocco)
da'wā	dispute
dukhūl	penetration, consummation of marriage
faqīh	expert in *fiqh*, Islamic jurist
fasād	corruption
fāsid	corrupt, irregular marriage
faskh	annulment
fātiḥa	first *sura* of the Koran; unregistered marriages (in Morocco)
fatwa	religious decree, a legal opinion issued by a *mujtahid*
fiqh	Islamic jurisprudence
ghaiba	absence, grounds for divorce in Morocco
ghīyābī	absence; divorce effected in the wife's absence (in Morocco)
ḥaḍāna	care, custody
ḥadīth	tradition, sayings attributed to the Prophet Muhammad
ḥajr	abandonment of marital duties, grounds for divorce
ḥākim-i shar'	Islamic judge (in Iran)
ḥalāl	licit, lawful
ḥarām	forbidden
ḥijāb	cover, code of dressing
ḥuḍūrī	presence; divorce effected in the wife's presence (in Morocco)
ḥukm	judgment
ḥurmat	a bar created by doing a 'harm' act
'ibādāt	ritual acts
'idda	waiting period that all divorced or widowed women must observe
iftidāḥ	scandal
ihmāl al-'usra	neglect of family (in Morocco)
ījāb	offer
ijmā'	consensus
ijtihād	independent judgment in legal and theological matters
ikrāh	reluctance
ilā'	oath, a form of repudiation in which the husband takes an oath to cease sexual intercourse with the wife

ilghā'	annul, cancel
ʿilm	knowledge
imtināʿ	defiance
intifāʿ	use, benefit
īqāʾ	unilateral act
iqrār	confession, acknowledgment of paternity
irjāʿ al-hawāʾij	demand made by the wife for return of her matrimonial goods (in Morocco)
ʿiṣmā	authority, control
isnād	chain of transmitters of a tradition
istibrāʾ	emptiness, freedom of womb
istiftāʾ	request for a legal opinion
istihlāq	attachment of paternity
istimtāʿ	sexual enjoyment
jabr	compulsion, the guardian's constraining power to suppress a woman's consent to marriage
jahīz	trousseau or dowry (in Iran)
jalsat al-bahth	Inquiry Session in Moroccan courts
jalsat al-ʿumūmiyya	Public Session in Moroccan courts
kālīʾ al-ṣadaq	remainder of dower (in Morocco)
kātib al-ʿumūmī	public scribe
khāhān	plaintiff, petitioner
khalwa	sexual intimacy
khānda	defendant, respondent (in Iran)
khilāf-i sharʿ	in contradiction to Shari'a rules
khulʿ	a type of divorce initiated by a woman in which she gives her husband a kind of compensation in return for his consent
kināsh al-hāl al-madaniyya	Civil Status Booklet (in Morocco)
lafīf	notarized document (in Iran)
lāzim	binding, indissoluble
liʿān	imprecation, a procedure by which a man denies the paternity of a child born to his wife
Mahkamat al-Ibtidāʾiyya	Court of First Instance (in Morocco)
Mahkamat al-ʾIstiʾnāf	Court of Appeal (in Morocco)
Mahkamat al-Tawthīq	Notary Court (in Morocco)
mahr	dower, brideprice
mahr al-mithāl	exemplary dower
mahr al-musammā	defined dower
mahram	lawful, permitted
makrūh	reprehensible, disapproved
maʿlūm	definite, specified

maqāl	petition
mas'ala	literally, 'question', legal clause in a treatise
milkiyyat	possession, ownership
muʿāmilāt	contracts, division of Islamic law dealing with social transactions
mubāḥ	neutral, permissible
mubārāt	a form of divorce initiated by women in which the compensation does not exceed the dower
muddaʿī	plaintiff, petitioner
muddaʿa ʿalaihi	defendant, co-respondent
mujtahid	an Islamic jurist who exercises *ijtihad*
musāʿada al-qaḍāʾiyya	legal aid (in Morocco)
mutʿa	temporary marriage (in Iran); compensation to which a divorced woman is entitled (in Morocco)
nafaqa	maintenance
nafaqat al-ḥaḍāna	maintenance for a child in custody
nafaqat al-ḥaml	maintenance for a pregnant woman
nafaqat al-ʿidda	maintenance after divorce (during waiting period)
nasab	filiation, paternity
nāsāzigārī	lack of cooperation (in Iran)
nāshiza	rebellious, a woman who abandons her marital duties
nikāḥ	marriage
niyyat	intention
nushūz	rebellion, abandonment of marital duties
qabūl	acceptance
qāḍī	judge
qāḍī al-tawthīq	notary judge
qāʾid	district authority (in Morocco)
qāʾim	custodian, a court courier (in Morocco)
qānūn	law, secular law as opposed to Shari'a
qānūnī	legal (in Iran)
qiyyās	analogy
raʾī	decision, judgment (in Iran)
raqqad	sleeping foetus (in Morocco)
rasmī	legal
rujūʿ	husband's right to return to marriage
ṣadaq	dower (in Morocco)
sharʿī	valid according to the Shari'a
shawār	trousseau (in Morocco)

shināsnāma	identity certificate (in Iran)
shīrbahā	literally 'price of milk', a kind of marriage payment (in Iran)
shubha	semblance, marriage by error
shūrā	trousseau (in Morocco)
si'at al-akhlāq	ill-temper
ṣīgha	in colloquial Persian: temporary wife; in legal terminology: a formula by which a contract is made (in Iran)
ṣulh	peace
sunna	practice of the Prophet
sūra	a chapter in the Koran
ṭalab	request, demand made in petitions
ṭalāq	a man's right to unilateral termination of marriage contract; repudiation
ṭalāq al-bā'in	irrevocable divorce
ṭalāq al-bidʿā	disapproved form of *talaq* procedure
ṭalāq al-mumālik	an irrevocable type of *talaq* (in Morocco)
ṭalāq al-rajʿī	revocable divorce
ṭalāq al-sunnā	approved form of *talaq* procedure
ṭalāq al-thalāth	third successive *talaq*
tamkīn	obedience; submission
tanāzul	withdrawing a petition
taqlīd	emulation, imitation; denotes the following of the dictates of a *mujtahid*
tashtīb	cancelling a petition
ṭatlīq	divorce by court action initiated by women
taʿzīr	discretionary punishment awarded by the Qadi
thubūt al-nasab	proof of paternity
thubūt al-zawjiyya	proof of marriage
ṭuhr	state of purity betwen menses
ʿudūl	notaries (in Morocco)
ujrat al-ḥadāna	custody wage
ujrat al-riḍāʿ	suckling wage
umma	community of believers
ʿurs	wedding (in Morocco)
wājib	obligatory act
wājibāt al-ṭalāq	divorce dues (in Morocco)
walad al-firāsh	literally, 'child of bed', legitimate child
walad al-zinā	literally 'child of fornication', bastard
walī	guardian
waqf	endowment

wilāya	authority, father's right to custody
yamīn	oath
yamīn al-hāsima	decisive oath
yamīn al-mukāmala	complementary oath
zarūrat	necessity (in Iran)
zawjiyyat-i dā'im	permanent marriage (in Iran)
zawjiyyat-i muvaqqat	temporary marriage (in Iran)
zihār	oath of continence taken by the husband which results in making marital intercourse illicit
zinā	fornication

Bibliography

ʿAbd Al ʿAti, H. 1977. *The Family Structure in Islam*. Indiana: American Trust Publication.

Adam, A. 1968. *Casablanca*, 2 vols. Paris: CNRS.

Afshar, H. 1987. 'Women, Marriage and State in Iran', in H. Afshar (ed.), *Women, State and Ideology*. London: Macmillan.

Ahmad, K. 1974. *Family Life in Islam*. London: The Islamic Foundation.

Ahmed, L. 1992. *Women and Gender in Islam*. New Haven: Yale University Press.

Ait-Zai, N. 1990. 'L'Enfant Illégitime dans la Société Musulmane', *Droit de l'Enfance et de la Famille*, XXIX: 287–303 (Special Issue: La Convention Internationale des Droit de l'Enfant).

Akesbi-Msefer, A. 1985. *Servages et Interdépendance*. Casablanca: Editions Maghrébines.

Alayli, B. 1980. *La Réglementation des Rapports Sexuels en Droit Musulman Comparé*. Thesis for Doctorat d'Etat, Université de Droit et d'Economie et de Sciences Sociales, Paris.

Algar, H. *see* Khomeini.

Allami, N. 1989. *Voilées, Dévoilées: Etre Femme dans le Monde Arabe*. Paris: L'Harmattan.

Ameer Ali, S. 1925. *Student's Handbook of Mahommedan Law* 7th edn. Calcutta & Simla: Thacker, Spink & Co.

Amin, S. H. 1985. *Middle East Legal Systems*. Glasgow: Royston Ltd.

Amirian, A. M. 1937. *Le Mouvement Legislatif en Iran et le Mariage en Droit et en Fait – Sa Reforme*. Paris: Librairie Générale de Droit et de Jurisprudence.

— 1938. *Le Mariage en Droit Iranien et Musulman Comparés avec le Droit Français*. Vol. 1. Paris: Librairie Générale de Droit et de Jurisprudence.

Anderson, J. N. D. 1950 and 1951. 'Recent developments in Shariʿa Law I & II', *The Muslim World*, XL (4): 244–56 and XLI (1): 34–48.

— 1958. 'Reform of Family Law in Morocco', *Journal of African Law*, II (3): 146–59.
— 1959. *Islamic Law in the Modern World*. New York: New York University Press.
— 1968. 'The Eclipse of the Patriarchal Family in Contemporary Islamic Law', in J. N. D. Anderson (ed.), *Family Law in Asia and Africa*. London: George Allen & Unwin.
— 1970. 'The Islamic Law of Marriage and Divorce', in A. M. Lutfiyya and C. W. Churchill (eds.), *Readings in Arab and Middle Eastern Societies and Cultures*. The Hague: Mouton.
— 1976. *Law Reform in the Muslim World*. London: The Athlone Press.
Antoun, R. T. 1980. 'The Islamic Court, The Islamic Judge, and the Accommodation of Traditions: A Jordanian Case Study', *International Journal of Middle Eastern Studies*, XII (4): 455–67.
— 1990. 'Litigant Strategies in an Islamic Court in Jordan', in D. H. Dwyer (ed.), *Law and Islam in the Middle East*. New York: Bergin & Garvey Publishers.
Arberry, A. J. 1983. *The Koran Interpreted*. Oxford: Oxford University Press.
Arjomand, S. A. 1989. 'Constitution-Making in Islamic Iran: The Impact of Theocracy on the Legal Order of a Nation-State', in J. Starr and J. Collier (eds.), *History and Power in the Study of Law*. Ithaca and London: Cornell University Press.
El-Awa, M. S. 1991. 'Approaches to Shariʿa: A Response to N. J. Coulson's "A History of Islamic law", *Journal of Islamic Studies*, II (2): 143–79.
Ayoob, M. (ed.). 1981. *The Politics of Islamic Reassertion*. New York: St Martin's Press.
Azari, F. (ed.). 1983. *Women of Iran: Conflict with Fundamentalist Islam*. London: Ithaca Press.
Al-Azmeh, A. 1988. 'Islamic Legal Theory and the Appropriation of Reality', in A. Al-Azmeh (ed.), *Islamic Law: Social and Historical Contexts*. London: Routledge.
Banani, A. 1961. *The Modernization of Iran, 1921–1941*. Stanford: Stanford University Press.
Baron, A. M. 1953. 'Mariage et Divorce à Casablanca', *Hespéris*, XL (3–4): 419–40.
Baron, A. M. and Pirot, H. 1955. 'La Famille Prolétarienne', *Les Cahiers de Faits et Idées*, I: 26–54.
Barth, F. 1973. 'Descent and Marriage Reconsidered', in J. Goody (ed.), *The Character of Kinship*. Cambridge: Cambridge University Press.
Bauer, J. 1983. 'Poor Women and Social Consciousness in Revolutionary Iran', in G. Nashat (ed.). *Women and Revolution in Iran*. Boulder, Colorado: Westview Press.
Behnam, J. and Bouraoui, S. (eds.). 1986. *Familles Musulmanes et Modernité: Le Défi des Traditions*. Paris: Conseil International des Sciences Sociales, Faculté de Droit de Tunis (CERP).
Belarbi, A. 1988. 'Salariat Féminin et Division Sexuelle du Travail dans la Famille: Cas de Femme Fonctionnaire', in F. Mernissi (ed.), *Femmes Partagées: Famille-Travail*. Casablanca: Edition de Fennec.

Ben-Miled, E. 1988. 'Violence et Contre Violence dans le Couple', in *Les Relations Interpersonnelles dans la Famille Maghrébine*. Proceedings of Colloquium. Tunis, Cahiers du CERES. Psychologie; 6. CRESM Coll. 116.0002.

Bercher, L. *see* Ibn Abi-Zayd Al-Qayrawani.

Berque, J. 1944. *Essai sur le Méthode Juridique au Maroc*. Rabat.

Betteridge, A. H. 1987. "Arousi: Wedding', *Encyclopaedia Iranica*, Vol. 2: 666–70. London: Routledge & Kegan Paul.

Betteridge, A. H. and Javadi, H. 1987. "Aqd: Marriage Contract Ceremony', *Encyclopaedia Iranica*, Vol. 2: 189–91. London: Routledge & Kegan Paul.

Bohannan, P. 1967. 'The Differing Realms of Law', in P. Bohannan (ed.), *Law and Warfare*. New York: The Natural History Press.

Borrmans, M. 1977. *Statut Personnel et Famille au Maghreb de 1940 à Nos Jours*. Paris: Mouton.

Bousquet, G. H. 1947. *Le Droit Musulman par les Textes (Précis de Droit Musulman*, Vol. 2). Algiers: La Maison de Livre.

— 1948. 'La Conception du Nikah Selon les Docteurs de la Loi Musulmane', *Revue Algérienne*, 63–74.

— 1950. *Précis de Droit Musulman Principalement Mâlékite et Algérien*, 3rd edn. Algiers: La Maison de Livre.

— 1966. *L'Ethique Sexuelle de l'Islam*. Paris: Maisonneuve et Larose.

Bousser, M. and Khelladi, A. 1942. 'Enquête sur le Trousseau (Choura) et le Sadaq au Maroc', *Revue Africaine*, XXXIX (1 & 2): 102–55.

Brunschvig, R. 1958. 'De la Filiation Maternelle en Droit Musulman', *Studia Islamica*, IX: 49–59.

Champayne, P. 1955. *Le Mythe de l'Enfant qui Dort chez la Femme Marocaine*. MD thesis, No. 78, Faculty of Medicine and Pharmacy, Bordeaux University.

Chehata, C. 1965. 'Faskh', *Encyclopaedia of Islam*. Vol. 2: 836. Leiden: E. J. Brill.

Cohen, A. 1974. *Le Coûte de Mariage à Fès*. BA dissertation, Department of Economics, University of Muhammad V, Rabat.

— 1975. 'Le Coûte de Mariage à Fès, *Lamalif*, LXIX: 121–44.

Cohen, R. 1971. *Dominance and Defiance: A Study of Marital Instability in an Islamic African Society*. Washington: American Anthropological Association.

Collier, J. F. 1975. 'Legal Processes', *Annual Review of Anthropology*, IV: 121–44.

Colomer, A. 1963. *Droit Musulman: Les Personnes, La Famille*. Rabat: Edition de la Porte.

Comaroff, J. L. (ed.). 1980. *The Meaning of Marriage Payments*. London: Academic Press.

Coulson, N. J. 1964. *A History of Islamic Law*. Edinburgh: Edinburgh University Press.

— 1969. *Conflicts and Tensions in Islamic Jurisprudence*. Chicago: Chicago University Press.

— 1971. *Succession in the Muslim Family*. Cambridge: Cambridge University Press.

Coulson, N. J. and Hinchcliffe, D. 1980. 'Women & Law Reform in

Contemporary Islam', in L. Beck and N. Keddie (eds.), *Women in the Muslim World*. Cambridge, Mass.: Harvard University Press.

Crapanzano, V. 1980. *Tuhami: Portrait of a Moroccan*. Chicago: Chicago University Press.

Decroux, P. 1962. 'Le Problème du Statut Personnel au Maroc', *Travaux et Jours*, IV (January–February). Beirut: Université Saint-Josep.

Djamour, J. 1966. *The Muslim Matrimonial Court in Singapore*. London: Athlone Press.

Dwyer, D. H. 1977. 'Bridging the Gap Between the Sexes in Moroccan Legal Practice', in A. Schlegel (ed.), *Sexual Stratification: A Cross Cultural View*. New York: Columbia University Press.

— 1978a. 'Women, Sufism, and Decision-Making in Moroccan Islam', in L. Beck and N. Keddie (eds.), *Women in the Muslim World*. Cambridge, Mass.: Harvard University Press.

— 1978b. *Images and Self-Images: Male and Female in Morocco*. New York: Columbia University Press.

— 1990. 'Introduction', in D. H. Dwyer (ed.), *Law and Islam in the Middle East*. New York: Bergin & Garvey Publishers.

Eickelman, D. 1989. *The Middle East: An Anthropological Approach*, 2nd edn. Englewood Cliffs, New Jersey: Prentice Hall.

Epstein, A. L. 1967. 'The Case Method in the Field of Law', in A. L. Epstein (ed.), *The Craft of Social Anthropology*. London: Tavistock.

Esposito, J. L. 1982. *Women in Muslim Family Law*. New York: Syracuse University Press.

Fagnan, E. 1909. *Sidi Khâlil: Mariage et Répudiation*. Translation with commentary. Algiers: Adolph Jourdan.

Fathi, A. 1985. 'Introduction', in A. Fathi (ed.), *Women and the Family in Iran*. Leiden: E. J. Brill.

Ferdows, A. K. 1985. 'The Status and Rights of Women in Ithna 'Ashari Shi'a Islam', in A. Fathi (ed.), *Women and the Family in Iran*. Leiden: E. J. Brill.

— 1986. 'Shariati and Khomeini on Women', in N. Keddie and E. Hoogland (eds.), *The Iranian Revolution and the Islamic Republic*. New York: Syracuse University Press.

Fischer, M. J. 1990. 'Legal Postulates in Flux: Justice, Wit, and Hierarchy in Iran', in D. H. Dwyer (ed.), *Law and Islam in the Middle East*. New York: Bergin and Garvey Publishers.

Fluehr-Lobban, C. 1987. *Islamic Law and Society in the Sudan*. London: Frank Cass.

Fyzee, A. A. 1964. *Outlines of Muhammadan Law*, 3rd edn. Oxford: Oxford University Press.

Geertz, C. 1983. 'Local Knowledge: Facts and Law in Comparative Perspective', in his *Local Knowledge*. New York: Basic Books.

Geertz, H. 1979. 'The Meaning of Family Ties', in C. Geertz, H. Geertz and L. Rosen, *Meaning and Order in Moroccan Society*. Cambridge: Cambridge University Press.

Gibb, H. A. R. and Kramers, J. H. 1953. *Shorter Encyclopaedia of Islam*. Leiden and London: E. J. Brill.

Gluckman, M. 1951. 'Kinship and Marriage among the Lozi of Northern Rhodesia and the Zulu of Natal', in C. D. Forde and A. R. Radcliffe-Brown (eds.), *African Systems of Kinship and Marriage*. London: Oxford University Press.
— 1965. *Politics, Law and Ritual in Tribal Society*. Oxford: Basil Blackwell.
Goody, J. and Tambiah, S. J. 1973. *Bridewealth and Dowry*. Cambridge Papers in Social Anthropology 7. Cambridge: Cambridge University Press.
Haeri, S. 1980. 'Women, Law and Social Change in Iran', in J. I. Smith (ed.), *Women in Contemporary Muslim Societies*. London: Associated University Press.
— 1989. *Law of Desire: Temporary Marriage in Iran*. London: I. B. Tauris.
Hamnett, I. 1977. *Social Anthropology of Law*. London: Academic Press.
Higgins, P. J. 1985. 'Women in the Islamic Republic of Iran: Legal, Social and Ideological Change', *Signs*, X (3): 477–94.
Hijab, N. 1988. *Womanpower: the Arab Debate on Women at Work*. Cambridge: Cambridge University Press.
Hill, E. 1978. 'Comparative and Historical Study of Modern Middle Eastern Law', *American Journal of Comparative Law*, XXVI (2): 279–304.
— 1979. *Mahkama! Studies in the Egyptian Legal System*. London: Ithaca Press.
Hillal Dessouki, A. E. 1982. 'The Islamic Resurgence: Sources, Dynamics and Implications', in A. E. Hillal Dessouki (ed.), *Islamic Resurgence in the Arab World*. New York: Praeger Publishers.
— 1987. 'Official Islam and Political Legitimation in the Arab Countries', in B. F. Stowasser (ed.), *The Islamic Impulse*. London: Croom Helm.
Hilli, Muhaqqiq N. 1364/1985. *Sharāyiʿ al-Islām* (Laws of Islam), Vol. II. Persian Translation by A. A. Yazdi, compiled by M. T. Danish-Pazhuh. Tehran: Tehran University Press.
Hinchcliffe, D. 1968a. 'Legal Reforms in the Shiʿi World – Recent Legislations in Iran and Iraq', *Malaya Law Review*, X (2): 292–305.
— 1968b. 'The Iranian Family Protection Act', *International and Comparative Law Quarterly*, XVII: 516–21.
Hoebel, E. A. 1965. 'Fundamental Cultural Postulates and Judicial Law-making in Pakistan', in L. Nader (ed.), *The Ethnography of Law*, special issue of *American Anthropologist*, LXVII (6) Part 2: 43–56.
Holy, L. 1989. *Kinship, Honour and Solidarity: Cousin Marriage in the Middle East*. Manchester: Manchester University Press.
Hourani, A. 1962. *Arabic Thought in the Liberal Age 1798–1939*. London: Oxford University Press.
Hunter, S. T. (ed.). 1988. *The Politics of Islamic Revivalism: Diversity and Unity*. Bloomington: Indiana University Press.
Hussein, A. 1985. 'Recent Amendments to Egypt's Personal Status Law', in E. W. Fernea (ed.), *Women and the Family in the Middle East: New Voices of Change*. Austin: University of Texas Press.
Husseini, S. (n.d.). *Izdivāj-i Muvaqqat dar Islām* (Temporary Marriage in Islam). Qum: Imam Sadiq Publishing House.
Imami, S. H. 1363/1984. *Huqūq-i Madanî* (Civil Law), Vols. 4 & 5. Tehran: Islamiyya Press.
Iran, 1360/1981. *Natāyij-i Āmārgîrî-yi Tihrān, 1359* (Tehran Census Results, 1980). Tehran: Iranian Statistical Centre.

Ja'fari-Langarudi, M. J. 1368a/1989a. *Tirminuluji-yi Huquqi* (Legal Terminology). Tehran: Ganj-i Danish Press.

— 1368b/1989b. *Huquq-i Khanivada* (Family Law). Tehran: Ganj-i Danish Press.

Jahir, H. and Bousquet, G. H. 1946. 'L'enfant endormi', *Cahiers Médicaux de l'Union Française, Revue Médico-Chirugical de la France d'Outre-Mer*, 1st year, No.1: 9–27.

Jansen, W. 1987. *Women Without Men: Gender and Marginality in an Algerian Town*. Leiden: E. J. Brill.

Jeffrey, A. 1959. 'The Family in Islam', in R. N. Anshen (ed.), *The Family*. New York: Harper.

Kandiyoti, D. 1991. 'Introduction', in D. Kandiyoti (ed.), *Women, Islam & the State*. London: Macmillan.

— 1992. 'Islam and Patriarchy', in N. Keddie and B. Baron (eds.), *Women in Middle Eastern History*. New Haven: Yale University Press.'

Katouzian, N. 1368/1989. *Huquq-i Madani-yi Khanivada* (Family Civil Law). Tehran: Tehran University Press.

Khalil, Ibn Ishaq *see* Fagnan and Perron.

Kellul, A. 1958. 'Le Serment en Droit Musulman, Ecole Mâlékite', *Revue Algérienne, Tunisienne et Marocaine de Legislation et de Jurisprudence*, LXXIV (1): 18–53.

Khamlichi, A. and Moulay Rchid, A. 1981. 'La Moudaouana après un Quart de Siècle de son apparition', *Revue Juridique Politique et Economique du Maroc*, 10: 31–63.

Khatib-Chahidi, J. 1981. 'Sexual Prohibitions, Shared Space and Fictive Marriages in Shi'ite Iran', in S. Ardener (ed.), *Women and Space: Ground Rules and Social Maps*. London: Croom Helm.

Khayat-Bennai, G. (n.d.). *Le Monde Arabe au Féminin*. Casablanca: Edition Populaire.

Khomeini, R. 1981. *Islam and Revolution: Writings & Declarations of Imam Khomeini*. Translated by H. Algar. Berkeley: Mizan Press.

— 1366/1987. *Risala-i Tawzih al-Masa'il* (Treatise on Explanation of Problems). Tehran: Markaz-i Nashr-i Farhangi-yi Rija'.

Lalu (ksiri), P. 1954. 'Le mythe de l'enfant endormi, occasion d'examen gynécologique', *Maroc Médical*, No. 344, 33rd year, pp. 642–3.

Lapanne-Joinville, J. 1951a. 'La Théorie des Nullités de Mariage en Droit Musulman Mâlékite', *Revue Algérienne*: 92–102.

— 1951b. 'L'Obligation d'Entretien (Nafaqa) de l'Epouse dans Rite Mâlékite', *La Revue Marocaine de Droit*: 102–10.

— 1952a. 'La Filiation Maternelle Naturelle en Droit Musulman Mâlékite', *La Revue Marocaine de Droit*: 256–67.

— 1952b. 'La Recision du Mariage en Droit Musulman Mâlékite', *La Revue Marocaine de Droit*: 431–50.

— 1956. 'Les Conflits de Paternité en Droit Musulman', *La Revue Marocaine de Droit*: 352–63.

Layish, A. 1975. *Women and Islamic Law in a Non-Muslim State*. Jerusalem and New York: Transaction Books.

— 1978. 'The Contribution of the Modernist to the Secularization of Islamic Law', *Middle Eastern Studies*, XIV (3): 263–7.

— 1982. *Marriage, Divorce and Succession in the Druze Family*. Leiden: E. J. Brill.

— 1991. *Divorce in the Libyan Family: A Study Based on the Sijills of the Shariʿa Courts of Ajdabiyya and Kufra*. New York: New York University Press.

Levy, R. 1975. *The Social Structure of Islam*, 2nd edn. Cambridge: Cambridge University Press.

Liebesny, H. 1967. 'Stability & Change in Islamic Law', *Middle East Journal*, XXI (1): 16–35.

— 1975. *The Law of the Near and Middle East, Readings, Cases and Materials*. Albany: State University of New York Press.

Linant de Bellefonds, Y. 1964. 'Le Divorce Pour Préjudice en Droit Marocain', *La Revue Marocaine de Droit*: 433–50.

— 1965a. 'Fasid wa Batil', *Encyclopaedia of Islam*, 2nd edn. Vol. 2: 829–33. Leiden: E. J. Brill.

— 1965b. 'Istibraʾ', *Encyclopaedia of Islam*, 2nd edn. Vol. 4: 253–4. Leiden: E. J. Brill.

Madelung, W. 1985. 'Shiʿi Attitudes towards Women as Reflected in Fiqh', in W. Madelung (ed.), *Religious Schools and Sects in Medieval Islam*. London: Variorum Reprints.

Mahdavi, S. 1985. 'The Position of Women in Shiʿa Iran: Views of the ʿUlama', in E. W. Fernea (ed.), *Women and the Family in the Middle East: New Voices of Change*. Austin: University of Texas Press.

Maher, V. 1974. *Women and Property in Morocco*. Cambridge: Cambridge University Press.

— 1976. 'Kin, Clients and Accomplices: Relations Among Women in Morocco', in D. L. Barker and S. Allen (eds.), *Sexual Divisions and Society: Process and Change*. London: Tavistock.

Mahmood, T. 1972. *Family Law Reforms in the Muslim World*. Bombay: N. M. Tripathi.

Malik, Imam. 1982. *Al-Muwatta*. Norwich: Diwan Press.

Mallat, C. and Connors, J. (eds.). 1990. *Islamic Family Law*. London: Graham & Trotman.

Maudoodi, A. A. 1983. *The Laws of Marriage & Divorce in Islam*. Kuwait: Islamic Book Publishers.

— 1986. *The Islamic Way of Life*. London: The Islamic Foundation.

Mayer, A. E. 1990. 'Reinstating Islamic Criminal Law in Libya', in D. H. Dwyer (ed.), *Law and Islam in the Middle East*. New York: Bergin & Garvey Publishers.

Mazandarani-Haeri, M. B. 1364/1985. *Izdivāj va Talāq dar Islām va Sāyir-i Adyān* (Marriage and Divorce in Islam and other Religions). Tehran: Private.

Mernissi, F. 1980. 'Le Divorce', *Alasas*, XVII: 50–2.

— 1985. *Beyond the Veil*. London: Al Saqi Books.

— 1986. *Le Maroc Raconté par Ses Femmes*, 2nd edn. Rabat: Société Marocaine des Editeurs Réunis.

— 1991. *Women and Islam: An Historical and Theological Enquiry*. London: Basil Blackwell.

Meshkini, A. 1366/1987. *Izdivāj dar Islām* (Marriage in Islam). Qum: Ilhadi Press.

Micadi, Z. 1988. *Al-ʾUsrat al-Maghribiyya bain al-Khatāb al-Sharʿī wa al-Khatāb al-Shaʿbī*. (Maghrebi Women Between Shari'a Discourse and Popular Discourse). Rabat: National Centre for Coordination and Planning of Scientific and Technical Research.

Millïot, L. 1953. *Introduction à l'Etude de Droit Musulman*. Paris: Recueil Sirey.

Mir-Hosseini, Z. 1986. 'Divorce in Islamic Law and in Practice: The Case of Iran', *Cambridge Anthropology*, XI (1): 41–69.

— 1989. 'Some Aspects of Changing Marriage in Rural Iran: the Case of Kalardasht, a District in Northern Provinces', *Journal of Comparative Family Studies*, XX (2): 215–31.

— 1993. 'Women, Marriage and the Law in Post-Revolutionary Iran', in H. Afshar (ed.), *Women in the Middle East: Perceptions and Struggles*. London: Macmillan.

Modaressi-Tabatabaʾi, H. 1984. *An Introduction to Shīʿi Law: a Bibliographical Study*. London: Ithaca Press.

Montgomery Watt, W. 1953. *Muhammad at Mecca*. Oxford: Clarendon Press.

— 1956. *Muhammad at Medina*. Oxford: Clarendon Press.

Moore, S. F. 1978. *Law as Process: An Anthropological Approach*. London: Routledge & Kegan Paul.

Morocco. 1986. *Code du Statut Personnel et de Succession (Moudawana)*. Arabic Text with French translation by F. P. Blanc and R. Zeidguy. Casablanca: Sochepress.

— 1989. *Femme et Condition Féminine au Maroc*. Rabat: Statistical Directorate, CERED.

— n.d. *Code de Procédure Civile*. Rabat: Ministry of Justice.

Moulay Rchid, A. 1985. *La Condition de la Femme au Maroc*. Rabat: Edition de la Faculté des Sciences Juridiques Economiques et Sociales de Rabat.

— 1986. 'Le Projet de Code de Statut Personnel', *Le Parlement et la Pratique Législative au Maroc*. Rabat: Toubkal.

— 1987. 'Changement Juridique et Changement Social à Travers la Condition des Femmes au Maroc', *Collection Approches: Portrait de Femmes*. Casablanca: Edition Fennec.

Muhaqqiq-Damad, S. M. 1365/1986. *Barrasî-yi Fiqhî-yi Huqūq-i Khānivāda* (Investigation of the Islamic Jurisprudence of Family Law). Tehran: Nashr-i ʿUlum-i Islami.

Mundy, M. 1988. 'The Family, Inheritance, and Islam: A Re-examination of the Sociology of Faraʾid Law', in A. Al-Azmeh (ed.), *Islamic Law: Social and Historical Contexts*. London: Routledge.

Murata, S. 1358/1989. *Izdivāj-i Muvaqqat (Mutʿa va Sīgha)* (Temporary Marriage (Mutʿa and Sigha)). Tehran: Hamdami Press.

Mutahhari, M. 1981. *Nizām-i Huqūq-i Zan dar Islām* (The Rights of Women in Islam), Anon. English translation. Tehran: World Organization for Islamic Service.

Naamane-Guessous, S. 1988. *Au-delà de toute Pudeur: La Sexualité Féminine au Maroc*, 2nd edn. Mohammedia (Maroc): Soden.

Najmabadi, A. 1991. 'Hazards of Modernity and Morality: Women, State and Ideology in Contemporary Iran', in D. Kandiyoti (ed.), *Women, Islam and the State*. London: Macmillan.

Naqavi, A. R. 1967. 'The Family Protection Act', *Islamic Studies*, VI: 241–66.

Nashat, G. 1980. 'Women in the Islamic Republic of Iran', *Iranian Studies*, XIII (1–4): 165–95.

— 1983. (ed.), *Women and Revolution in Iran*. Boulder, Colorado: Westview Press.

Nasir, J. J. 1990. *The Islamic Law of Personal Status*. London: Graham & Trotman.

Nassehi-Behnam, V. 1985. 'Changes in the Iranian Family', *Current Anthropology*, XXVI: 557–62.

Pascon, P. and Bentahar, M. 1971. 'Ce Que Disent 296 Jeunes Ruraux', in A. Khatibi (ed.), *Etudes Sociologiques sur le Maroc*. Rabat: Publication du Bulletin Economique et Social du Maroc.

Payman, H. 1349/1970. *Tahavvul-i vazʿ-i Zanāshūʾi dar Īrān* (Evolution of Marital Conditions in Iran). Tehran: University of Tehran, Institute of Social Studies.

Pearl, D. 1987. *A Textbook on Muslim Personal Law*, 2nd edn. London: Croom Helm.

Perron, M. 1848. *Précis de Jurisprudence Musulmane, ou Principes de Législation Musulmane, Civil et Religieuse, Selon le Rite Mâlékite, Khâlil Ibn Ishak*, 6 vols. Paris.

Pesle, O. 1936. *Le Mariage Chez les Mâlékites de l'Afrique du Nord*. Rabat: Edition Félix Moncho.

— 1937. *La Répudiation chez les Mâlékites de l'Afrique du Nord*. Rabat: Edition Félix Moncho.

— 1946. *La Femme Musulmane dans le Droit, la Religion et les Moeurs*. Rabat: Edition Félix Moncho.

Powers, D. S. 1990a. 'Fatwas as Sources for Legal and Social History: A Dispute over Endowment Revenues from Fourteenth-Century Fez', *Al-Qantara*, XI: 294–341.

— 1990b. 'The Islamic Inheritance System: A Socio–Historical Approach', in C. Mallat and J. Connors (eds.), *Islamic Family Law*. London: Graham & Trotman.

Al-Qayrawani, Ibn Abi-zayd. 1960. *La Risala ou Epitre sur les Elements du Dogme et la Loi de l'Islam Selon le Rite Mâlékite*. Arabic text with French translation by L. Bercher. 5th edn. Algiers: Carabonal.

Qurbani, F. 1370/1991. *Majmūʿa-i Kāmil-i Qavānin va Muqarrarāt-i Khānivāda va ʿMadanī-yi Khāssʾ* (Complete Collection of Family Laws and Procedures and 'Special Civil Act'). Tehran: Ferdowsi Press.

Rahman, A. 1986. *The Role of Muslim Women in Society: Women in the Quran and Hadith*. London: Seerah Foundation.

Ramadan, S. 1961. *Islamic Law: Its Scope and Equity*. London: Macmillan.

Rassam, A. 1980. 'Women and Domestic Power in Morocco', *International Journal of Middle East Studies*, XII: 171–9.

Rodinson, M. 1961. *Mohammad*. Harmondsworth: Penguin Books.

Rosen, L. 1984. *Bargaining for Reality: the Construction of Social Relations in a Muslim Community*. Chicago: University of Chicago Press.

— 1989. *The Anthropology of Justice: Law as Culture in Islamic Society*. Cambridge: Cambridge University Press.

Rosenthal, E. I. J. 1965. *Islam in the Modern National State*. Cambridge: Cambridge University Press.

Russell, A. D. and A. M. Al-Suhrawardy, 1906. *First Steps in Muslim Jurisprudence, Consisting of Excerpts from Bakurat al-Saʿd of Ibn Abu-Zayd*. London: Luzac & Co.

Ruxton, F. H. 1916. *Maliki Law: a Summary from French Translations of Mukhtasar Sidi Khalil*. London: Luzac & Co.

Sabah, F. A. 1984. *Women in the Muslim Unconscious*. New York: Pergamon Press.

Sbai, N. 1987. *L'Enfant Endormi*, 2nd edn. Rabat: Edino.

Schacht, J. 1929a. 'Zina', *The Encyclopaedia of Islam*. Vol. IV: 1227–8. Leiden: E. J. Brill.

— 1929b. 'Talak', *The Encyclopaedia of Islam*. Vol. IV: 636–40. Leiden: E. J. Brill.

— 1932a. 'Mutʿa', *The Encyclopaedia of Islam*. Vol. III: 774–6. Leiden: E. J. Brill.

— 1932b. 'Nikah', *The Encyclopaedia of Islam*. Vol. III: 912–4 Leiden: E. J. Brill.

— 1959. *The Origins of Muhammadan Jurisprudence*. Oxford: Oxford University Press.

— 1960. 'Problems of Modern Islamic Legislation', *Studia Islamica*, XII: 99–131.

— 1964. *An Introduction to Islamic Law*. Oxford: Clarendon Press.

Sebti Lahrichi, F. 1985. *Vivre Musulmane au Maroc*. Paris: Librairie Générale de Droit et Jurisprudence.

Shahid-i Awwal. 1368/1989. *Kitāb-i Lamʿih*, Vol. 2. Compiled by A. R. Fayiz and A. Muhazzab. Tehran: Tehran University Press.

Sharabi, H. 1988. *Neopatriarchy: a Theory of Distorted Change in Arab Society*. Oxford: Oxford University Press.

Shariff, A. H. 1977. *Why Polygamy is Allowed in Islam*. Tehran: A Group of Muslim Brothers.

Shayegan, D. 1989. *Le Regard Mutilé: Schizophrénie Culturelle: Pays Traditionnel Face à la Modernité*. Paris: Albin Michel.

Smith, R. 1973. 'The Matrifocal Family', in J. Goody (ed.), *The Character of Kinship*. Cambridge: Cambridge University Press.

Starr, J. 1978. *Dispute and Settlement in Rural Turkey: an Ethnography of Law*. Leiden: E. J. Brill.

Starr, J. and Collier, J. F. 1987. 'Historical Studies of Legal Change', *Current Anthropology*, XXVII (3): 367–72.

— 1989. 'Introduction: Dialogues in Legal Anthropology', in J. Starr and J. F. Collier (eds.), *History and Power in the Study of Law: New Directions in Legal Anthropology*. Ithaca and London: Cornell University Press.

Stern, G. 1939. *Marriage in Early Islam*. London: Royal Asiatic Society.

Stowasser, B. F. (ed.). 1987. *The Islamic Impulse*. London: Croom Helm.

Tabari, A. and Yeganeh, N. 1982. *In the Shadow of Islam: the Women's Movement in Iran*. London: Zed Press.

Tapper, R. L. (n.d.). '"Islamic Anthroplogy" and "the Anthropology of Islam"'. Paper presented at Middle East Studies Association of North America Annual Meeting, 23–26 November 1991, Washington.

Tapper, R. L. & Tapper, N. S. 1993. 'Marriage, Honour and Responsibility: Islamic Theory and Customary Practice', *Cambridge Anthropology*, xvi (2): 1–12.

Tibi, B. 1988. *The Crisis of Modern Islam: a Preindustrial Culture in the Scientific–Technological Age*. Translated by J. Von Sivers. Salt Lake City: University of Utah Press.

— 1987. 'Islam and Arab Nationalism', in B. F. Stowasser (ed.), *The Islamic Impulse*. London: Croom Helm.

Toledano, H. 1981. *Judicial Practice and Family Law in Morocco: the Chapter on Marriage from Silmasi's al-Amal al-Mutlaq*. New York: Columbia University Press.

Vatani, M. H. 1366/1987. *Majmūʿa-i Kāmil-i Qavānīn va Muqarrarāt-i Umūr-i Khānivāda* (Complete Collection of Laws and Regulations of Family Affairs). Tehran: Ferdowsi Pres.

Verma, B. R. 1971. *Muslim Marriage and Dissolution*. Allahabad: Law Books Co.

Vesey-Fitzgerald, S. G. 1955. 'Nature and Source of the Shariʿa', in M. Khadduri and H. J. Liebesny (eds.), *Origins and Development of Islamic Law*, Vol. 1. Washington: The Middle East Institute.

Weiskopf-Bock, S. 1985. 'The Working Iranian Mother', in A. Fathi (ed.), *Women and Family in Islam*. Leiden: E. J. Brill.

Westermarck, E. 1914. *Marriage Ceremonies in Morocco*. London: Macmillan.

Index

Authors